BRITISH TRANSPORT POLICE

A DEFINITIVE HISTORY OF THE EARLY YEARS
AND SUBSEQUENT DEVELOPMENT

Front Cover: A group of North Eastern Railway Policemen pose for a photograph at Tyne Dock, South Shields in County Durham (now Tyne and Wear) circa 1910.

Back Cover: Ambergate Station Junction Signal Box in Derbyshire during the railway strike of 1911. A Midland Railway Policeman, standing guard, is flanked on either side by four armed guards from the Royal Dublin Fusiliers. A railway porter is present to attend to their needs. The signalman standing inside the signal box is one of many railwaymen who worked through the strike to keep the railways running.

BRITISH TRANSPORT POLICE

A DEFINITIVE HISTORY OF THE EARLY YEARS
AND SUBSEQUENT DEVELOPMENT

MALCOLM CLEGG

PEN & SWORD
TRANSPORT
AN IMPRINT OF PEN & SWORD BOOKS LTD.
YORKSHIRE – PHILADELPHIA

First published in Great Britain in 2022 by
Pen and Sword Transport
An imprint of
Pen & Sword Books Ltd.
Yorkshire - Philadelphia

Copyright © Malcolm Clegg, 2022

ISBN 978 1 39909 547 1

The right of Malcolm Clegg to be identified as author of this work has been asserted by him in accordance with the Copyright, Designs and Patents Act 1988.

A CIP catalogue record for this book is available from the British Library.

All rights reserved. No part of this book may be reproduced or transmitted in any form or by any means, electronic or mechanical including photocopying, recording or by any information storage and retrieval system, without permission from the Publisher in writing.

Typeset by SJmagic DESIGN SERVICES, India.

Printed and bound in the UK by CPI Group (UK) Ltd., Croydon. CR0 4YY.

Pen & Sword Books Ltd incorporates the imprints of Pen & Sword Books Archaeology, Atlas, Aviation, Battleground, Discovery, Family History, History, Maritime, Military, Naval, Politics, Railways, Select, Transport, True Crime, Fiction, Frontline Books, Leo Cooper, Praetorian Press, Seaforth Publishing, Wharncliffe and White Owl.

For a complete list of Pen & Sword titles please contact

PEN & SWORD BOOKS LIMITED
47 Church Street, Barnsley, South Yorkshire, S70 2AS, England
E-mail: enquiries@pen-and-sword.co.uk
Website: www.pen-and-sword.co.uk

or

PEN AND SWORD BOOKS
1950 Lawrence Rd, Havertown, PA 19083, USA
E-mail: Uspen-and-sword@casematepublishers.com
Website: www.penandswordbooks.com

CONTENTS

Acknowledgments	vi
About the Author	vii
Preface	viii
List of Abbreviations	xi
Introduction	xii
Chapter 1 Development of the Railways	1
Chapter 2 Development of the Police Service	12
Chapter 3 Railway Construction and the Navvies	28
Chapter 4 Early Railway Policemen	35
Chapter 5 Nineteenth Century Railway Crime	51
Chapter 6 Railway Accidents and Liability	74
Chapter 7 Crimes Committed Against Passengers	85
Chapter 8 Dangers Facing Nineteenth-Century Railway Policemen	98
Chapter 9 Analysis of Nineteenth Century Crime	111
Chapter 10 Beyond the Nineteenth Century	118
Chapter 11 A Pictorial History of the Transport Police	126
Appendix A Railway Byelaws	181
Appendix B British Transport Police - Constituent Forces	190
Appendix C Nineteenth Century Railway and Dock Policemen Killed on Duty	210
Appendix D List of Chief Constables	226
Bibliography	228
Notes	229
Index	232

ACKNOWLEDGMENTS

The author would like to offer his sincere thanks and appreciation to the following organisations and individuals who provided information, material and assistance used in writing this book, including copyright permission for photographs, images and the reproduction of documents and other information.

British Transport Police; History Group. (www.btphg.org.uk).

National Railway Museum York.

British Newspaper Archives.

Peter Cookson; Retired school-master, author and railway historian.

Viv Head; Retired British Transport Police.

Richard Stackpoole-Ryding; Retired British Transport Police.

Martin McKay; Retired British Transport Police.

Ed Thompson; Retired British Transport Police.

Kevin Gordon; Retired British Transport Police.

Stephen Beamon; Retired British Transport Police.

ABOUT THE AUTHOR

After leaving school, Malcolm Clegg enjoyed a thirty-year career with the British Transport Police. He served both in uniform and in CID, working mainly in South Wales, policing the railway network. He did however work for a number of years as a Docks Constable at Cardiff and Newport Docks and later worked for several years as a Uniform Sergeant at Swansea and Port Talbot Docks. In addition, almost a decade of his career was spent working at various locations in London.

The final ten years of his service were spent as a Detective Sergeant based in Swansea, investigating crimes committed on the Docks and Railway premises over an extensive area of South and West Wales which included Fishguard Harbour, incorporating the then Sealink passenger ferry services which operated between Fishguard and Rosslare in Ireland.

After his retirement, he became an active member of the British Transport Police History Group (www.btphg.org.uk). He has carried out extensive research on behalf of the group and has written a number of articles.

He has written three other books: *British Steam Locomotives before Preservation*, *The Last Days of British Steam* and *LMS and LNER Steam Locomotives*, each published by Pen & Sword.

PREFACE

This book gives an insight into the origins of the British Transport Police, a modern specialist police force which provides a service to staff and passengers of the various train operating companies which make up Network Rail, Britain's national railway operating company. The services of the British Transport Police, which formerly embraced numerous ports, docks, harbours and canal networks, currently extends to cover the London Underground Network, Docklands Light Railway, Croydon Tram Link, Midland Metro Tram System, Tyne and Wear Metro, Glasgow Subway, Eurostar, High Speed 1 and the Emirates Air Line, which is a Transport for London cable car service operating between the Greenwich Peninsula and the Royal Victoria Dock.

In total, the British Transport Police is responsible for the safety of some 8.6 million passengers who travel each day, as well as policing over 10,000 miles of railway track and more than 3,000 railway stations and depots. With an annual budget of some £280 million, the force deploys over 3,000 police officers and 362 police community support officers. They, in turn, are supported by 300 special constables. In addition, the force employs almost 1,700 civilian staff members.[1]

As a cost-effective arrangement for the British taxpayers, the total budget allocated to fund the British Transport Police is met by the Network Rail train operators, Transport for London and the other aforementioned companies who use the services of the force.

Unlike most British police forces, the British Transport Police is not overseen by the Home Office and throughout its history it never has been. The British Transport Police is directly accountable to the British Transport Police Authority, which is an independent body, the members of which are appointed by the Secretary of State for Transport. The duties of the British Transport Police Authority are similar to those of the Police and Crime Commissioners who operate in England and Wales and the Scottish Police Authority which operates in Scotland.

The British Transport Police Authority sets objectives for the policing of the railway before the beginning of each financial year and publishes a plan setting out the arrangements proposed for policing during the year. In addition, it publishes a plan every three years setting out medium-term and long-term strategies for railway policing and publishes an annual report on policing of the railways. The British Transport Police Authority is directly accountable to the Department for Transport, although close contact is maintained between the British Transport Police Authority and the Home Office to ensure that officers from both the Home Office police forces and the British Transport Police are kept on the same footing for training and for operational purposes including the possession and use of firearms.

The main aim of this book is to demonstrate just how the present-day British Transport Police Force evolved from its original roots, which were planted almost 200 years ago with the coming of the railways and the introduction of the first railway policemen. A national police force, similar to the British Transport Police of today, only emerged after the nationalisation of the railways, which took place in 1948, when the first ever national police force was formed in Britain, primarily from the amalgamation of four railway police forces which had policed the Big Four railway companies operating prior to that time. The four companies were the London, Midland and Scottish Railway (LMS), the London and North Eastern Railway (LNER), the Great Western Railway (GWR) and the Southern Railway (SR). These four companies had in turn, been founded in 1923, from the grouping and merging of no less than 120 different railway companies which had existed prior to that time. The majority of those railway companies employed railway policemen in varying numbers, all of whom were absorbed into the four railway police forces when they were founded in 1923.

Railway Policemen first appeared on the scene during the birth of the railways, when the Stockton and Darlington Railway opened in 1825, followed by the Liverpool and Manchester Railway in 1830. Both companies employed railway policemen. During the 1830s and 1840s, railway growth expanded rapidly with new railways springing up all over Britain in quick succession. Almost all the emerging railway companies employed railway policemen to maintain law and order as well as performing operational duties to assist in the actual running of the railways. The terms Railway Policeman and Railway Policemen are used freely throughout this book, as they were during the nineteenth and early twentieth centuries. Women Police Officers did not exist and were not employed in any police force in Britain until after 1916.

The duties performed by early railway policemen have little or no resemblance to those carried out by their modern counterparts who serve in the British Transport Police, yet history provides a direct link between them. For this reason, a large part of this book is devoted to the nineteenth century, giving an insight into the day-to-day work which was carried out by early railway policemen, the type of crime which they encountered and the many changes and developments which occurred during the Victorian era.

The book goes on to explain the connection between railway policing and the policing of other transport institutions, such as Docks, Ports, Harbours and Canals and it describes how these undertakings also have direct links to the modern British Transport Police.

LIST OF ABBREVIATIONS

ABP	Associated British Ports.
BR	British Railways.
BTC	British Transport Commission.
BTP	British Transport Police.
GCR	Great Central Railway.
GER	Great Eastern Railway.
GNR	Great Northern Railway.
GWR	Great Western Railway.
H&B	Hull and Barnsley Railway.
LBSCR (LB&SCR)	London, Brighton and South Coast Railway.
LMS	London, Midland and Scottish Railway.
LNER	London and North Eastern Railway.
LNWR	London and North Western Railway.
LSWR	London and South Western Railway.
MR	Midland Railway.
NER	North Eastern Railway.
SR	Southern Railway.
TVR	Taff Vale Railway.

INTRODUCTION

Prior to 1921, the whole of Ireland was a part of the United Kingdom of Great Britain and Ireland. In May 1921, the island of Ireland was divided. Northern Ireland was created and continued to be governed from Westminster, whilst Southern Ireland became the independent sovereign state of the Republic of Ireland. Whilst the British Transport Police did in the past have a small number of officers stationed at North Wall Quay in Dublin (until the mid-1960s) and at Donegal Quay in Belfast (until the late-1980s), this book focuses upon the history of transport policing in England, Scotland and Wales and does not generally include events which took place on the island of Ireland, although Ireland is referred to in places.

The first Railway Policemen anywhere in the world appeared in Britain in the 1820s when construction of the first modern-day railways began. The railways quickly replaced the canal network as the principal method of transporting goods which were being mass produced in consequence of the industrial revolution, the transition to new manufacturing processes which took place in Britain over an eighty-year period from 1760 until 1840. The large-scale introduction of new machinery resulted in cottage industries and hand-made manufacturing, which had been a source of new production for centuries, giving way to large-scale methods of producing all manner of materials, ranging from iron and steel to textiles and glass. Improved efficiency in the use of water-power and in particular the development of steam power, led to an unbelievable increase in the mass production of a wide range of products. Steam driven agricultural machinery led to a boom in the farming industry and agricultural automation released many thousands of land workers to seek better paid employment in the growing industrial towns and cities, particularly in the Midlands and North of England.

Between 1750 and 1820, extensive canal networks were constructed throughout Britain by labourers known as navigators (commonly referred to as navvies), to enable these mass-produced products to be transported nationwide. Although transporting goods by canal barges was more satisfactory than transportation by horse and cart or horse-drawn wagons, it was slow, inefficient and an unsatisfactory form of transport, which certainly did not meet with the demands of the new industrial revolution. A new and more efficient form of transport was urgently needed.

A breakthrough came early in the nineteenth century when rapid improvements in steam technology led to the invention of the steam locomotive which was able to propel itself by using steam traction as a source of power. In addition, it was capable of pulling wagons and trucks along a railway track, which enabled the transportation of goods without the need for horses to pull road vehicles, railway vehicles or canal barges.

By the 1830s, thousands of navigators were once again employed in Britain, not to build more canals, but to build a vast railway network suitable to meet the needs of the ever-expanding industries in Britain. These new railways, which used steam instead of horsepower, enabled a wide and varied range of products, ranging from coal and other minerals, to parcels, livestock, agricultural products and even the Royal Mail to be speedily transported the length and breadth of Britain to places inaccessible by the canal network. Goods could be transported to docks and harbours for distribution by Britain's Merchant Navy fleet to all corners of the British Empire and beyond.

In addition, it was soon realised that the railways were ideal for transporting people. Passenger traffic was considered by many to be an extra bonus, but still an important aspect of the new railways. It enabled ordinary people the freedom to travel and visit places that a decade or so earlier they could only have dreamed about.

The 1840s were the boom years of railway construction which saw speculative frenzy dubbed Railway Mania as money poured in from speculators and investors trying to board the gravy train to make their fortunes. Inevitably, the bubble burst and many people lost their life savings to fraudsters and unscrupulous individuals, yet the lucky few did indeed make their fortunes.

This book gives an insight into the early construction period of the railways and the social changes brought about as a consequence of its development, whilst focusing upon the introduction and role of railway policemen, who were recruited to assist in the smooth operation of the industry as well as dealing with the safety and well-being of passengers and staff. The early railway policemen were also intended to allay concerns about travelling by train, railway safety and railway crime.

Although this book focuses mainly on the nineteenth century, when most of the radical changes in railway policing took place, it does extend to the twenty-first century, in order to follow the development of the various railway police forces as the years progressed, the creation of the modern British Transport Police in 1963 and its subsequent advancement to the present day.

The Railways Act of 1921 was an important piece of railway legislation as far as railway history is concerned, although at the time the act was created primarily to stem spiralling financial losses of the many railway companies which were operating at that time. These losses had been brought about by the effects of the First World War, when the railway network as a whole suffered severe neglect, largely through lack of maintenance whilst under government control.

There were no fewer than 120 different railway companies operating in Britain after the Great War, often in fierce competition with each other. The act brought about the merger and amalgamation of all the different railway companies into just four large companies, in order to make them more manageable and stop the unnecessary rivalry which was taking place between them. These changes took place when the act came into effect on 1 January 1923.

The Railways Act quickly became known as the Railway Groupings Act and the new companies which emerged in 1923 became known as the Big Four Railway Companies. The four companies concerned, in order of size and starting with the largest, were called: the London, Midland and Scottish Railway (LMS), the London and North Eastern Railway (LNER), the Great Western Railway (GWR) and the Southern Railway (SR).

Most of the railway companies which were amalgamated to form the big four companies already employed their own police personnel. In January 1923, all these serving police officers were absorbed into four new Railway Police Forces created to police the four new railway companies. The relative sizes of the four railway police forces differed from those of the railway companies, inasmuch as the LNER Police had the most officers (1,360), followed by the LMS Police (790), the SR Police (510) and the GWR Police (363).[2] Each of the four police forces were also given statutory powers to continue recruiting new police constables as and when necessary.

From 1923 onwards, the police forces of the big four railway companies worked closely together and as far as possible standardised their practices and procedures, including pay and conditions of service. The officer in charge of each force was given the title Chief of Police and each had an assistant. The rank structure in each force was identical, as were police uniforms and equipment (other than distinguishing features such as crests, buttons, badges and helmet plates). The four forces continued working alongside each other, exchanging information where necessary, until September 1939, when the railways were again taken under government wartime control, to be administered by a Railway Executive Committee, following the outbreak of the Second World War.

By 1945, the railways were in a worse state than they were after the First World War and were in no fit state to be handed back to the big four railway companies. Consequently, the post war Labour government decided to nationalise the railway network. The railways were nationalised on 1 January 1948 but continued to be managed by the Railway Executive Committee during a transition period of one year whilst a new body, the British Transport Commission (BTC), was created to oversee not only the newly nationalised railway network, but also the nation's docks, shipping, inland waterways, road transport, road haulage and a number of other subsidiary companies.

Britain's first national police force, the British Transport Commission Police (BTC Police), was also created by virtue of the British Transport Commission Act of 1949. The new force, headed by a Chief of Police, became responsible for policing all the newly nationalised transport institutions. Officers who had served in the big four railway police forces became an integral part of the BTC Police, but additional officers, who had served in former dock, and canal police forces, were also absorbed into the new force. The British Transport Commission Police officially became operational on 1 January 1949 and successfully policed the nationalised transport institutions throughout the 1950s.

In 1958, the British Transport Commission Police Force dispensed with the post of Chief of Police and replaced it with that of Chief Constable in line with most civil police forces in Britain. In December of that year, the London Transport Police, the body responsible for policing the underground rail network and buses in the capital, was also absorbed into BTC Police Force. At its heyday, the British Transport Commission Police Force had over 4,000 serving police officers and was the third largest police force operating in Britain, after the Metropolitan Police and the Lancashire Constabulary.

In 1962, the British Transport Commission was abolished after it was no longer considered to be fit for purpose, having incurred serious financial losses and having failed in its attempt to develop a cohesive transport system in Britain. Harold MacMillan's Conservative Government replaced the Commission with five new bodies, namely the British Railways Board, the British Transport Docks Board, the British Waterways Board, the London Transport Board and the Transport Holding Company.

Effective from 1 January 1963, with the operating body of the British Transport Commission having been abolished, the British Transport Commission Police was re-named the British Transport Police and it carried on policing the five new administrations without any immediate changes.

During the years that followed, however, many changes did take place within the British Transport Police and not all of the changes were welcome. Some dark times lay ahead. In 1963, Richard Beeching, the Chairman and Head of the new British Railways Board which had been set up to operate the railway network, published a report entitled The Reshaping of British Railways. The report, which later became known as the Beeching Report or the Beeching Axe, concluded that much of the railway network was under-used and should be closed down. The report proposed a massive programme which would involve the closure of 2,363 railway stations and over 5,000 miles of track. The government backed the closures and most of them were implemented during the next few years. As a result of these large-scale closures, the British Transport Police saw its railway jurisdiction slashed by a massive thirty per cent of track miles and fifty-five per cent of railway stations, almost overnight.

Also in the 1960s, the British Waterways Board decided to terminate their policing agreement with the British Transport Police. In January 1964, a Private Security Force was set up to patrol the canals and docks on the inland waterways as a cheaper alternative to being policed by the British Transport Police. As a result, the BT Police Force withdrew their services from the inland waterways later that year. This was a further reduction to the size and jurisdiction of the British Transport Police and a sad loss for the force.

The Thatcher years of the 1980s was another bad decade for the fortunes of the British Transport Police as things went from bad to worse. The British Transport Docks Board was privatised by the Thatcher government in consequence of the Transport Act of 1981. A new company, which succeeded the British Transport Docks Board, traded under the name Associated British Ports (ABP) and took immediate control of twenty-one ports throughout Britain. The British Transport Police had, in the past, policed most of these ports which included Hull, Grimsby, Southampton and five South Wales ports at Newport, Cardiff, Barry, Port Talbot and Swansea. Initially, Associated British Ports retained the services of the British Transport Police, before introducing private security firms onto their premises, in part due to cost cutting measures. In 1985, ABP severed their policing arrangements with the British Transport Police entirely and all serving officers were withdrawn from the docks later that year. A considerable number of these former Dock Police Officers faced the prospect of redundancy but fortunately were deployed elsewhere.

In 1984, Sealink British Ferry Services, a large passenger shipping company, was sold by the British Government in another privatisation plan. Policing of the company had previously been carried out by the British Transport Police, with officers stationed at such places as Dover (Western Dock), Folkestone, Fishguard Harbour and Holyhead. The British Transport Police discontinued policing all the ferry services the following year. The year 1984 also witnessed the London buses withdrawing from their policing agreement with the British Transport Police who had been responsible for policing the system for over thirty-five years.

As the twenty-first century approached, the British Transport Police had in some respects reverted back to where it first started, that of solely policing the railways, a far cry from the numerous undertakings which were within its jurisdiction in the 1950s and early 1960s. As the force entered the twenty-first century, it seemed as if calmer waters lay ahead until an unexpected turn of events took place on the political arena which could further reduce the overall size and jurisdiction of the British Transport Police.

In 1999, a Scottish Parliament was set up in Edinburgh as a result of the Scottish electorate voting for Scottish devolution in a referendum which took place in 1997. In 2016, the responsibility for policing the railways in Scotland was handed over to the Scottish Parliament who decided that the railway police structure in Scotland would become a part of the Police Service of Scotland (Police Scotland) which had been formed in 2013. It was provisionally agreed that Police Scotland would maintain a specialist railway policing structure under the control of the Chief Constable of Police Scotland and accountable to the Scottish Police Authority, based upon the skills, knowledge and experience of the British Transport Police. Arrangements would therefore be made to integrate the British Transport Police officers serving in Scotland into Police Scotland.

The matter has since been the subject of numerous discussions after it was realised that the concept of integrating a part of the British Transport Police into Police Scotland was not as simple and straightforward as initially thought, for a number of reasons. After over five years of discussions and debates, the future of the British Transport Police still hangs in the balance as far as Scotland is concerned and it is still not known whether or not the proposed changes will ever be implemented. It does seem quite likely, but only time will tell.

Having said that, the predecessors of the British Transport Police Force were originally founded and developed to police the railways, and little has changed in that respect. Today, the British Transport Police, a professional body, is still responsible for policing a large and busy railway network, including the London Underground. The force currently employs over 5,000 members of staff which includes more than 3,000 serving police officers under the command of a Chief Constable and it appears to have a bright future.

Despite the fact that the early creation and development of railway policing in the nineteenth century is well and truly confined to the history books, it is difficult to comprehend that Railway Policemen have been around for almost 200 years. Today, officers policing the railway network work on a par with police officers serving in all other police forces in Britain. They are no longer routinely referred to as Railway Policemen. The duties carried out by their early predecessors, who were true Railway Policemen, were altogether different from duties performed today, although the duties they did carry out, back in the day, were considered at the time to be equally as important.

The modern British Transport Police is still the only national police force in Britain. The force is currently well trained, well equipped and well established, but more importantly, seems well poised for a long and successful future. For just how long? Who knows, with a bit of luck and a fair wind, perhaps another couple of hundred years?

Chapter 1

DEVELOPMENT OF THE RAILWAYS

When discussing the topic of railways, people frequently ask which is the world's oldest railway or when was the first public railway built? Simple questions? Perhaps, but the answers are not so simple because they are very much based on interpretation and matters of opinion.

Britain was certainly in the driving seat when it came to the construction of railways and the development of steam locomotives. Wagonways or tramways had been used in Britain since the seventeenth century for transporting coal and other minerals relatively short distances. They were far more efficient than using horse and carts or horse drawn wagons on roads, as the smooth wheels on smooth rails caused far less friction resulting in much bigger loads being transported using the same power. Horse drawn wagonways continued to be built throughout the eighteenth century, mainly to transport coal from collieries to local rivers, canals, and docks for distribution further afield by ships and barges. These wagonways or tramways were the fore-runners of modern-day railways.

One such wagonway, built in 1758, was the Middleton Wagonway at Hunslet near Leeds in West Yorkshire. The wagonway ran a distance of approximately one mile (1.6km) from Middleton to the river Aire in Leeds and the gauge of the wagonway (the distance or width between the two running rails) was 4ft 1in (1245mm). The purpose of the Middleton Wagonway was to transport coal which was being extracted from a number of bell pits (a type of shallow or surface mining) at Middleton, to coal barges on the river Aire in Leeds. Horses were initially used to pull the coal wagons along the track. The building of the wagonway itself was authorised by an Act of Parliament secured by Charles Brandling, a local landowner, and was the first Act of Parliament ever enacted in Britain specifically to authorise the construction of a wagonway or railway.

The Middleton Wagonway introduced steam locomotives to replace horses in 1812, after which it became referred to as a railroad or railway. The first steam locomotive introduced onto the railway was a twin cylinder engine named *Salamanca*, built by Matthew Murray. Steam locomotives were successfully used to work coal trains from Middleton to coal barges on the

River Aire for many years. The railway was converted to a standard gauge railway of 4ft 8½in (1435mm) in 1881, when it was officially classified as a light railway. The Middleton Railway is today a popular Heritage Railway run by volunteers and it is an important part of the nation's railway history. It operates a passenger service for visitors at weekends and bank holidays from Moor Road Station in Hunslet, to Park Halt in Middleton. A number of people consider the Middleton Railway to be the world's oldest continuously working railway and the first ever commercial railway to use steam locomotives. The Middleton Heritage Railway Trust, who own the railway, also advertise and promote the railway to that effect.

Whilst the Middleton Railway Trust may make certain claims, the railway itself started life as a narrow gauge wagonway built for transporting coal, loaded onto horse drawn wagons. It was not officially converted to a standard gauge light mineral railway until 1881, by which time there were almost 13,000 miles of standard gauge railway track in Britain with over 5.5million passengers being conveyed on the railways annually. Whilst most people would recognise the importance of the Middleton Railway in historical terms, relatively few consider it to be the world's first public or modern railway, although it is a matter of opinion.

On 21 February 1804, the world's first ever steam locomotive took to the tracks to travel a distance of 9.5 miles (15 km) from Pen-Y-Darren Iron Works in Merthyr Tydfil, South Wales, to the Merthyr and Cardiff Canal at Abercynon on rails made from cast iron. The locomotive, an un-named, single cylinder steam engine which was later referred to as *Uncle Dick's Puffer*,[3] was designed and built by Richard Trevithick, a Cornish mining engineer. It hauled five railway wagons containing eleven tons (9979.03 kilograms) of iron and seventy men. The locomotive reached a top speed of five miles per hour (eight kilometres per hour) and completed the journey without stopping for water. It used two hundredweight (101.6 kg) of coal for fuel which was carried on a small coal tender. Unfortunately, the locomotive and loaded wagons were too heavy for the brittle cast iron rails to support, causing several broken rails during the journey. The locomotive made at least three trial runs which were partially successful but problems with fractured rails persisted and eventually the railway scheme was abandoned. Some people consider the Pen-Y-Darren Railway as being the world's first but again it is a matter of opinion.

Another contender for the world's first public railway is sometimes said to be the Oystermouth Railway (no longer in existence) which was also in South

Wales. There is little doubt that this was the world's first public fare-paying passenger railway. Construction of the railway began in 1804 and it covered just over five miles (8 km) from Swansea to Oystermouth. Originally, the railway was built as a four-foot gauge mineral railway (converted to standard gauge in 1855). Officially named the Oystermouth Railway and Tramroad Company, it was designed and built to transport coal and limestone to the port town of Swansea from surrounding areas. The railway opened in 1806 and horse-drawn goods wagons were used to transport mineral traffic. The following year, some of the wagons were modified to be used as passenger carrying vehicles and fare-paying passengers were introduced onto the railway in 1807. The railway continued carrying fare-paying passengers for over 150 years, until its closure in 1960.

Steam traction replaced the horse-drawn vehicles in 1877 and steam locomotives were used to haul passenger train services. The railway was renamed the Swansea and Mumbles Railway in 1898, when the line was extended from Oystermouth to Mumbles Pier to enable passenger trains to provide services for visitors and holidaymakers arriving in Mumbles via the busy Paddle Steamers and Ferry Services operating to and from there.

In 1928-29 the railway was electrified, using an overhead pantograph system and a fleet of thirteen new electric double-decker tramcars, each capable of carrying more than 100 passengers, were introduced into service by 1930. The railway at that time stretched some eleven miles (17.7 km) from Swansea to Mumbles Pier and served ten stations along the seafront of Swansea Bay. More than 3 million fare paying passengers a year were using the Mumbles Railway (as it was locally known) by 1950.

Sadly, during the 1950s, the South Wales Transport Company set up in fierce competition with the Mumbles Railway when it started to operate an ever-increasing number of local bus services running adjacent to the railway, whilst at the same time buying up most of the railway company shares. It had acquired ninety per cent of the shares by 1958. The use of public roads also ensured that the bus company had an unfair advantage over the railway by avoiding many of the maintenance and operational costs incurred to run and maintain the railway. Despite strong local public opposition, the railway closed in January 1960. Most of the track bed of the former Mumbles Railway is now a public footpath and cycle track. Quite a number of people consider the Mumbles Railway to be the world's first public railway but once again, it is a matter of opinion.

Several railways are well placed to stake a claim as being a world's first, but as far as public opinion is concerned, just two railway companies stand head and shoulders above the rest, the first being the Stockton and Darlington Railway and the other the Liverpool and Manchester Railway, with public opinion seemingly favouring the latter.

The Stockton and Darlington Railway opened on 27 September 1825, when large crowds, estimated at some 40,000 people, turned out to see George Stephenson at the controls of his new-fangled steam engine *Locomotion* (Number 1), as it hauled a train consisting of a purpose built passenger coach named *Experiment*, which seated company directors and VIPs, eleven wagons laden with coal, four wagons laden with flour and a further twenty coal wagons, fitted with seats, to carry workmen and other passengers. The train ran for nine miles (14.4 km) from Shildon to Darlington at an average speed of 4mph, reaching a top speed estimated to be 15mph. Stephenson's brothers Ralph and James were alongside him at the controls of the locomotive, feeding coal into the fire-box.

Although the Stockton and Darlington Railway was originally built as a horse-drawn railway, improvements in steam technology at the time led to a decision being made to use steam traction, as well as horses. Steam locomotives had turned from a dream to reality and although horse-drawn trains were initially used on the Stockton and Darlington railway as well as steam, they were phased out by 1833.

Exactly five years after the opening of the Stockton and Darlington Railway, another milestone was reached in railway history. September 1830 saw the opening of the Liverpool and Manchester Railway, which a great many people deem to be the birth of modern railways. A double track railway connected the port town of Liverpool to the rapidly expanding industrial town of Manchester, a distance of some thirty-five miles. This railway was the world's first solely reliant upon steam locomotives for conveying both goods and passengers by train. It was also the first double track public railway to connect two major towns. The company employed a number of railway policemen from the outset and viewed their duty as one of great responsibility. During the construction of the railway, houses and huts were built at intervals along the track (approximately one mile apart) which were occupied by railway constables to ensure the safe and unimpeded running of locomotives and trains.

Directors of early railway companies were aware they had a duty of care and protection towards passengers and staff as well as a strong need for the protection and security of their railways and as a result, they began to employ railway policemen specifically for this purpose.

***Locomotion Number** 1.* Built at Newcastle, County Durham in 1823 by father and son, George and Robert Stephenson and driven by George Stephenson at the opening of the Stockton & Darlington Railway in 1825.

Whilst the directors of the Liverpool and Manchester Railway were conscious of the dangers and pitfalls of running a railway, nothing had prepared them for an infamous incident which occurred during the opening ceremony of the railway on 15 September 1830. To mark the event, a special train ran from Liverpool to Manchester. The train was full of VIPs and special dignitaries which included the prime minister Arthur Wellesley, the first Duke of Wellington. One of the dignitaries travelling on the train was the Right Honourable William Huskisson, MP for Liverpool, Board of Trade President and a former cabinet minister.

The train travelled from Liverpool to Parkway Railway Station, approximately halfway between Liverpool and Manchester, where it made a scheduled stop to take on water. All passengers had been previously instructed by staff that under no circumstances should they alight from the train until it arrived at its destination in Manchester. During the excitement, however, approximately fifty of the elite passengers, including William Huskisson, got off the train when it stopped at Parkside to stretch their legs and take a break.

Huskisson walked along the railway track, with a view to shaking hands with the Duke of Wellington who was in another carriage. However, as he tried to open the door on the Duke's carriage, the door swung open and struck Huskisson, causing him to fall backwards onto the adjacent track where he was struck by the famous *Rocket* locomotive which was passing by. He later died as a result of the accident.

A memorial tablet was subsequently placed alongside the railway line at Parkside where the accident took place and has remained there ever since. His death immediately highlighted the dangers of walking on the railway and railway legislation was later introduced creating the criminal offence

Depiction of the 1830 railway fatality involving the Right Honourable William Huskisson MP.

of railway trespass, whilst at the same time, affording powers to railway policemen and other members of staff to deal with it.

Whilst the world's first fatal railway accident is often attributed as being that of Huskisson, historically that is not the case. Whilst Huskisson has the unfortunate infamy of being the first passenger to be fatally injured on the railway, a number of other fatal accidents had already taken place prior to 1830.[4]

As far as can be ascertained, the first three railway fatalities all took place on the Middleton Railway. The first written record of a railway fatality was published in a newspaper article, which appeared in the *Leeds Mercury* in February 1813. It was reported that a 13-year-old boy by the name of John Bruce was struck and killed by a steam locomotive whilst he was running alongside it on the Middleton Railway in Leeds. Some five years later, on 28 February 1818, another fatality occurred on the Middleton Railway when the driver of the steam locomotive *Salamanca* was killed after the boiler of the locomotive exploded. The driver was seen tampering with the safety valves on the locomotive prior to the explosion which may have caused it. In the early days of steam engines, a small number of drivers sometimes jammed objects such as pieces of wood into the safety valves of locomotives for a short period of time to prevent the valves from opening and discharging excess steam. This resulted in additional steam pressure building up inside the boiler, providing extra power, which enabled an increase in acceleration and speed of the locomotive. This was a highly dangerous practice which could, and in some cases did, result in boiler explosions which usually proved fatal for anyone in close proximity to the locomotive.

Another fatal accident on the Middleton Railway occurred during the afternoon of Wednesday, 5 December 1821 as David Brook, a carpenter, was returning home from work in Leeds. He often took a short cut home by walking along the railway line. Whilst walking along the track towards Middleton, he put up an umbrella to prevent sleet beating into his face. The umbrella partially obscured his vision, and he didn't see or hear a coal train which passed over his lower extremities, mangling his legs and thighs. He died in the infirmary later that evening. He left a widow and six children.

Early railway fatalities were not however confined to the Middleton Railway. Records in the parish register at Eaglescliffe Parish Church in County Durham refer to an unnamed female, believed to have been a blind beggar, being killed by a steam locomotive on the Stockton and Darlington Railway in 1827.

The following year saw another two people killed in separate incidents on the Stockton and Darlington Railway. On 19 March 1828, the boiler of Stockton and Darlington Railway locomotive Number Five exploded, killing one person. On 1 July 1828, the boiler of Stockton and Darlington Railway engine *Locomotion No.1* exploded and driver John Cree suffered severe injuries. He died just two days later.

It is not known how many accidents, fatal and non-fatal, occurred during the actual construction of Britain's railways but the numbers are thought to be considerable. The primitive methods used by the navvies in building massive structures such as bridges, tunnels and viaducts resulted in many accidents ranging from minor to fatal. It is known that during the construction of the Liverpool and Manchester Railway in 1829, at least one fatal accident involving a workman occurred as a result of a landslip. Several horses were also killed. Between 1838 and 1841, in just one large scale building project, an estimated 100 navvies were killed during construction of the two mile long Box Tunnel on the Great Western Railway in Wiltshire.

Whilst the unfortunate accident to William Huskisson dampened the carnival atmosphere at the opening of the Liverpool and Manchester Railway, the railway itself was a huge success, paving the way for fierce competition in the race to build more railways.

Throughout the 1830s, railway construction continued and in 1836 alone, a total of 1,126 miles of new railway was sanctioned by the legislature in parliament. The following decade saw a frenzy as railway share prices rocketed towards a record high, along with new proposals being laid before parliament for the building of more railways.

The situation of Britain's railways by the end of 1844 was 2,235 miles (3597 km) of track in operation and an additional 855 miles (1376 km) in various stages of construction, having been approved by parliament, making a grand total of 3,090 miles (4983 km). A total of 104 different railway companies had been founded and were operational. Some investors were being offered as much as ten per cent interest return on their capital if they invested in railway shares, as money continued pouring in from speculators.

In 1845, no less than 383 applications were presented to parliament for the building of new railways. The following year, 1846, saw the pinnacle of Railway Mania when a staggering 560 new railway schemes were laid before parliament, 270 of which were authorised and received Royal Assent, authorising the construction of an additional 4,540 miles (7,306 km) of new track.[5]

As the year 1846 came to a close, however, people started to sell their railway shares when it became apparent that the large dividends which they had been promised were not forthcoming. There were also rumours involving fraud and over-investment, some of which were exposed in the highly respected and well-thought-of newspaper, *The Times*.

Between 1847 and 1850, the gravy train came to a halt and the Railway Mania bubble burst. Share prices dropped dramatically and many people lost their life savings. Others were declared bankrupt. Almost 100 new railway construction schemes which had already been approved by parliament or given Royal Assent were abandoned due to lack of finance. The golden years for railway investors seemed to be at an end.

Without a doubt, the most infamous of all the early railway speculators and fraudsters of the railway boom years was George Hudson, dubbed the Railway King. George Hudson was born at Howsham near York in 1800. At the age of fifteen, he moved to York to start work as an apprentice linen draper with the firm Bell and Nicholson, in College Street. He completed his apprenticeship in 1821, after which he married Elizabeth, the daughter of Richard Nicholson, one of the business partners. Later, the other business partner, William Bell, retired and George Hudson was given his share of the business and the firm became Nicholson and Hudson.

In 1827, George Hudson, who was by then already a wealthy man, received a bequest of £30,000 from a great-uncle, Matthew Bottrill, a gentleman farmer. In 1833, he decided to invest the money in a venture which proposed the building of a railway from Newcastle to London via York. An enabling Act of Parliament was passed in 1837, and the York and North Midland Railway Company was subsequently founded. George Hudson was the largest shareholder in the company, and he became the Company Chairman.

George Stephenson, the famous locomotive engineer, was appointed Chief Engineer of the company. In November that year, Hudson was appointed Lord Mayor of York before going on to become a Tory Member of Parliament for Sunderland. Hudson soon became a millionaire and continued investing his fortunes in railway companies hence the un-official title of the Railway King. He also purchased land and several private estates within his home county of Yorkshire.

George Hudson was well established as the Railway King by 1844, when he owned over 1,000 miles of railway track. He continued to buy shares in railway companies and it was alleged that he distributed several thousand pounds in bribes to politicians and others, in order to promote the railway

George Hudson, 'The Railway King'.

companies in which he had financial interests. Although the mid-1840s saw the zenith of railway mania, it was about to yield unwelcome changes to the good fortunes of George Hudson.

George Stephenson had become suspicious of Hudson's business methods and no longer wished to be a part of them, so he resigned his position with the York and North Midland Railway Company. By the late 1840s, cracks began to appear in George Hudson's empire after he was found to have been paying dividends out of company capital, which was unlawful (Railway Clauses Consolidation Act 1845, Section 121). As his empire crumbled around him, he fled to France to avoid his creditors. He later returned to Britain where he was arrested and imprisoned for three months in his home city of York. Criminal proceedings against Hudson for his fraudulent activities would have caused a great deal of embarrassment, both for the government and his many influential friends, so he was able to stave off prosecution by offering financial settlements to investors who had lost money as a result of his actions. In one respect, George Hudson was a very lucky man. His power, influence and friends in high places had undoubtedly prevented him from serving a very lengthy prison sentence. After his release from prison, Hudson lived a sedate life in a modest property in London. With his vast fortune gone, he died in 1871, leaving an estate worth a mere £200, a far cry from the rich pickings of the former millionaire.

The misdeeds of George Hudson were just the tip of the iceberg when it came to fraud and malpractice involving railway companies at that time. Many other types of railway fraud became commonplace on the railways as the nineteenth century progressed and railway policemen were given the task of investigating them. Consequently, a considerable number of railway police man-hours were spent investigating and dealing with a variety of frauds on the railways throughout the nineteenth century and a considerable number of people were convicted of fraudulent activities.

Officers investigating early railway frauds, frequently worked in civilian clothes rather than in uniform and although the introduction of the first official detective departments did not take place until the early 1860s, the officers conducting these investigations were, to all intents and purposes, the first ever Railway Detectives.

Chapter 2

DEVELOPMENT OF THE POLICE SERVICE

In Britain during the Middle Ages, it was the responsibility of the reigning monarch to maintain the peace, oversee the administration of justice and ensure that the common laws of the land which had been passed down since time immemorial were upheld. Lords of the Manor, the landholders of rural estates, were given legal powers to maintain law and order and dispense justice within their estates.

During the twelfth century, the office of High Sheriff was introduced, whereby noblemen were appointed by the king to maintain law and order and administer justice within the shires of the kingdom on his behalf. Medieval Britain also saw the first watchmen appearing in communities around the country. These watchmen were unpaid volunteers from within the local community who would patrol the streets to deter crime, keep the peace and afford protection to local citizens. They often patrolled during the hours of darkness, carrying a lantern and armed with a stout stick and a bell to attract attention where necessary.

The title Constable or Petty Constable was used as early as the thirteenth century to describe a member of the king's army who was appointed on a local basis where necessary to control behaviour, as any breaches of law and order were monitored under the watchful eye of the army or local militia (reserve forces). This enabled military personnel to be mustered quite quickly where necessary, to quell any serious disturbances which included looting and rioting.

The sixteenth century saw the appearance of a different type of Constable, namely the Parish Constable who was not attached to the military. Civil parishes appointed Parish Constables to maintain law and order. These Parish Constables were initially chosen and appointed by local parishioners but by the second quarter of the seventeenth century, although still chosen by parishioners, they had to be sworn in and appointed by local magistrates. Parish Constables played an important role in society for many years and on the whole were successful in maintaining law and order until the continual increases in the population of towns and cities during the late eighteenth and early nineteenth centuries made it impossible for them to fulfil the demands placed upon them. This was just another step towards more modern policing which was introduced in earnest during the nineteenth century.

Modern policing is thought by many to stem from a concept which started in 1749 when, as a result of a surge of crime in London due to an increase in the population there, magistrate and author Henry Fielding founded a small band of six men who were attached to the Bow Street Magistrate's office in London, to patrol the streets in order to catch criminals and preserve the peace. Initially the men were dressed in ordinary civilian clothes but later, as their numbers increased, they were issued with scarlet waistcoats and blue greatcoats in order to distinguish them from ordinary members of the public. The patrols did achieve considerable success and the force of men continued to increase in number, reaching sixty-eight in 1800, by which time they had earned themselves the nickname and unofficial title of the Bow Street Runners. In 1805, a mounted brigade consisting of fifty-four additional men on horseback was created to swell the ranks and increase their efficiency even further. In 1834, parliament recommended that the Bow Street Runners should be absorbed into the new Metropolitan Police Force which had been founded five years earlier. The recommendations were enacted into law by the introduction of the Police Act of 1839, after which the Bow Street Runners were disbanded.

At the turn of the eighteenth/nineteenth century, not only was the population of London rapidly increasing but there was a marked increase in the population of towns elsewhere, in part as a result of the industrial revolution. The increased population was particularly noticeable in the towns of Northern England where people were arriving from other parts of the country to make new lives for themselves and their families by securing employment in the large number of new mills and factories which were being built. Jobs were plentiful and workers were able to earn significantly more money than agricultural workers. This increase in population inevitably brought about an increase in crime and whilst the practice of using constables and watchmen had yielded adequate protection in the past, the system was struggling to cope with the events of the day, which necessitated a more modern approach to policing and a significant increase in the number of constables to adequately enforce law and order.

Scotland, it could be argued, was at the forefront of establishing modern police forces in Britain at that time. As early as 1800, Glasgow had formed its own police force, followed by Edinburgh (1805), Paisley (1806), Perth (1811) and Aberdeen (1824). The forces mentioned were all established by virtue of Acts of Parliament which preceded the Metropolitan Police by quite a number of years. In Northern Ireland, Belfast had also introduced a police force as early as 1800.

There is little doubt that the examples set by Scotland in the early nineteenth century were followed south of the border as increasing numbers of constables were sworn in by local authorities in England and Wales which set the cornerstone of modern-day policing as we know it. From 1830 onwards, policing methods became more standardised as new police forces started to emerge. The Municipal Corporations Act of 1835 ordered all incorporated boroughs in England and Wales to create a Police Force which was accountable to a local watch committee and in 1856, policing, which was by then funded from the Central Government Treasury Department, was made compulsory throughout England and Wales. As the end of the nineteenth century approached, over 180 separate municipal or civil police forces were operating in Britain, employing some 60,000 officers. As Britain entered the twentieth century, modern civil policing had been well and truly established.

Large profit-making organisations such as the railways, docks and canal networks rapidly expanded in the nineteenth century, coinciding with the expansion of municipal police forces. However, it was not the responsibility of the British taxpayer to fund the security and policing of these commercial organisations and it was not the job of civil police officers to routinely police them. These commercial administrations had an obligation to provide their own safety and security measures for staff, passengers and other members of the public using their premises. In order to fulfil these obligations, private police forces and other forms of private security were introduced. The organisations who opted to employ their own police forces tended to be the railways, docks, harbours and canal companies. The policemen whom they engaged were not surprisingly referred to as Railway, Dock and Canal Policemen. Industrial premises and other large institutions tended to engage watchmen and security officers which were a much cheaper option, yet quite adequate to suit their needs.

To enable police constables to carry out their duties on what was essentially private property, legislation was introduced by parliament specifically for private police forces. Enactments created criminal offences exclusive to places such as railways, docks and canals, together with the necessary police powers, to enable railway, dock and canal policemen to function. The types of offences which related specifically to railway policing included trespassing, railway obstruction, stone throwing, wilful damage and fare evasion. Additional offences for use on docks, ports, harbours and canals mainly involved shipping. Numerous Railway, Dock and Canal Byelaws were also introduced. These byelaws governed what people were allowed to do and not allowed to do whilst on the property to which they related. The byelaws contained a list of criminal offences, penalties for transgressors and police powers to implement them. Examples of railway byelaws used during the nineteenth century can be found in Appendix A.

In the summer of 1826, history was made when the world's first ever railway policeman was appointed to work as a constable on the Stockton and Darlington Railway. He was Joseph Sedgwick, a local man from Stockton.[6] Three other railway constables were engaged shortly afterwards. The four constables were required to wear police uniforms which consisted of a dark blue dress coat with high collar and matching trousers, a stovepipe or top-hat and a greatcoat. Their normal working hours were from 6am to 8pm, Monday to Saturday and four hours on a Sunday. They also had to work nights or other shifts if called upon to do so. A number of gatekeepers were also employed by the police department in order to avoid policemen being confined to static duties.

After the police department was established, a Superintendent was appointed to take charge. He was also required to wear a uniform and hold weekly meetings with the Railway Board of Directors to update them of the work being carried out by his officers, as well as providing the board with full details of any fatal accidents which had taken place on the railway. As the Stockton and Darlington Railway later increased in size, the police numbers increased accordingly. The Stockton and Darlington Railway Police operated successfully until 1863 when all the serving officers became part of the North Eastern Railway Police after the Stockton and Darlington Railway Company amalgamated with the North Eastern Railway Company.

Following the Stockton and Darlington Railway, the Liverpool and Manchester Railway, which opened in 1830, was the second railway company to employ railway policemen. They were engaged from 1828, whilst it was still in the final stages of construction. They also wore police uniforms with top-hats, similar to the uniforms worn by officers in the Stockton and

Darlington railway police. The Liverpool and Manchester Railway only operated for fifteen years before being absorbed into the Grand Junction Railway in 1845, in a prelude to merging with two other companies, the Manchester and Birmingham Railway and the London and Birmingham Railway. The merger of the three companies created the London and North Western Railway Company which was founded in 1846. All former Liverpool and Manchester railway policemen were absorbed into the new London and North Western Railway Police Force that year. The LNWR Company itself went on to become the largest pre-grouping railway company in Britain, absorbing over 100 smaller railway companies in the process. The LNWR Police Force consisted of approximately 400 officers when it became part of the London, Midland and Scottish Railway Police during the railway groupings which took place in 1923, although when constables were performing such duties as signalling and crossing keeper duties in the early 1850s, the LNWR Company alone employed in the region of 700 constables.[7]

It was a fortunate coincidence that both the early railway police forces and civil police forces happened to be founded around the same time, developing side by side throughout the nineteenth century, as it enabled them to work closely together, assisting each other where necessary and exchanging ideas on how emerging police forces could best develop. There were many similarities in the way the two types of forces operated and the rank structures in both police forces were, in the most part, compatible. Railway constables, however, did have a number of different types of duties to perform, which their civil police counterparts did not have to contend with. These were mainly operational matters involving the day to day running of the railways and enforcing the many enactments of specific railway legislation which were progressively appearing on the statute books.

Police uniforms were worn by both civil and railway police officers to give a visible presence and make them instantly recognisable. The most popular colour for police uniforms was dark blue which was the colour adopted by the Metropolitan Police Force in London. However, some early railway, municipal and dock police forces, opted to wear different colour uniforms. The London and Birmingham Railway Police, the Great Western Railway Police and the London, Brighton and South Coast Railway Police, initially wore rifle green uniforms which was the dark green colour worn by British Army riflemen. The Bute Dock Police in Cardiff also wore green uniforms as did officers in the Lancashire County Constabulary. Early constables working on the London and Southampton Railway, and their successors in the London and South Western Railway Police, wore tail-coats that were chocolate brown in colour. Uniform Inspectors in the Great Western Railway Police wore a red stripe on the outside of their trouser legs to distinguish them from other ranks. This idea was based on various military uniforms using red stripes to signify rank. It was generally accepted however that military style uniforms and military type tactics should not be used by any police force in Britain as it was acknowledged by most politicians that policing should be by public consent and any suggestion of military style policing would alienate members of the public. As the nineteenth century progressed, the design and style of uniforms still continued to vary slightly but as the century wore on, they became more standardised as an ever-increasing number of forces based their designs on the one used by the Metropolitan Police.

The earliest Metropolitan Police Constable's uniform consisted of a dark blue swallow tail-coat with high collar and a stovepipe or top hat which was reinforced with cane. Constables were issued with two pairs of trousers, one being dark blue to match the tailcoat, the other pair being white. The blue trousers were worn during winter months (and during the hours of darkness), whilst the white were worn during the summer months. Some forces however reserved their white trousers for ceremonial use and other special occasions, wearing blue trousers in both summer and winter. Black boots were the standard issue for constables. Most railway police forces had also embraced these designs by the eighteen-fifties.

Accoutrements issued to early police constables consisted of a wooden truncheon or baton, a wooden rattle, handcuffs and a bullseye type oil lamp for use at night. Railway constables were also individually issued with pocket watches, as time played an integral part in operating a railway. Most passengers, particularly third-class, travelling by train in the mid-nineteenth century did not carry or even possess watches and frequently approached railway constables to ask the time when travelling. This led to a well-known saying in Victorian times, 'If you want to know the time, ask a policeman'.

The size of a police truncheon usually ranged from approximately twelve inches (30.5cm) to eighteen inches (46cm) in length and they were made of hardwood which was frequently lignum vitae or mahogany. Most early truncheons were elaborately painted with gold and other bright colours, often on a black background. They usually bore the royal crown and the initials of the reigning monarch such as WR (William IV) or VR (Queen Victoria) and a coat of arms or crest which signified the city, town or borough to which it related. Railway police truncheons were similarly adorned, sometimes with

Three nineteenth-century railway police truncheons. Two Taff Vale Railway Police Truncheons numbered five and six. In the centre is a rare South Wales Railway Police Truncheon. The South Wales Railway was built in 1850 and only existed for thirteen years before amalgamating with the Great Western Railway in 1863.

the crown, but instead of bearing a civic coat of arms they displayed the name and crest of the railway or docks company in which the police officer to whom the truncheon was issued served. Some also bore the collar number of the officer to whom it was issued. Firearms were not issued routinely to police, but revolvers were sometimes available, should they be required.

Although swords have traditionally been issued in the police service to high-ranking police officers as a part of their ceremonial uniforms for performing duties in connection with royalty and on other special occasions, swords and cutlasses were never issued for general use as a weapon in any British police force after the turn of the twentieth century.

In the nineteenth century, however, things were different. Both swords and cutlasses were used by a number of police forces, both civil and private, to afford protection for officers, usually during the hours of darkness. The basic difference between the sword and the cutlass issued to police was that a sword was a long straight-bladed weapon with a hilt, designed to stab, or cut, whilst the cutlass tended to be a shorter, broader, slashing type weapon, usually with a curved blade. Cutlasses were popular as a naval sword, also favoured by pirates for close combat. In essence, a cutlass is a nautical name for a sabre. When issued to nineteenth-century police officers, cutlasses were commonly referred to as hangers, hanger sword or hunting sword.

Although a number of nineteenth century police constables were routinely trained in the use of swords and cutlasses, stringent restrictions were in place as to their day-to-day use and most forces who did routinely carry them restricted their use to officers performing night duty patrols. Use at any other time was ordinarily confined to times of civil unrest, serious public disorder and riotous behaviour.

During the second half of the nineteenth century, some changes were made to police uniforms and equipment. Swallowtail coats were replaced by longer frock coats in some police forces and high dog-collar fitted tunics in others. Capes, which began to appear in the 1840s, were becoming more popular, whilst white trousers were no longer considered suitable and dispensed with, although some forces retained them for ceremonial use, royal duties and other special events. Stovepipe or top hats were initially replaced in some forces by

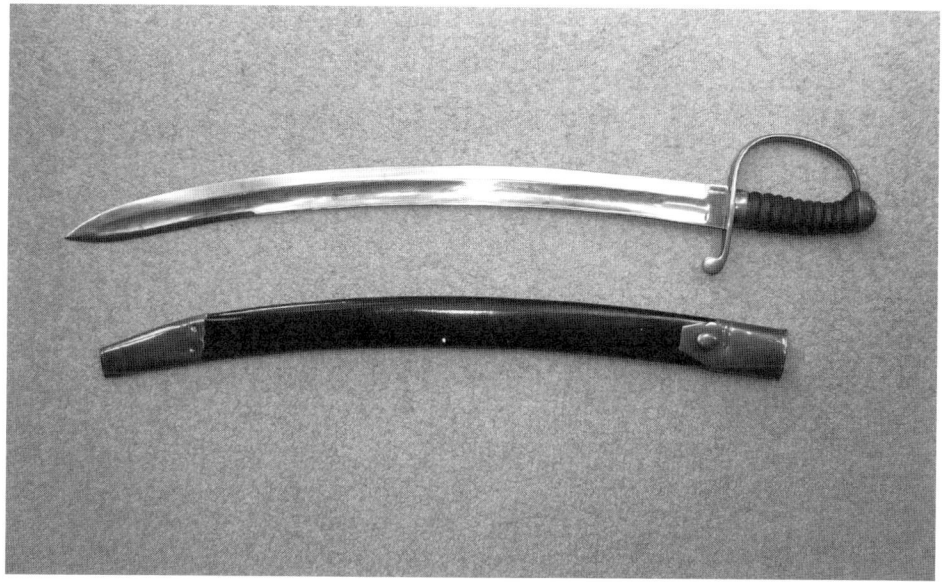

An original naval style police cutlass, issued to officers of the Bute Docks Police from 1860 until 1887. The Bute Docks Police were the force responsible for policing Cardiff Docks for much of the nineteenth and early twentieth century.

dark blue caps until a new type of reinforced police helmet was introduced. These helmets, which were first introduced into the Metropolitan Police in 1863, were based on the design of pickelhaube military helmets, worn by soldiers of the Prussian army. They were well received by officers of all forces as they offered a great deal of protection and proved to be a great success. Helmets were soon adopted by many police forces nationwide, including railway police forces.

By the late 1880s, wooden rattles, which had been used for many years to attract attention, had been replaced by police whistles. Policemen were instructed to give three short, sharp blasts on their whistles to attract attention and summon assistance. Towards the end of the nineteenth century, dark blue uniforms had become the standard issue for almost all British police forces, although the Bute Dock Police in Cardiff for example, who were proud to wear their green uniforms, managed to retain them until as late as 1922. A few individual railway police officers also continued to wear top hats throughout the nineteenth century, apparently without any admonishment from their supervisors who, it appears, turned a blind eye to such practices.

Below is a pictorial comparison of Civil and Railway Police Uniforms, both from the 1850s, showing the similarities in design.

The police ranking system adopted by municipal police forces and railway police forces in Britain during the nineteenth century was similar but not identical, although all railway forces subsequently made the necessary changes during the twentieth century to bring their rank structure in line with the one used by home office forces.

The rank of Police Constable or Constable was the lowest, yet the most numerous of the police ranks adopted by all British police forces in the nineteenth century and has remained

An unknown Metropolitan Police Constable wearing an early style uniform consisting of a top hat and a tunic with a leather belt during the 1850s. A number of railway police forces based their uniform design upon those worn by the Metropolitan Police.

Development of the Police Service • 21

Police Constable John Wallbridge of the Taff Vale Railway Police, pictured in the 1850s, wearing a uniform based upon that of the Metropolitan Police, as shown in the previous picture. PC Wallbridge is wearing white 'summer issue' trousers in this picture, although blue trousers matching the tunic were worn in winter months.

Above left: **A nineteenth century** North Eastern Railway Policeman's wooden truncheon or baton, elaborately painted and typical of the design adopted by both railway and civil police forces at that time.

Above middle: **A pair** of Lancashire and Yorkshire Railway Police Hiatt handcuffs. They were issued to all constables of the Lancashire and Yorkshire Railway Police during the nineteenth century.

Above right: **A wooden** police rattle, used to summon assistance or attract attention. Rattles were used from the 1830s until the late 1880s, by which time they had been replaced by whistles. A few early pea whistles were used by some forces in the 1860s and 1870s until the standard Metropolitan police whistle, which was invented by Joseph Hudson of Birmingham, appeared in 1884. Its loud piercing screech could be heard for over half a mile, twice the distance of a rattle. Whistles soon became standard issue for all forces and remained in use until the late twentieth century when radios rendered them obsolete.

Left: **A nineteenth** century bullseye police oil lamp or lantern for use during the hours of darkness.

in constant use ever since. Police Constables have always been the mainstay of all British police forces.

The rank of Police Sergeant was adopted by all nineteenth century police forces. It was based upon the army rank of the same name and the duties were similar. It was the only military rank title to be used in any British police force. Police sergeants were responsible for the close supervision of constables, their personal appearance, cleanliness and conduct as well as ensuring that they performed their duties efficiently and effectively.

The rank of Police Inspector was a supervisory rank, adopted by all nineteenth century police forces. He was in charge of all the sergeants and police constables under his command. He had overall responsibility for the conduct and discipline of his staff and acted as a link and means of communication between the lower and high-ranking officers.

The rank immediately above that of inspector is a Chief Inspector, yet not all police forces adopted the rank. It varied from force to force both in railway forces and in municipal forces. Some forces also used the rank at intermittent times during their history. The tradition of use, non-use and partial use of this rank continued well into the twentieth century. When founded in 1829, the Metropolitan Police did not initially recognise the rank of Chief Inspector but introduced the rank into the force almost forty years later in 1868. Since the early 1930s, each division of the Metropolitan Police has had two chief inspectors, one in charge of administration and the other in charge of crime.

In 1992, the British Home Secretary, Kenneth Clarke, commissioned the Sheehy Inquiry to examine the rank structure of police forces in England and Wales. The inquiry recommended that the rank of Chief Inspector should be abolished. The report was widely condemned by the police, and it was eventually decided that the rank should be retained.

In home office or municipal police forces, the rank of Police Superintendent has always been the rank above Chief Inspector (or inspector in the absence of a chief inspector). The word Superintendent was originally derived from a sixteenth century ecclesiastical word of Latin origin (superintendere) meaning to supervise or oversee. A total of eight police superintendents were appointed in the Metropolitan Police when it was founded in 1829.

Railway police forces differed somewhat when it came to the rank of superintendent. When railway police forces were first introduced, the officer in overall charge was given the title Superintendent. As the nineteenth century progressed, a number of superintendents changed their titles to that of Chief of Police which became more common. The post of superintendent was still retained, but from 1923 onwards, it had become a rank below that of chief of police (and assistant chief) which had, by that time, been formally accepted as being the highest rank in all railway police forces.

Although non-existent in the nineteenth and early twentieth century, the rank of Chief Superintendent was first introduced into the Metropolitan Police in 1949. It soon became popular with other forces and is now widely used in all British police forces.

Commissioner of Police or Police Commissioner is the highest-ranking police officer and usually the head of an entire police force. The name has been adopted worldwide. In a few countries however, the name is sometimes used to denote the head of a single police station.

When the Metropolitan Police was founded in 1829, it was decided that not one, but two officers would be jointly in charge of the force and they were both given the rank or title of police commissioner. Lieutenant-Colonel Sir Charles Rowan KCB became the First Joint Commissioner and Sir Richard Mayne KCB was appointed as Second Joint Commissioner of the Force. They were both directly accountable to the Home Secretary. The practice of having two commissioners lasted until 1856, when both posts merged into just one. After that date, each Commissioner was provided with an Assistant Commissioner to assist him in his duties and take command of the force in his absence.

The square mile of the City of London, which is the primary central business district and the former historical Roman Londinium settlement area of London, has traditionally remained independent from the rest of the capital. In 1832, the City of London formed its own police force named the London City Police. Attempts were made almost immediately to merge the force with the new Metropolitan Police Force upon which it had been shaped. In order to stave off this threat, the City of London Police Act of 1839 was introduced which approved an independent police force for the City of London and the new City of London Police Force was founded. Like the Metropolitan Police, the chief police officer was given the title Commissioner of the City of London Police. All remaining municipal police forces in England and Wales are under the command of a Chief Constable and have never used the rank of Police Commissioner.

Railway Police Forces did not adopt the rank of Chief Constable in England and Wales during the nineteenth century but decided to introduce Chiefs of Police as their highest-ranking officers.

In Scotland however, things were slightly different. The first railway police force in Scotland was founded in 1838 on the Garnkirk and Glasgow Railway.

It is known that during the mid-nineteenth century, chief constables of some municipal police forces in Scotland were also appointed Chief Constable of their local Railway Police Force. William Anderson, Chief Constable of the Aberdeen Rural Constabulary for example, also served as Chief Constable of the Great North of Scotland Railway Police in the mid-nineteenth century.

Police forces with a chief constable in charge, invariably had an assistant chief constable (ACC) or a deputy chief constable to assist him or assume command in his absence. It was not until 1958 that a railway police force, namely the British Transport Commission Police, appointed its first chief constable. The rank has been continually used ever since and is still used by the British Transport Police.

The highest-ranking police officer in many countries, including the USA and Canada, is the Chief of Police, sometimes referred to as Police Chief, Chief Officer or just Chief. In Britain however, the rank of Chief of Police was not initially used by any police force. Directors of the Railway Companies who established their own private railway police forces in the nineteenth century opted to use Superintendent or Police Superintendent as the title for their most senior police officer. The title superintendent was also used to denote the heads of all railway departments and was in common use for heads of departments in most other organisations and industries for much of the nineteenth century.

Almost immediately, some of the railway police superintendents considered that as officers in charge of a police force, their rank should be more akin to those of their municipal or civil police counterparts, than the name used by the heads of railway and other industrial departments. As a result, some superintendents decided to change their titles. However, instead of adopting the title of Chief Constable or Police Commissioner, they preferred to use the title Chief of Police.

The first written evidence of this occurred in the eighteen forties, when an appointed superintendent, Thomas Manton, officer in charge of the Stockton and Darlington Railway Police, changed his title from Superintendent to that of Chief of Police. Later, in a routine letter sent to the Directors of the Railway Company, informing them that a man by the name of George Watkinson had been sentenced to fourteen years transportation for breaking into a railway cabin and stealing a coat, he referred to himself as Chief of Police. The letter dated 1 March 1848 was signed by Thomas Manton, Police Superintendent Chief of Police. The letter in question has been preserved in the National Archives.[8] As time progressed, more officers in charge of railway police forces changed their title to Chief of Police and some were referred to as both Superintendent and Chief of Police. Some such examples are mentioned in old newspapers which can be accessed via the newspaper archives.

During the early twentieth century, the title Chief of Police was quite widespread amongst railway police forces, so much so that when the railway groupings took place in 1923, the big four Railway Police Forces that emerged were each structured to be under the command of a Chief of Police and his assistant. The rank of superintendent was then officially retained as a rank below that of assistant chief of police. The rank Chief of Police was abolished in 1958 during the era of the BTC Police (see below), after the force decided to replace it with that of Chief Constable, in line with Home Office police forces.

Nationalisation of the railways and other private institutions in 1948 led to a new national police force emerging in Britain. Its purpose was to police the large number of transport undertakings, including the railways, docks, harbours, ports, canals and various other transport institutions and subsidiary companies. This national police force which became operational on 1 January 1949 was given the title the British Transport Commission (BTC) Police.

Initially, the most senior ranking officer of the BTC Police was that of Chief of Police, which had been the highest rank in the big four railway police forces prior to nationalisation. The Chief of Police selected to be in charge of the BTC Police Force was William Bertram Richards MVO, the former Chief of Police of the London, Midland and Scottish (LMS) Railway Police Force. Richards had over 4,000 officers under his command when he took charge of the BTC Police, which was the third largest police force in the country at that time. He retired from the force in 1955 and was replaced by Colonel Norman McKay Jesper MC, DSO, OBE, ERD, who had previously served as Chief Police Officer of the Southern Region of the BTC Police. Colonel Jesper himself retired in 1958 and Arthur Charles West OBE, KPM, the Chief Constable of the Portsmouth City Police, was appointed the first ever Chief Constable (replacing the title Chief of Police), of what was still primarily considered to be a railway police force. The BTC Police force was re-named the British Transport Police in 1963 and retained the title of Chief Constable for its highest-ranking officer. The British Transport Police still operates today under the command of a Chief Constable.

Because the British Transport Commission Police Force was a national police force with a jurisdiction covering the whole of England, Scotland, and Wales, it was divided into six regions, geographically similar to those of newly nationalised British Railways, which was founded on 1 January 1948.

A Regional Chief of Police (with an assistant) was placed in charge of each region, directly accountable to William Richards, the new Chief of Police for the whole force. Each region was then divided into Police Divisions, Police Sub-Divisions, Police Stations and Police Posts. The Regions of the BTC Force were later re-named Areas and the officers in charge of the former Regions, became Area Chiefs of Police and the title Regional Chief of Police was abolished. The title Area Chief of Police (and Assistant Area COP) was used for quite a number of years after the British Transport Police was founded in 1963, until that title too was abolished, in favour of the title Chief Superintendent, once again, in line with the ranks of Home Office Forces. Structural reforms continued for the remainder of the twentieth and into the twenty-first century, until, in April 2014, even more radical changes were introduced, which finally resulted in the structure of the British Transport Police Force as it is today.

The force currently operates under the control of a Chief Constable based in the Force Headquarters at Camden in North West London. The force consists of just three divisions, B, C and D, each of which is under the command of a chief superintendent. The three divisions (together with sub-divisions), cover geographical areas set out as follows: B covers London and the South East of England; C (the largest division), covers Pennine, Midlands, the whole of Wales and South West England (includes the cities of Birmingham, Leeds and Manchester); and D covers the whole of Scotland, with officers working under Scottish law and legislation. Since the formation of the British Transport Police in 1963, the force has seen a multitude of changes during its continuing development, yet it still remains the only exclusive railway police force in Britain.

Civil police forces have also experienced many changes and developments to keep pace with fluctuations in our society over the years, yet officers from both the British Transport Police and the Home Office forces have continued to work side by side. They train together and frequently work together, assisting each other where necessary. It could even be said that modern police officers, in all forces, have closer ties now than at any time in the past two hundred years, when it all started. In any event, hundreds of different police forces have existed in Britain since the early nineteenth century and countless numbers of devoted officers have dedicated their working lives to carry out a job intended to protect the public at large, fittingly described in the Gilbert and Sullivan operetta *The Pirates of Penzance*, written in 1879, 'When constabulary duty's to be done, to be done, a policeman's lot is not a happy one (happy one)'.

Chapter 3

RAILWAY CONSTRUCTION AND THE NAVVIES

The eighteen-thirties and forties saw a rapid expansion in railway construction. Thousands of navvies, some of whom were descendants of the former navigators who had constructed the canal networks a few decades earlier, were drafted in to build the railways. They were joined by local labourers and ex-soldiers from the Napoleonic wars. There were also vast numbers of immigrants from Ireland, many of whom were escaping poverty and later, fleeing the effects of the potato famine of 1845-1850. These navvies were often rough, hard drinking and sometimes violent individuals, who were forced to live in huts, shacks and tents alongside the railway. Many had brought their wives and children with them.

A butty gang of railway navvies laying railway track during the nineteenth century.

Whilst working, the navvies were divided into gangs called butty gangs which usually consisted of twelve men. There was no official gang foreman and all the men were considered to be of equal status. They did however jointly elect one member of the gang as an unofficial leader and spokesperson. He had the task of keeping the gang in check and collecting wages from the site superintendent to distribute equally amongst the men. The gangs were left to their own devices to sort out shirkers and lazy workers, which was usually done by fisticuffs.

The contractors who employed the navvies on behalf of the railway companies engaged site superintendents to oversee the work being carried out by the navvies as well as being responsible for their conduct and discipline. Any breaches of discipline or sub-standard workmanship was usually punished by instant dismissal. Most of the site superintendents were themselves tough men, very experienced and hard taskmasters. Their reputations often preceded them as they moved from site to site over the years.

As the railways expanded, these navvies moved through the length and breadth of the country, often wreaking havoc in their wake. Some large-scale

Nineteenth Century Navvies take time out to pose for a photograph.

projects, such as the building of tunnels or viaducts, often took several years to complete and whole shanty towns sprang up around these construction sites to accommodate the workers and their families. There was often rivalry and animosity between the Irish, English, Scottish and Welsh navvies, which frequently led to disturbances, fighting and sometimes rioting.

The railway companies frequently employed railway policemen and special constables during these turbulent times. Railway policemen often faced overwhelming numbers when dealing with incidents involving railway navvies and it was not uncommon for them to seek assistance from their local civil police colleagues, the local militia and in some cases the military itself when their own personal safety came under threat.

One such incident occurred during the height of railway construction in Britain, just outside Fushiebridge, about eleven miles south of Edinburgh in Scotland. This incident culminated in the murder of Police Constable Richard Pace, a police officer in the Edinburgh-Shire Constabulary, which existed at that time, and serious injury being inflicted upon Police Constable John Veitch, a railway policeman who was with him.

At about midnight on Saturday, 7 March 1846, two Irish navvies who were employed in the construction of a North British Railway branch line from Edinburgh to Hawick were arrested alongside the railway near Fushiebridge and taken into custody where they were charged with stealing watches belonging to non-Irish railway workers, who were also involved in the construction of the railway. They were lodged in the cells at the County Police Station at Gorebridge. Word of their arrest quickly spread amongst the community of Irish navvies, who resided in huts alongside the railway.

In the early hours of Sunday, 8 March, approximately 300 navvies armed with pickaxes, clubs and other weapons stormed the police station, demanding the release of their work colleagues. On duty inside the police station and in charge of the prisoners were Sergeant Brown, a railway police officer, and Constable Christie from the local County Constabulary. One of the navvies pointed a pistol to the head of Sergeant Brown and threatened to shoot him unless the prisoners were released. Police Constable Christie intervened but was attacked, sustaining extensive injuries in a severe beating by some of the men. Sergeant Brown still refused to unlock the cell, but the navvies broke open the cell door and released their comrades. The intruders and prisoners left the police station and marched in the direction of Fushiebridge some half a mile away, where they were met by Police Constable Richard Pace, the local

County Constabulary district patrol officer, who was being accompanied by John Veitch, a railway constable.

The two officers immediately came under a savage attack from the navvies and were both subject to serious assaults. One of the men struck Constable Pace on the back of his head with a pickaxe handle, causing a severe fracture to his skull which was split wide open. Constable Veitch was kicked and severely beaten before passing out on the side of the road. A short time later, two members of the public who were passing by found both officers lying unconscious. They summoned assistance from local residents and Police Constable Pace was carried home where he died shortly afterwards as a result of his injuries. Police Constable Veitch luckily survived the attack.

Later that morning, Sheriff Spiers and Sheriff Jamerson, two Sheriff Principals (Scottish court judges, also responsible for the administration of local justice), arrived at the scene, together with Superintendent List and officers of the Edinburgh-Shire County Police Force. They were accompanied by approximately twenty officers from the Edinburgh City and Railway Police Forces and sixty Scottish Dragoon Guardsmen from Edinburgh Castle Garrison. In total, some nineteen Irish navvies were arrested by police and with the assistance of the dragoons, they were escorted to Edinburgh gaol.

About forty dragoons and a large police presence remained in the area of the crime scene for the remainder of the day and throughout the Sunday night to prevent any further outrages taking place. This was due in part to a large number of Scottish and English workers threatening to take action against the Irish navvies to avenge their countrymen.

At about 8am on Monday, 9 March 1846, Scottish and English workers began to assemble in Edinburgh, determined to extract revenge on their Irish counterparts. Approximately 100 local pit workers from the Marquis of Lothian's coal mines joined them. They formed into a procession of over 1,000 in number, having armed themselves with a variety of weapons which included pick-shafts, spades, bludgeons and hammers. To the sound of music from bagpipes and bugles, the men marched south from Edinburgh. As the procession approached Fushiebridge, the Irishmen, seeing the large procession coming their way, took to their heels and fled. Disappointed in not having a fight with the Irish, the Scottish and English started to burn down the huts in which the Irish navvies were living alongside the railway. At Crichton Moor, they burned six or eight, before proceeding to Borthwick Castle where they burned a further dozen or so.

Although some thirty to forty police officers were present, owing to the overwhelming numbers of railway labourers they did not intervene but merely observed the riotous behaviour as the men continued to burn down the Irish huts. Fortunately, the wives of the Irish navvies were left alone and not harmed or molested by the mob. The women salvaged what few personal belongings and household utensils they could, before sitting down, dejected, beside the smoking ruins of their homes. The Scottish and English workers, having completed their work of destruction, disbanded and returned quietly to their homes by different routes.

Police and Dragoon Guardsmen spent another night at Fushiebridge to prevent any further incidents. In the meantime, a large number of Irish navvies who had earlier fled the Scottish and English workers began to congregate in the Cowgate public house in Edinburgh where they discussed paying the Scots and English back with interest.

Between eight and nine o'clock the following morning, the navvies began to pour from the Cowgate pub into the nearby streets. Most were under the influence of drink. They were armed with heavy sticks as they made their way along the public road towards Dalkeith, spreading fear and trepidation amongst the local population.

Having been advised of their movements in advance, the Sheriff, supported by a strong police and military presence, met the mob several miles from Edinburgh. The Sheriff remonstrated with them as to the impropriety of their conduct which, he said, would not be tolerated, advising them to return to Edinburgh and disband or suffer the consequences of their actions. After speaking to them at some length, they eventually capitulated. They were escorted part of the way back to Edinburgh by Superintendent List and the officers under his command.

The labourers eventually agreed to allow consultations between representatives acting on their behalf and the railway contractors who employed them, to try and settle their grievances and reach an amicable agreement to prevent further atrocities taking place. A further nine arrests were made that day in connection with burning the huts of the Irish, taking the total number of arrests to twenty-eight. Thirteen Irish navvies were also in custody for being engaged in the riot which ended in the murder of Police Constable Pace and the serious assault on Police Constable Veitch. Sheriff Spiers of Edinburgh later circulated details of two Irish Labourers wanted for questioning in relation to the murder of Constable Richard Pace and a reward of £50 (£6,000 today) was offered for information leading to their apprehension. The two suspects, who had left the area after the murder, were named as Patrick (Pat) Reilly and Peter Clark.

In the aftermath of the North British Railway riots of 1846, meetings were held between railway officials and contractors. Wilson and Moore were the contractors who employed the Irish workers and Graham and Sandison were responsible for employing the Scottish and English workers. Agreements were eventually reached for both sets of workers to return to work. The two men, Patrick Reilly and Peter Clark, who were thought to have carried out the brutal murder of PC Pace and the attempted murder of PC Veitch, were never seen or heard of again.

On 12 May 1846, nine of the Scottish and English contract workers named McQueen, McKillop, McLean, Grant, MacKay, McCracken, Morrison, Shaw and Henry Brown, appeared before the High Court in Edinburgh, charged with mobbing and rioting, fire-raising (burning the Irish huts), malicious mischief and assault. The charges against McLean were dismissed. The other accused were all convicted and sentenced to terms of imprisonment ranging from eight months for Shaw to two years for Henry Brown.

Navvies and horsepower were the order of the day when this picture was taken in the nineteenth century. Unfortunately, many of these fine animals were killed and injured by accidents in the quest to build Britain's railways.

It is a popular misconception that all railway navvies were men. Whilst the large majority were men, women workers also played a part in building the railways and there is little doubt that the rather large ladies in this picture would not take lightly to being referred to as the weaker sex.

In June that year, four Irish navvies appeared before the High Court in Edinburgh. They were all convicted of taking part in the first riot, which led to the murder of PC Pace. Lord Justice Clerk sentenced each of the men to seven years transportation.

Although the murder of PC Pace had close links to the railway and was undoubtedly committed by railway navvies, it was never officially classified as a railway murder as it did not occur on railway property.

Chapter 4

EARLY RAILWAY POLICEMEN

After the opening of the Liverpool and Manchester Railway in 1830, other railway companies started to emerge, quickly spreading all over the country. The two main railway companies founded in the 1830s were the London and Birmingham Railway which opened in 1838 and the Great Western Railway which opened in stages between 1838 and 1842. Both companies were given statutory powers to appoint police constables to serve on their respective railways. Section 213 of the London and Birmingham Railway Act of 1833 gave the company powers to appoint regular policemen and almost identical provisions were granted to the GWR by virtue of the Great Western Railway Act of 1835. Both Acts of Parliament stated that Railway Directors would nominate the constables they wished to appoint, who were then sworn in under oath by Justices of the Peace who actually made the appointments. The directors did however have sole powers to dismiss officers without the need to consult the justices. These two pieces of legislation were the first time that statutory powers had been granted to railway companies to appoint their own police officers. Neither the Stockton and Darlington Railway nor the Liverpool and Manchester Railway had been awarded such powers. Instead, they had used other enactments to appoint Special Constables to police their railways.

The railway construction era of the 1830s coincided with the introduction of the Special Constables Act of 1831. This Act of Parliament established the modern principles of employing special constables in Britain and gave them the necessary police powers to work alongside regular constables. The act effectively rendered previous legislation obsolete, but was tailor made for the new emerging railway companies wishing to employ police personnel and they wasted little time in taking full advantage of it. Unlike today where special constables are unpaid volunteers, the early railway police special constables were paid the same rates of pay as any other constable. Many of the smaller railway companies with the need for police in the early nineteenth century had no option other than to employ special constables because they were not specifically authorised by act of parliament to employ regular constables. In practice however, it made little difference, as the name special (as in special constable) was seldom used and the specials or special constables who policed the railways were routinely referred to simply as constables, railway constables, or railway policemen which is what they were perceived to be by ordinary members of the public. Railway special constables were routinely issued with the same uniforms and accoutrements as regular constables and, in reality, there was little difference between them.

By the mid-1840s, railway policemen in uniform were a common sight for travelling members of the public but the life of the early railway uniform constable was somewhat different to that of a modern British Transport Police Constable. Their duties certainly did not reflect those of a modern police officer and most of their time was spent engaged as uniformed railway officials assisting in the day to day running of the railways, rather than performing

Above left: **Depiction of** a London and South Western Railway Policeman wearing an early police uniform with a top hat. He is carrying an elaborately painted baton. Circa 1841.

Above right: **Picture depicting** a Great Western Railway Policeman operating an early slotted arm semaphore signal, circa 1844.

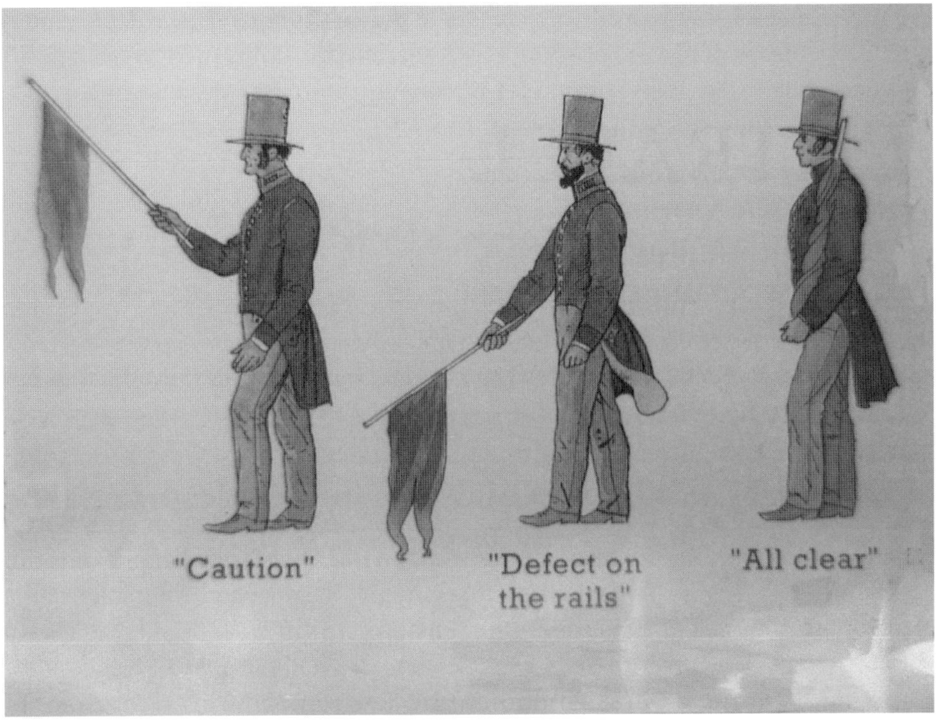

Early Railway Policemen • 37

One of the many early visual aids used by railway policemen. This one demonstrates some of the flag warning signals which were given to locomotive drivers by railway policemen during the 1830s and 1840s.

Depiction of an early Railway Policeman giving a white night-lamp signal to a locomotive driver. The lamp is being waved side to side, indicating that the line is clear to proceed. Railway lamps had a tricolour aspect. White (clear glass), red and green and the following simple associated rhyme explaining the colours was taught to railway staff. White is right (line clear), red is wrong (stop), green is gently go along (proceed with caution).

what people of today would consider to be police duties. When the Liverpool and Manchester Railway opened in 1830, railway policemen were posted alongside the railway line at regular intervals, approximately one mile apart, to ensure that the track was kept clear and free from any obstructions. They were responsible for controlling the movements of locomotives and trains with hand signals and later by using red and green flags. Early mechanical semaphore signals at the side of the track and level crossing gates were also operated by railway policemen.

As well as carrying out signalling duties, policemen operated track-side levers which controlled points at railway junctions. They were sometimes referred to as switchmen or pointsmen. This part of their job became known as point duty and railway policemen continued to perform this task for a number of years, until the introduction of efficient mechanical signalling systems rendered it unnecessary.

Many years later however, policemen and traffic wardens were once again performing point duty in cities and towns nationwide, not to control traffic on the railways, but in an effort to control the vast amounts of traffic introduced to our roads and highways. History repeated itself and point duty for constables directing road vehicles became obsolete as reliable mechanical signals in the form of traffic lights were introduced at busy road junctions to control road traffic.

As the nineteenth century railway network expanded further, more railway policemen were recruited, many of whom were stationed at level crossings where they were responsible for the opening and closing of crossing gates. Many hundreds of railway level crossings were built during the nineteenth century, so much so that a new post of crossing keeper was specifically introduced in the second half of the century which released railway policemen from these static to more fitting duties. The new job of crossing keeper was considered to be a very responsible job which ensured the safe and smooth running of the railways, so much so that houses were often built alongside level crossings for the use of crossing keepers and their families. These houses were rent free as they came with the job, to ensure that the crossings were manned twenty-four hours a day where necessary. Specific manning arrangements were agreed between each crossing keeper and the railway company who employed him. The company also ensured that relief crossing keepers could be made available at very short notice, to cover in the event of sickness or other unforeseen circumstances.

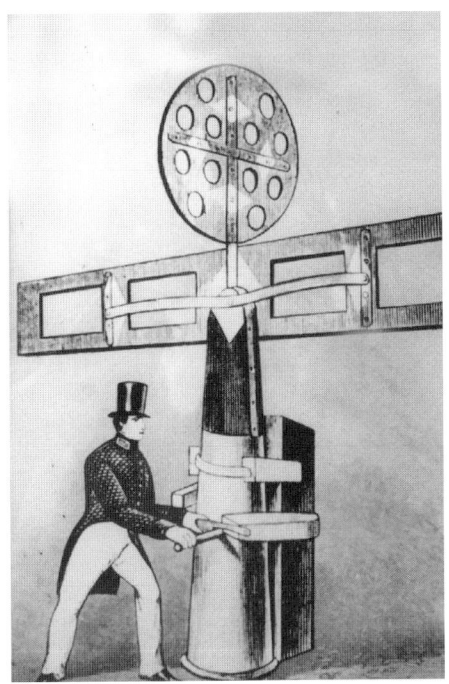 

Above left: **A Great** Western Railway Policeman operating a Brunel disc and crossbar signal in 1844. The disc was mounted on a spindle at right angles to the crossbar. When facing the locomotive, the disc indicated that the line was all clear and the crossbar was a signal to stop. This type of signal was introduced onto the GWR in 1838.

Above right: **A Railway** Policeman performing tunnel entrance duties with one arm outstretched, indicating that the line is clear, c.1844.

Early railway policemen performed other fixed post duties at locations such as tunnel entrances, approaches to bridges, viaducts and other strategic points. Lineside police sentry boxes were sometimes placed at these locations, to afford protection and shelter to the constables from the weather. These police sentry type boxes were very basic and whilst they gave shelter from heavy rain, they were inadequate for extreme cold and other adverse weather. One heart-rending incident took place at Taunton in Somerset on New Year's Eve in 1848. A Great Western Railway Constable, John King, effectively froze to death after spending a twelve-hour night shift inside a police sentry box on what was a bitterly cold winter's night. His body was discovered the following morning, New Year's Day 1849. No cause of death was formally

Above: **Depiction of** two Railway Policemen on the London to Birmingham Railway, shortly after it opened in September 1838. One is performing static bridge duties at Regent's Canal Railway Bridge, Camden Town and the other is guarding the train by sitting on top of it. A specific job of train guard was later introduced to replace policemen in this role. Guards were deemed to be in overall charge of the train and provided with a guard's van fitted with a hand-brake to assist the engine driver to slow down or stop where necessary.

Left: **An early** nineteenth-century railway police lineside sentry box, to afford protection from the weather for policemen performing fixed lineside duties. The box shown in the photograph is a replica which is on public display at the Didcot Centre Railway Museum.

established but it was believed that extreme cold led to his death. Accidental hypothermia was not generally recognised in the mid-nineteenth century and as a result, not attributed in this case. Police Constable King left a wife and four children.[9]

Lineside policemen were considered invaluable to successful train movements in the very early years of railway development. In 1841, the famous railway engineer Isambard Kingdom Brunel proudly told a Parliamentary Select Committee that there was an average of one and a half policemen per mile (including policemen at stations) on the whole of the Great Western Railway line from London to Bristol.

Whilst most lineside duties carried out by railway policemen were considered essential for maintaining railway safety during the early railway era, people were working tirelessly behind the scenes to create new mechanical innovations which would retain safety standards, whilst releasing railway policemen from the necessity to perform time consuming and costly static duties.

A major breakthrough, and what is considered by many to be the most important advancement in railway technology during the 1840s, was the introduction of the world's first successful electric telegraph system. This transformed the railways virtually overnight by enabling lineside signal boxes to communicate with each other to track the precise location of trains, as well as paving the way for modern signalling to be introduced. This new invention eventually allowed the static lineside duties performed by railway policemen to be dispensed with. Railway stations, depots and other railway departments also took full advantage of this new technology, which gave them instant interdepartmental communication to which distance was no barrier.

The first recognised commercial telegraph system in the world had been introduced onto the Great Western Railway in 1833 by Sir William Fothergill Cook and Charles Wheatstone. The system stretched some thirteen miles from Paddington to West Drayton. The cables used to operate the system were installed in an underground conduit. After proving to be an initial success, the insulation on the underground cables deteriorated and the telegraph system began to fail.

Undeterred by the failure, a new telegraph system was speedily installed, this time using overhead cables supported by telegraph poles. The first section of the new system was installed between Paddington and Slough, a distance of some 20 miles (32km), and was completed in 1843. It proved

Above left: **Photograph of** Sir William Fothergill Cook, early pioneer of the electric telegraph, 1830s.

Above right: **Photograph of** Charles Wheatstone, early pioneer of the electric telegraph, 1830s.

to be a complete success and by 1850, similar telegraph systems had been introduced on more than half of Britain's railway network.

The general public became aware of the true value of this new communications device a year after it had been installed, when on the 6 August 1844 a message was passed by the Great Western Railway telegraph system that Queen Victoria had given birth at Windsor Castle to her second son, Alfred, who would later become the Duke of Edinburgh. The message was quickly received in London to the jubilation of anxious Ministers and members of the public.

Although primarily designed for the day-to-day running of the railways, it was soon realised that the electric telegraph system had a wide range of other benefits to the country as a whole, which included detecting crime by affording assistance to police officers in their pursuit of dangerous criminals, particularly over long distances. In an ironic twist of fate, the GWR telegraph system itself was used for precisely that purpose, to solve a serious local crime which was committed at Slough, shortly after the electric telegraph had been installed on the Great Western Railway. The crime in question, a serious murder, entered the history books as being the first ever crime solved as a direct result of using the electric telegraph.

On New Year's Day 1845, a married man, John Tawell, murdered his mistress Sarah Hart by poisoning her, administering a quantity of hydrogen cyanide (prussic acid), which was contained in a medicinal compound, Scheele's acid, used in the treatment of varicose veins. Tawell had visited the home of Miss Hart in Salt Hill near Slough and laced a glass of stout with cyanide which she drank as they toasted the New Year. As the poison began to take effect, Tawell left the cottage and made his way to Slough railway station to catch a train home to London, leaving Miss Hart alone to suffer an agonising death. After he had left the cottage, Miss Hart somehow managed to raise the alarm by contacting the Reverend E.T. Champnes, her neighbour and a local vicar. She gave a description of Tawell to the reverend on her deathbed and as a result, he immediately made his way to Slough Railway Station. He arrived at Slough station just in time to see a man who he assumed to be Tawell boarding the 7.42pm train to London Paddington.

Without further ado, the reverend immediately summoned Mr Howell, the station master at Slough, who acted astutely and arranged for what was to become an historic telegraph message to be sent to Paddington. The message read:

> A murder has just been committed at Salt Hill and the suspected murderer was seen to take a first-class ticket for London by the train which left Slough at 7.42pm for London. He is in the garb [clothing] of a Quaker with a brown greatcoat on, which reaches down to his feet. He is in the last compartment of the second first-class carriage.

A short time later, the telegraph clerk at Slough received a reply to the telegram which read as follows:

> The up train has arrived and a person answering in every respect the description given by telegraph came out of the compartment mentioned. The man got into a New Road omnibus and Sergeant Williams into the same.

In the meantime, having received the original message at Paddington, the quick-thinking telegraph clerk handed the message to a telegraph messenger-boy, who ran to Police Sergeant Bill Williams of the Great Western Railway Police and handed him the message. Sergeant Williams placed a civilian coat over his uniform and met the train when it arrived from Slough. Sergeant Williams saw a person matching the description he had been given alight from a first-class compartment of the train. Tawell left the station and boarded a horse drawn bus, followed by Sergeant Williams. After travelling across London, Tawell alighted from the bus on the corner of Princess Street in the City and eventually entered a lodging-house in Scott's Yard near Cannon Street. Sergeant Williams followed discreetly, taking care not to arouse Tawell's suspicions.

After satisfying himself that the lodging house was Tawell's home, Sergeant Williams returned to Paddington to confirm the authenticity of the telegram and ensure that a murder had in fact taken place. After confirming these facts, Sergeant Williams liaised with Inspector Wiggins of the Metropolitan Police at Paddington Green police station.

The following morning, Inspector Wiggins, in company with Sergeant Williams, visited the lodging house in Scott's Yard but Tawell was not at home. Shortly afterwards, Sergeant Williams spotted Tawell having breakfast in the nearby Jerusalem Coffee House. Inspector Wiggins entered the coffee house and escorted Tawell from the premises, whilst Sergeant Williams waited outside. Tawell denied being in Slough the previous day and also denied knowing anyone who lived there. He denied all knowledge of the murder which had taken place. Sergeant Williams identified Tawell as the person he had seen alighting from the train at Paddington the previous day and who he followed to the address in Scott's Yard. As a result, Inspector Wiggins arrested Tawell.

John Tawell appeared before the Aylesbury Assize Court on 12 March 1845, where he pleaded not guilty to a charge of the wilful murder of Sarah Hart. He was subsequently found guilty by the jury and sentenced to death by hanging. On the 28 March the sentence was carried out at Aylesbury before a crowd of over 2,000 spectators. Prior to the execution taking place, Tawell made a full written confession in the presence of a priest, which included the fact that he had made another unsuccessful attempt to murder Miss Hart the previous September. John Tawell had made history as being the first criminal ever to have been apprehended as a direct result of the electric telegraph.

The electric telegraph played a huge part in the success of the railways in Britain and as a result of instant communication nationwide, the concept of time in Britain changed as people knew it. The question of time in relation to

Artist's impression of John Tawell, hanged for murder in 1845.

travel had been studied during the 1830s whilst Cook and Wheatstone were perfecting their electric telegraph system. It was quickly realised that when transmitting messages over long distances, the person sending the message and the person receiving it could well be in different time zones which was still being calculated by the relative position of the sun. For example, if a message was sent on the Great Western Railway telegraph system from Paddington to Bristol, the time difference was ten minutes. This anomaly was not conducive to operating railway timetables for running trains. As a result, the Great Western Railway introduced what was called Railway Time onto the

Great Western Railway in 1840. Railway time was based on Greenwich Mean Time which was set in London by the Royal Observatory in Greenwich. All clocks on the Great Western Railway network were synchronised to railway time in November of that year.

Other railway companies were quick to follow suit and, by 1848, all the railways in Britain were operating on railway time, though it took a further decade before all the towns and cities had adopted railway time as being the official time in Britain. In 1880 however, a letter was published in *The Times* newspaper from a clerk to the justices suggesting that railway time had no legal status in law. This resulted in the swift passage through parliament of the Statutes (Definition of Time) Act 1880, which received royal assent the same year. The act officially adopted Greenwich Mean as the official standard time for the whole of the UK. The term Greenwich Mean Time was soon embraced by people all over Britain and Railway Time was quickly forgotten before being confined to the history books. By the end of the 1850s, railway policemen were no longer seen at regular intervals along the track, neither were they waving flags or giving hand signals to train drivers. Instead, their focus was to protect members of the public and railway staff whilst concentrating on maintaining law and order, assisting passengers and dealing with accidents.

The trackside buildings initially occupied by policemen were replaced by signal boxes which were built in an elevated position, affording excellent views of the railway and surrounding areas. Mechanical signal levers and cables were able to operate a number of signals and track points from one signal box and the various signal boxes had instant communication with each other by the telegraph system which afforded instant control over traffic movements.

By 1852, over 7,000 miles of track had been laid in Britain.[10] This continued to expand rapidly, reaching 22,000 miles by the turn of the century,[11] by which time the railway network housed over 130 separate railway companies[12] which employed over 3,000 railway policemen. The civil police, which evolved simultaneously with the railway police over the same 70-year period, had amassed 181 separate police forces[13] which employed over 60,000 police officers.[14]

The increases in population of the towns and cities in the second half of the nineteenth century, and the increase in the size of the railway network during the same period, inevitably led to an increase in crime. It had become apparent as early as the 1830s that police forces could no longer rely upon

Early Railway Policemen • 47

Depiction of a Railway Signal Box being operated by a railway policeman in 1851. After the introduction of the electric telegraph system and more advanced signalling techniques, highly trained signalmen were introduced to replace railway policemen who were no longer required to perform signalling duties by the end of the decade. Early signal boxes, consisting of an elevated hut on a platform like the one illustrated above, were introduced from 1846 onwards to operate signals. The more traditional British railway two storey structures with mechanical leavers to operate both signals and points upstairs, above a room which housed the interlocking mechanism, evolved in the 1860s.

the visible presence of uniformed officers alone to control and prevent crime. Additional resources were needed to deal exclusively with investigating unsolved crimes and detecting the offenders. This resulted in the introduction of policemen dressed in civilian clothes as opposed to uniforms. They were given the titles detectives or plain clothes policemen and they operated out of detective departments.

The Metropolitan Police set up a detective department in 1842 when they appointed eight detectives to investigate unsolved crimes and from the mid-nineteenth century onwards, other forces followed suit. The first police force to use the name Criminal Investigation Department (CID) was the Nottingham Borough Constabulary when they established one in 1854. The department was initially manned with a superintendent and four detective constables. Other forces soon started to establish their own CID. It was not until 1878 that the Metropolitan Police created a CID to replace their detective department, although in reality, it was little more than a name change.

The railway police forces started using plain clothes constables and detectives in the early 1840s to investigate frauds and other unsolved crimes. These officers were initially used on an ad hoc basis by different railway forces until more formal standardised departments were created in the 1860s. These departments were referred to by two different names depending on the force they belonged to. Most railway forces created detective departments in which detectives were employed. These were fashioned on the one being used by the Metropolitan Police. The first railway police force to set up a formal detective department was the London and North Western Railway police in 1863. Some railway forces however, decided to refer to their plain clothes departments as special departments and officers serving in the special departments were referred to as special police (not to be confused with special constables who were uniformed officers). The first special department was set up by the Great Western Railway police in 1864. Both of these departments were later renamed Criminal Investigation Departments (CID) in line with civil police forces, rendering the names special and detective departments obsolete. By the late nineteenth century, Criminal Investigation Departments were well and truly established in all forces throughout Britain and they were an important aspect of British policing, as were the detectives working within those departments.

Railway detectives in the nineteenth century spent their time investigating serious crimes such as robbery, serious assaults and endangering the safety and lives of passengers, as well as fraud, thefts, forgery and revenue offences.

They were also involved in investigating serious accidents and other major incidents.

Detectives continued to work into the twentieth century using the same methods to detect crime as they had done in the nineteenth. In 1902, however, things were about to change when Harry Jackson appeared before the Central Criminal Court (the Old Bailey) in London, where he was sentenced to seven years imprisonment after being found guilty of an offence of burglary. Jackson's conviction was based solely on fingerprint evidence; the first person ever to have been convicted in a British Court of Law on fingerprint evidence alone. This case was unique and a game changer for detectives engaged in the investigation of crime. Other convictions involving fingerprint evidence quickly followed and fingerprint evidence has continued to be the bread and butter for detectives involved in the solving of crimes ever since.

Advances in forensic science continued, resulting in the discovery and use of Deoxyribonucleic Acid (DNA) Profiling, which first appeared on the scene in the mid-1980s. This is a much more sophisticated method of identifying criminals than the use of fingerprinting. DNA is considered by many to be the greatest forensic science discovery of all time and is now an integral part of forensic science, medical science and other important scientific developments worldwide.

Whilst the railway detectives moved into the twentieth century, anticipating little change to their day-to-day duties, the uniformed railway policemen had little or no idea what lay ahead, after having experienced a multitude of changes during the nineteenth century.

During the nineteenth century and in particular the early years of the railways, it must have seemed like mayhem at times for railway policemen starting work for the first time. After being sworn in as a constable, little initial police training was given and few guidelines were issued as to what their job actually entailed. Railway policemen were just thrown in at the deep end and expected to perform a multitude of different jobs as the need arose. They issued train tickets, worked as ticket collectors, train guards, crossing keepers, timekeepers and signalmen. They were expected to deal with accidents, maintain law and order and investigate crime. They were without doubt Jacks of all trades, a far cry from what people today would consider to be policemen. Having said that, their work at that time was considered essential and a vital part of keeping the railways running.

Fortunately, those early Jacks became Bobbies as the nineteenth century progressed and the railways developed further. Many of their early duties were abolished as a result of new technology and automation. New members of staff were specifically trained to work as booking clerks, ticket collectors, crossing keepers, train guards and signalmen. Railway policemen were then able to concentrate on their main aim which was maintaining law and order, preserving the peace, protecting lives and property as well as preventing and detecting crime.

During the twentieth century, the role of the railway policemen became much more defined and railway police forces became more professional. Many changes continued to be made during the twentieth century, as one would expect, and police training improved considerably. Practices were standardised amongst the various railway police forces and close cooperation and exchanges of ideas took place.

After 1923, the Big Four railway companies emerged, each with their own police force, yet the serving officers within those forces faced anguish, as they struggled to deal with industrial unrest and large-scale public disorder, leading up to the General Strike of 1926. Police morale was low and continued as such whilst officers struggled to cope through the Great Depression of the late 1920s and early 1930s. After this, officers serving in the railway police forces experienced some happier times as the railways began to flourish and they experienced what many consider to be the golden years of the railways. Unfortunately, this jubilant period was short lived and soon interrupted by the outbreak of the Second World War in September 1939. In 1948, the railways were nationalised and the stage was set for the creation of the first ever national railway police force in Britain - the British Transport Commission Police.

-

Chapter 5

NINETEENTH CENTURY RAILWAY CRIME

One of the most important jobs of a policeman is the prevention and detection of crime and for the nineteenth century railway policemen there was an abundance and wide variety of crime for them to deal with. One of the earliest forms of crime on the railway was that of theft, or larceny as it was called in the nineteenth century. The fact that the railways were originally built for the transportation of goods meant that all manner of goods in transit were left unattended and as such were easy pickings for anyone intent on stealing them. This was one of the reasons why railway policemen were engaged in the first place.

Modern railways can pick and choose what type of goods, if any, they transport and are free to select the types of customers they deal with. For the early railway companies, things were very different. In 1830, the passing of the Carriers Act proclaimed railway companies to be common carriers of goods upon the railway. The act stipulated that railway companies were bound to accept certain goods whenever offered, to be transported upon the railway and in the event of them being lost for any reason (which included being stolen), they were obliged to pay compensation. After all, the railways were purpose built for transporting goods and freight in order to obtain their revenue. The thought of carrying people on the railway was not really considered when railways were planned and certainly was not a determining factor when they were built.

The subsequent thirst for travel on the railways by ordinary members of the public occurred after the railways became operational and was an unexpected windfall for the railway companies and an added bonus for investors. Railway companies were more than happy to accommodate eager passengers wishing to travel, even though the transportation of passengers brought about some additional problems which railway policemen usually had to deal with. Unattended items of luggage and personal belongings being carried by passengers became an easy target for thieves who were quick to take advantage of the situation. As a result, early railway policemen were committed to investigating both thefts of luggage and personal effects from passengers as well as goods in transit.

The first ever goods recorded as being stolen in transit by train on a public railway anywhere in the world were stolen from the Stockton and Darlington Railway in 1826. Two separate parcels were stolen on 14 November 1826, just over twelve months after the railway opened. Both items were being transported by train to Bishop Auckland in County Durham. One of the items, a bale of drapery linen, was being sent to William Barratt and the other was a parcel being sent to Richard Spencer, both of whom lived in Bishop Auckland. A brief mention of the incidents appeared in the *Durham County Advertiser* on 18 November that year.[15] Although these two matters may seem minor and insignificant, they were just the start of what was to become a serious problem for all railway operating companies and railway policemen alike. Thefts of items in transit by train soon became a very serious problem indeed.

As early as the 1830s, railway policemen quickly became aware that this new type of crime not only attracted career criminals and opportunists but also railway officials and employees who could not resist the temptation to steal items which were passing through their hands in the course of their daily duties. One such example of so-called trusted employees abusing their position occurred in November 1880, when detectives of the Manchester, Sheffield and Lincolnshire Railway Police performed night observation duties at the parcels depot at Manchester London Road Railway Station (now Manchester Piccadilly), following complaints of goods missing in transit.

The two people whom the detectives suspected of being involved in these crimes were Thomas Wilson and John Lee, both employed as clerks in the parcels depot. On two successive nights, detectives watched as the two men closely inspected almost every single parcel that passed through the depot. On the third night, the men were seen interfering with some boxes which contained perishable goods in transit. They were in fact, shellfish. Wilson and Lee began to remove some oysters from a package and started eating them, before throwing the shells into the fire. Later that evening, Wilson left the office and Lee, being alone, was seen to open another parcel and steal a musical accordion from a box. When Wilson returned to the office, both men were arrested on suspicion of stealing goods in transit. Early the following morning, a search of their homes was carried out and a large quantity of items believed to have been stolen from the railway were recovered.

As enquiries continued, railway detectives turned their attention to the local railway carters who were employed to drive horse drawn wagons and carts around Manchester delivering parcels which had arrived by train and collecting consignments to be sent by train from Manchester to other destinations. One such carter was Albert Earnshaw, who was being observed by detectives as he opened a parcel of books in the back of his van. He had picked up the books earlier from the firm of Messrs J. Heywood & Co. to be taken to the parcels office for despatch by train.

Earnshaw was later arrested and questioned in relation to other items which had been stolen after leaving the parcels depot for local delivery. One particular item was a gold watch in transit which had arrived by train at the parcels office for local delivery by road to its destination in Brown Street, Manchester. After being received at the parcels office, it had subsequently gone missing and was never delivered. Earnshaw eventually admitted stealing the watch which he gave to his girlfriend as a gift. She did not know that the watch was stolen. The watch was later recovered by detectives.

On Thursday, 25 November 1880, the three men appeared in court in Manchester. Wilson and Lee both pleaded not guilty to a number of charges of stealing items in transit. Wilson was found guilty on two counts of larceny and Lee was found guilty on three similar counts. Wilson was sentenced to six months imprisonment with hard labour and Lee was sentenced to eight months imprisonment with hard labour.

Albert Earnshaw, who had been employed by the Company for eleven years, pleaded guilty to stealing the gold watch and other items. He was sentenced to nine months imprisonment with hard labour. All railway employees convicted of such offences were instantly dismissed.

Not all goods stolen in transit involved railway employees, far from it. Goods in transit on the railways were often considered easy pickings for a wide range of individuals, ranging from opportunists to professional or semi-professional thieves and even organised gangs of thieves.

Perhaps the most common method used to steal goods in transit on the railways during the nineteenth century was to simply enter a goods yard, depot or railway sidings, break any seals or padlocks on vans and wagons stabled there and just remove a variety of items whilst they were unattended. These offences were often carried out by gangs of thieves who frequently targeted such items as cigarettes, wine, spirits and beer which were easily disposed of. Many of the gangs were career criminals who planned raids on vans very carefully, usually operating after dark, particularly at weekends and bank holidays when the chances of being disturbed by railway staff was minimal.

It should also be remembered that the quantity of goods transported by rail today is just a fraction of the freight which was carried during the nineteenth and early twentieth centuries. There were no motorways until the end of the 1950s and the amount of goods transported by road was miniscule compared with the railways.

Millions of wagons and vans were in constant use on Britain's railway network at any given time during the nineteenth century. Some were empty but large numbers which were loaded with all manner of goods were often left standing unattended in railway sidings at various stages of transportation, awaiting shunting into train formations for particular destinations. Railway road vehicles collecting and delivering goods in towns and cities were at their most vulnerable whilst stationary and unattended, luring thieves, which was a constant cause of concern for both the railway companies and railway policemen alike.

It was not just stealing goods from vans or wagons which was of concern, an array of goods were regularly stolen from all over the railway network and in some cases it was the most unlikely items that went missing. Who, in their right mind for example, would want to steal a bale of hay from the railway or curtains from train compartments? It did happen.

On 10 November 1828, Mr Longstaff, a carter on the Stockton and Darlington Railway, left twelve bales of hay on the railway just outside Darlington. When he returned the following day, he discovered that one of the bales was missing. Enquiries were made and it was established that someone had witnessed two men making up small bundles of hay from one of the bales shortly after it had been left there. After tying the bundles with rope, the men were seen to place them into an empty railway wagon which was stabled nearby. A search of the wagon was subsequently made, and a number of bundles of hay were found. It appeared that they had been placed in the disused wagon to conceal them. Thomas Edwards, aged 27, and William Hilton, aged 26, from the village of Heighington, near Darlington, were subsequently arrested by railway police after they later returned to the scene to collect the stolen hay. They were charged with stealing the bale of hay and a quantity of rope. Both denied the offence and pleaded not guilty in court but were committed to stand trial at the next quarter sessions.

On Tuesday 13 January 1829, Edwards and Hilton appeared before the Durham Epiphany Sessions (Quarter Sessions) in Darlington, charged with stealing the hay and rope from the Stockton and Darlington Railway. After the hearing, the jury delivered a guilty verdict against both defendants. The court heard that Edwards had previously been convicted of a felony. He received seven years transportation. Hilton, who was of previous good character, was imprisoned in the house of correction for six calendar months. The severity of sentencing a person to seven years transportation for stealing some hay seems extremely harsh and inconceivable in today's society.

It also seems quite bizarre that someone would want to steal a pair of curtains from a railway carriage, but they did. In March 1877, a seamstress was arrested by Lancashire and Yorkshire Railway Police investigating the theft of curtains which were occurring from railway carriages. It transpired that the woman had been stealing the curtains in order to use the material to make clothing which she later sold. Her downfall was brought about when she tried to pawn a skirt which bore the Lancashire and Yorkshire Railway crest on the front of it. She was sentenced to three months imprisonment by Liverpool Magistrates.

Unattended parcels stacked on barrows on railway platforms was another common sight on all railway stations during the nineteenth and twentieth centuries and something that many opportunists could not resist. Usually, people would use some discretion to ensure that the coast was clear before helping themselves, unless they were really stupid, or perhaps had consumed one drink too many!

On Sunday 28 September 1889, Police Constable Boulton of the Barry Railway Police was on duty in uniform at Cadoxton railway station, near Penarth in South Wales, when he saw Thomas Bumford pick up a parcel from a barrow on the station platform and walk away with it. William Regan, a railway porter, also witnessed the incident. Constable Boulton arrested Bumford, who, when questioned about the parcel, said, 'I've been drinking. I don't know anything about it.' The parcel which was being conveyed on the railway contained a suit of clothes. Bumford was sentenced to two months hard labour.

It was not only adults who stole from the railways, a great many children were also apprehended. Sentences for children varied. Some justices were compassionate towards children, whilst others did not believe in a lenient approach and considered the short sharp shock of corporal punishment to be the answer, as 9-year-old Joseph Cleaver was to become all too painfully aware after his brush with the law. On Friday 9 August 1872, Cleaver was caught stealing a small quantity of coal from a railway wagon belonging to the Newport Pagnell Railway Company. He appeared before Newport Pagnell Magistrates a week later where he was sentenced to be flogged with eight strokes of the rod and imprisoned for one day. The sentence was later carried out.

Stealing coal from the railway was extremely common during the nineteenth century and there was an abundance of coal on the railway to steal; it seemed to be lying about everywhere. Large scale thefts of coal were quite rare, the reason being, that coal was plentiful and used by almost every household in the land. Coal was delivered on horse drawn carts by local coal merchants and anyone attempting to sell large quantities of cheap stolen coal would quickly attract attention to themselves. It followed therefore that most of the coal stolen was generally stolen in small quantities for household consumption, often by people who could ill afford to buy it or as a means of saving money.

Although stealing coal from the railway was commonplace, one must not forget the potential dangers involved. One such example came to light at Newport in South Wales in 1891 when a housewife appeared in court for stealing coal from the railway because she could not afford to buy it.

On 20 May 1891, Mrs Helena Stamburgh appeared before Newport Magistrates Court, charged with stealing coal from the Dock Street Sidings of the Great Western Railway on 20 April that year. The court heard that Mrs Stamburgh was picking up coal which had fallen from the top of coal wagons, when she was caught between the buffers of two wagons which had been put in motion by shunting operations. As a result, she suffered two broken ribs, a crushed arm and had been laid up for one month under the care of a doctor. She pleaded guilty to stealing coal but told the court that she could not afford to buy it, her husband was out of work at the time and because of her injuries, she considered that she had already suffered enough. The court agreed and after reiterating the dangers of going on to the railway, sentenced her to just one day imprisonment.

Stealing or interfering with the Royal Mail has always been considered to be a serious offence wherever it has taken place and some harsh sentences have been handed out to transgressors. When the first railways were built, they seemed tailor-made for transporting the Royal Mail and the Post Office wasted little time in making full use of them.

Royal Mail horse drawn coaches started operating between Bristol and London in 1784 and other routes soon followed. In 1830, however, the monopoly of using horse-drawn coaches to transport the nation's mail was about to change. September 1830 saw the opening of the Liverpool to

Manchester railway and it took just less than three weeks before the Royal Mail was conveyed by railway for the first time, following an agreement between the Liverpool and Manchester Railway Company and the Post Office. The construction of other railways quickly followed and railway company directors sought the lucrative trade of transporting the Royal Mail by offering their services to the Post Office. The Railways (Conveyance of Mails) Act of 1838 set out the procedures to be adopted in transporting Royal Mail by railway. It gave powers to the Postmaster General and set out obligations to the railway operating companies. A rapid increase in mail being transported by trains took place during the late 1830s and 1840s, which resulted in the withdrawal of the last main horse-drawn mail coaching route to Norwich in 1846. Whilst a few regional royal mail horse-drawn carriages continued to operate into the 1850s, they were soon phased out completely and replaced by the railways.

With the acceptance of Royal Mail onto the railways came the responsibility of protecting it. This, in the main, became another important task to fall within the remit of the various railway police forces. Fortunately, there were no serious problems with security surrounding the Royal Mail during the nineteenth century due in part to the high number of railway and postal staff in the vicinity of the many thousands of mailbags which were being transported daily. Mailbags were left unattended on station platforms, usually for short periods of time and although opportunist thieves did take advantage of this fact on occasions, it was a risky business as they immediately aroused suspicion if they were seen carrying a mail bag for even a short distance. A number of mailbags were however stolen, often by railway employees or former employees and despite using their inside knowledge, many were apprehended and invariably received sentences of imprisonment.

During the early twentieth century, the Royal Mail continued to be transported by train without any serious problems and railway detectives worked closely with post office investigation branch officials in an endeavour to apprehend any criminals who were actively involved in stealing it. Nonetheless, from the mid-1950s, thefts of mailbags from the railway started to steadily increase, until it did become a serious concern for both Post Office officials and officers of the British Transport Commission Police, the body responsible for policing the railways at that time.

In the early 1960s, a special team of detectives dubbed the mail bag squad, operating from the BTC Police Force Headquarters in London, was set up to combat the stealing of mail bags. However, following a large increase in post office losses on the railway, it soon became apparent that a few specialist gangs of thieves were repeatedly targeting the railway networks specifically to steal the Royal Mail. The worst affected area was on the Southern Region of British Railways, where trains operating between London and the South Coast were being repeatedly targeted by one specific gang of thieves who police labelled the South Coast Raiders.

The British Transport Commission Police was renamed the British Transport Police from 1 January 1963. The new regime continued policing the railways in the same vein as the BTC Police had done and incidents involving the thefts of post office mailbags continued to be a major concern. This concern was well founded, as members of the South Coast Raiders were already joining forces with another mob. Their ultimate target was the Glasgow to Euston mail train. This combined gang of thieves began to plan their future and moved their activities from the Southern Region of British Railways to the London Midland Region. Their first target was the Irish Mail train which carried high-value mail from London, Euston, to Holyhead, bound for Ireland by ferry. The train consisted of fourteen coaches. Twelve were compartment passenger coaches with a sleeping car coach in front and a guard's coach at the rear of the train. The guard's coach contained the post office mailbags, including the high value mail.

The gang had established that during the train journey, shortly after leaving Euston, the guard would lock his van and walk through the corridor of the train with a ticket collector, to examine the tickets of passengers. The guard's van was locked and unattended for about forty-five minutes. It was decided that, during this time, members of the gang would break into the guard's van and steal items of value from the mail bags. In the meantime, other gang members would cover a green signal light on the railway track at a location near Hemel Hempstead in Hertfordshire and place a red lamp next to it, to stop the train. When the train came to a halt the gang members on the train would alight with their ill-gotten gains and make good their escape. The plan was simple, yet ingenious.

At 8.40pm on Wednesday, 20 February 1963, the Irish Mail Train departed Euston on time. The plan to steal the mail was put into action but the weather conditions were atrocious with heavy snowfalls. As a result of the adverse weather, there were very few passengers on the train that evening. Consequently, the train guard Hywel Owen and the ticket collector Tom Thomas had checked all the tickets and returned to the guard's van within about twenty minutes instead of the usual forty-five. Guard Owen immediately realised that the guard's van door had been forcibly opened and upon entering, followed by ticket collector Thomas, they disturbed the gang rifling the mailbags. The two men were beaten and tied up by gang members inside the van. Shortly afterwards, other gang members on the lineside were successful in stopping the train and even though the gang members on the train had been disturbed by Owen and Thomas, they alighted from the train, having successfully stolen cash and some diamonds estimated to have been valued at about £3,000 (approximately £66,000 today). The gang did make good their escape, together with their ill-gotten gains. As far as the gang members were concerned, the Irish Mail Train robbery was largely a success and they continued their plans to execute their ultimate assignment, the infamous Great Train Robbery, referred to by many people as the crime of the twentieth century.

On Thursday, 8 August 1963, the audacious gang carried out their next attack on the Glasgow to Euston Travelling Post Office mail train at Ledburn in Buckinghamshire and made off with approximately 100 mailbags containing £2.6 million in used banknotes (over £56 million today). Full details of the Great Train Robbery have been the subject of so many films, books and documentaries that I do not propose to repeat the specific facts in this book, except to say that although the bulk of the money was never recovered, eleven men were later convicted of offences involving conspiracy to rob the Royal Mail, for which they received heavy sentences of up to thirty years imprisonment. These sentences reflected the seriousness attached to stealing Her Majesty's Royal Mail.

In the aftermath of the robbery, British Transport Police officers manned all Travelling Post Office trains for a number of years to prevent any re-occurrence taking place, although this course of action was deemed by many as closing the stable door after the horse had bolted. The Post Office stopped using the railways for transporting the Royal Mail in 2004, due to rising costs. It is now transported by road.

Another form of stealing which nineteenth-century railway policemen often encountered was the removal of items from the person, or pickpocketing as it was commonly called. Pickpocketing was an extremely common crime in the nineteenth century, occurring on an almost daily basis. Pickpockets were usually found wherever crowds of people gathered, such as fairgrounds, markets, race meetings, theatres and of course, railway stations. Many of the railway pickpockets were career criminals often well known to police as they travelled up and down the country, stealing from unsuspecting members of the public at every opportunity.

The art of pickpocketing was often practised by boys from a young age in the nineteenth century as famously portrayed in the 1838 novel *Oliver Twist* by Charles Dickens. These impoverished boys often continued their criminal activities throughout their lives and were generally well known to police. Railway pickpockets were no exception. They favoured the railways due to the crowds of people who travelled daily. Young men frequently travelled on crowded trains which were taking passengers to and from race meetings and other sporting events where rich pickings could be found. Football supporters became easy targets towards the end of the nineteenth century as they returned home from matches after celebrating success or drowning their sorrows in defeat. Some pickpockets preferred to work alone whilst others worked in teams or gangs. The judiciary viewed pickpockets with contempt and severe sentences were often handed out to persistent offenders.

A typical example of early pickpocketing and subsequent sentencing which occurred on the railway took place in September 1849 when Mrs Elizabeth Young travelled by train from Croydon to London Bridge on the London, Brighton and South Coast Railway. Shortly after leaving London Bridge Station, she felt a tug on her clothing. She turned around and saw two men. One of the men introduced himself as a railway detective and the man with him was Michael Daley who was under arrest. The officer told Mrs Young that Daley had stolen her purse whilst she was leaving the railway station. Mrs Young checked and found that her purse containing 8 shillings and 10 pence had indeed been stolen. The purse and contents were found in the possession of Daley. It transpired that Daley was part of a gang of pickpockets operating on London Bridge Station that day and as a result of a number of recent complaints from members of the public, railway detectives had been observing the station in an attempt to apprehend offenders. Daley had been seen approaching several female passengers before removing the purse of Mrs Young. Michael Daley, who had several previous convictions for pickpocketing, appeared before the Surrey Quarter Sessions on Thursday 25 October 1849 and was sentenced to seven years transportation.

Transportation as a punishment in Britain was abolished after the Penal Servitude Act of 1857, although some convicts continued to be transported until 1868 when the last ever transportation took place from Britain. After that, incarceration with hard labour or penal servitude as it was called was a favoured sentence handed out to criminals convicted of what were considered to be serious crimes, including that of pickpocketing.

As mentioned earlier, pickpockets often started their trade at a tender age and whilst the majority of these pickpockets were young boys, girls were sometimes found to be the culprits. Ordinary railway passengers may view some young men with suspicion but would seldom give a young girl a second glance if she was tagging along behind or alongside another female passenger. One young girl used this trait, together with the hustle and bustle of Glasgow Buchanan Street Station, to her advantage. An inconspicuous 13-year-old, Janet Macfarlane, was sent to Glasgow Reformatory for five years in July 1899, after stealing purses containing substantial sums of money, by picking the pockets of well-dressed ladies as they passed through the station. A police spokesman told the court that despite her tender years, she was one of the most expert pickpockets they had ever encountered.

Of the numerous pickpockets operating on the railways during the nineteenth century, some were very successful, making a lucrative living out of the proceeds. Many however were not as clever or as accomplished as the professionals yet continued to ply their trade. Railway Police forces often had teams of plain clothes constables or detectives specially trained for detecting and apprehending pickpockets, or dips as they were often referred to, and these teams of officers had considerable success in apprehending perpetrators. For obvious reasons, pickpockets did not usually operate in close proximity to police officers in uniform. Having said that, some uniformed officers did apprehend pickpockets.

One such example occurred at Sunderland in 1894, when an experienced and vigilant uniform sergeant from the North Eastern Railway Police was carrying out his daily duties. On Monday 29 January 1894, an elderly-looking man, Robert Knight, appeared before the Sunderland Magistrates, charged with attempting to pick pockets at Sunderland Central Railway Station the previous Saturday night. Knight pleaded guilty to the charge against him.

Sergeant James Smith of the North Eastern Railway Police told the court that he was on duty at the station on the night in question when he became suspicious of the prisoner's movements. He saw him go amongst a crowd of people near the third-class waiting room and make two unsuccessful attempts to pick ladies' pockets. Sergeant Smith was aware that a lady had reported £2 10s stolen from her pocket earlier that evening. Knight was arrested and admitted attempting to steal the two purses but denied any knowledge of the earlier incident.

The court officer then informed the magistrates that the prisoner was a very bad character. He had been sentenced to seven years penal servitude

A North Eastern Railway Police Sergeant pictured in 1894. Possibly Sergeant James Smith, the officer who arrested Robert Knight for attempting to pick pockets at Sunderland on 29 January 1894.

for larceny of a purse at Durham. At the same court he was given eighteen months imprisonment and twenty lashes for assault and robbery. At Birmingham he had been sentenced to six years penal servitude for felony. At Manchester he received fifteen months for shop-breaking and at Newcastle he was sentenced to nine months for larceny. The prisoner also had similar convictions elsewhere. He was sentenced to serve twelve months in the county gaol and led from the dock.

Later that day, the prisoner was re-called to court to be advised that the court had made an administrative error. Robert Knight should have been informed of his right to be tried before a jury if he so desired. He had not been informed but was then offered that right, to which he replied, 'Let it be as it is.' He was then led from the court again, this time to serve his gaol sentence.

Pickpocketing was a huge social problem in the nineteenth century but fortunately, due in part to less poverty and an improvement in social conditions, the offence went into decline in the twentieth century, although police dip squads have continued to operate in the British Transport Police, particularly on the London Underground where the offence is still quite commonplace, with many of the unfortunate victims being foreign tourists visiting London.

Having mentioned various different methods of stealing which were dealt with on a daily basis by both uniformed and detective officers serving in railway police forces, offences involving fraud were of particular concern to both railway policemen and the directors of the railway companies themselves. Fraud, which includes passenger fare evasion, is the category of crime which financially had the most adverse effect on the railway companies as a whole. It is impossible to know the vast amounts of money stolen, or loss of revenue incurred, by the early railway companies as a result of fraudsters, because so many such offences went undetected, although it was considerable.

Ticket offences and fare evasion have always been numerically the most common examples of fraud committed against any railway company, resulting in a direct loss of revenue. In the early years of the railways, these offences were often investigated and dealt with by detectives. However, as the years passed, the numbers of ticket offences being committed became so numerous that specific departments were set up to deal with them. Some were manned by railway police, others by railway revenue staff. This eased the burden on detectives who were then able to concentrate on the more serious types of frauds as well as other serious offences which were being committed.

Railways, by their very nature and structure, were always susceptible to frauds in one form or another. Amongst the large numbers of staff employed, some corrupt or dishonest members of staff could not resist exploiting their position in order to make money. Even a few usually honest individuals would sometimes succumb to temptation for various reasons.

Within the traffic department of the railways, booking clerks spent all their working lives handling cash in the form of revenue from members of the public in exchange for issuing tickets. Ticket collectors also collected money from passengers for unpaid and excess fares. Railway Company Directors relied upon the honesty of their staff to ensure that all money was recorded, paid in and accounted for, yet it was a relatively simple matter for booking clerks and ticket collectors to pocket some of the money passing through their hands.

To combat this, all the big railway companies had audit departments where professional teams of accountants and auditors were based. It was their job to ensure that all transactions ran smoothly, and all money was accounted for. Many railway departments handled vast sums of money, ranging from estate departments responsible for buying or selling land and property, to civil engineering departments who spent millions of pounds to purchase materials for large scale building projects and day to day maintenance of the railways. A whole range of other materials were purchased by the railway companies to meet their operational needs, everything from office furniture and stationery to bars of soap and toilet rolls. Each of these purchases involved financial transactions which needed to be carefully monitored to prevent crimes such as theft, fraud and embezzlement taking place.

Other types of fraud aimed at the railways centred on legal tenders and contracts between railway companies and outside firms. Some firms secured tenders and contracts with railway companies by offering bribes, gifts or other inducements to railway officials. Such occurrences often involved criminal offences of bribery and corruption which could be rather complex cases and often difficult to prove.

Fraud involving railway officials usually came to light as a result of routine audit checks being carried out by auditors and accountants. After uncovering suspicious activities, auditors would usually report the matter to the railway police detective department and they would work together, until, hopefully, a satisfactory conclusion was reached. Generally, if criminal activities were suspected, detectives would take charge of the investigation with a view to criminal proceedings being instituted against the person or persons concerned and accountants or other audit officials would assist where necessary.

After the railway boom years of the 1840s, which is often considered to be the golden years of the railway fraudsters, it was recognised that procedures surrounding the issuing of stocks and shares were a cause for concern and prone to fraudulent activities. Significant amounts of money were swindled from railway companies and there is no doubt that a large number of these offences went undetected. Possibly the worst type of fraud involving share certificates is when a person in authority, employed by a particular railway company, abuses their position of trust to promote criminal activities for personal gain. Such an individual could expect no sympathy or mercy from the judiciary. One such person was John Duncan, Secretary & Chairman of the Greenock Railway Company, who appeared before Lord Young at the Glasgow Circuit Court in Scotland on Monday 23 December 1878. There was to be no Christmas cheer for Mr Duncan, who pleaded guilty to issuing false share certificates from the Railway Company of which he was the Chairman. The court heard that Mr Duncan netted himself £11,444 (almost £1,400,000 today) by issuing false shares over a nine-year period whilst he was the secretary of the company. Lord Young said it was the worst case of fraud he had ever dealt with. He then sentenced Duncan to penal servitude for life.

A considerable number of railway ticket collectors were prosecuted for fraudulent activities during the nineteenth century. This usually involved offences of embezzlement as a result of pocketing money received from passengers to pay their fare. An early example of this type of offence occurred in the small picturesque village of Hele in North Devon in 1850.

Robert Walters was employed as a porter/ticket collector at Hele Railway Station in North Devon. He had worked on the railway for seven years. Hele Station was located on the main Bristol to Exeter railway line between Taunton and Exeter. Walters, however, was not the honest and polite railway servant that he purported to be, and he exploited his position in order to embezzle cash from his employer.

His downfall resulted from the vigilance of Superintendent Blackmore of the Bristol and Exeter Railway Police, who happened to alight from a Bristol train at Hele railway station one chilly autumn morning in 1850. As he was leaving the station, a passenger in front of him presented a ticket to Walters. The ticket was issued at Bristol that morning for a journey to Taunton. Walters charged the passenger the excess fare between Taunton and Hele, then put the money and the Bristol to Taunton ticket in his pocket. Superintendent Blackmore's suspicions were aroused by the actions of Walters. As a result, Superintendent Blackmore ordered some ticket tests to be carried out on him.

Over the next few weeks, undercover officers of the Bristol and Exeter Railway Police purported to be members of the travelling public. They alighted from trains at Hele station when Walters was on duty and either presented him with a ticket which required excess payment, or they stated that they had travelled from stations without having purchased a ticket and offered to pay the outstanding fare. In all cases, Walters accepted fare payment or excess fare payment without issuing a ticket or giving a receipt. The results of the ticket tests were later analysed, and the suspicions of Superintendent Blackmore were proved to be well founded. Walters had failed to pay any of the money to his employer, or account for it. He had pocketed the cash for himself. Walters was arrested for embezzlement and committed for trial by local magistrates. In December 1850, Robert Walters, having pleaded guilty to offences of embezzlement, was sentenced to ten years transportation after the judge told him he would not tolerate a man in a position of trust stealing from his employer.

Other railway employees who handled revenue on behalf of their employers were railway booking clerks who issued tickets from station booking offices. A small number of these trusted employees abused their position to make money. The most common form of dishonesty involving booking clerks also involved the embezzlement of cash, although, on occasions, more ingenious scams were carried out. One dishonest booking clerk came under suspicion after a number of counterfeit coins began circulating in London during the 1870s.

Arthur Keen, aged 32, was employed as a booking clerk by the Metropolitan Railway Company at Edgware Road railway station in London. In the spring of 1875, a barman in his local public house introduced Keen to John Neave and his fiancé Annie Bolwell. The barman informed Keen that John Neave, who was a shoemaker by trade, may be able to put some money his way. Keen listened to what Neave and Bolwell had to say, and he agreed to go along with the idea. It transpired that Neave, a shady individual, was engaged in the production of counterfeit coins of the realm. The coins were of different denominations. An agreement was reached between the two men that Neave would supply counterfeit coins to Keen, who would exchange the coins for an equivalent amount of genuine money from the booking office. Keen would then hand out the counterfeit coins, together with genuine coins as change to unsuspecting passengers who had purchased tickets. Thousands of people were purchasing tickets from Edgware Road booking office every day, most of whom were in a hurry and just put change into their pockets without making a close examination of it. There were also occasions when Keen worked at other booking offices, in particular Westbourne Park, which would enable the source of the distribution to vary.

The devious scheme was put into action and a considerable number of counterfeit coins began to circulate in London. As time went on, Keen distributed more and more counterfeit coins into public circulation without arousing any suspicion. Eventually, some members of the public started complaining that they had received bad money from the Metropolitan Railway Company. Detectives from within the company started an investigation in which they began visiting booking offices, buying tickets and checking the coins handed back in change. One detective received a bad shilling in change after tendering half a crown to buy a ticket at Edgware Road station. Consequently, Edgware Road booking office was soon identified as a possible source from where the coins were emanating. Detectives carried out observations and quickly established a link between Keen and Neave. They saw both Neave and his fiancé Bolwell visit the booking office, either together or on their own, on a number of occasions and hand Keen a number of small packages, for which he gave them money. By 11 May 1875, detectives had enough evidence to incriminate Keen, Neave and Bolwell, who were subsequently arrested.

The three prisoners were charged with conspiring to counterfeit currency. It was estimated that Keen had been circulating approximately 500 counterfeit coins each week from the booking office. The three defendants pleaded guilty in court and John Neave was sentenced to seven years penal servitude, Annie Bolwell was given twelve months hard labour and Arthur Keen received two years hard labour. After the convictions, the circulation of counterfeit coins in the area abruptly stopped.

During the nineteenth century, most railway employees received staff travel concessions for use when travelling on the railway of the company which employed them. They would normally receive a small number of free journeys which were often extended to spouses and children to enable the family to take an annual holiday. Any additional travel would usually cost the employee a quarter of the normal passenger fare. Despite these generous travel concessions, a small number of railway staff members would still attempt to travel on the railway without paying, or use their own travel concessions to purchase a reduced price ticket on behalf of a friend or relative to enable them to save money by avoiding payment of the full fare, which was unlawful. Members of the staff found abusing their travel concessions were subject to instant dismissal and prosecution. Regular reminders were frequently circulated and exhibited on staff notice boards as a reminder and warning to all staff members.

Unfortunately, no amount of publicity will eradicate fare evasion on the railways. Members of staff and railway passengers alike, old or young, male or female, it makes no difference. People have even been known to evade paying fares for dogs. For whatever reason, fare evasion has occurred since the dawn of the railways and as long as the trains keep running, the fare dodging brigade will be lurking amongst the passengers.

The most important job for any police officer, whether railway or civil, is usually considered to be the protection of life and property. Railways, by their very nature, are, and always have been, susceptible to accidents involving trains and passengers. None more so than during the nineteenth century.

Apart from two trains colliding head on, perhaps the most dangerous accident which can occur on the railway is when a train, travelling at speed, encounters an obstruction on the track. Many obstructions on the railway are unavoidable. They can be caused by falling trees, landslides, floods, snow and other natural phenomena. Apart from the obvious physical danger to passengers and train crews when locomotives encounter objects on the track, widespread delays and disruption can be caused, often affecting whole

177

S 852]

CAUTION.

Transfer of Privilege Tickets.

This is a criminal offence.

A Passenger Porter at Halifax Station has been discharged from the service for transferring a Privilege Ticket Order (issued in favour of himself and wife) to his brother, who was not in the employ of the Company.

For accepting and using this Privilege Ticket Order, the brother was convicted at the Manchester City Police Court, and fined 40s. and costs, with the alternative of a month's imprisonment.

Extract from the Lancashire and Yorkshire Railway staff magazine of March 1891, warning railway staff members against the fraudulent use of staff travel concessions.

railway networks. Dealing with the simplest cases of railway obstruction invariably causes train delays and considerable expense to the operating companies involved.

Obstructing the railway can also be a very serious criminal offence. Deliberately placing objects on the railway line for whatever reason can lead to serious train derailments and in some cases widespread loss of life. The penalty for obstructing the railway with intent to endanger life is that of life imprisonment. Of course, there are varying degrees of railway obstructions which have been the subject of railway legislation for many years. Not all obstructions are carried out intending to cause loss of life or serious injuries to people. The criminal offence of obstructing the railway falls into various categories, some of which do not have to be intentional. A railway can be obstructed by neglect on behalf of an individual. For example, should a workman who is engaged in the maintenance or repair of a railway line forget to remove his tools after he has finished work and inadvertently leave them on the track thereby causing delay or accident involving a train, he would be guilty of a criminal offence of obstructing the railway by neglect.

Obstructing the railway by wilful omission is another example of criminal obstruction of the railway. If a person uses an unmanned railway crossing (of which there were many in the nineteenth century) and does not bother to close the gates, thus allowing animals to stray onto the railway line, thereby causing a train to slow down or stop, that person would be guilty of an offence of obstructing the railway by an act of wilful omission i.e., omitting to fasten the gates after use.

The obstruction itself does not have to be a physical obstruction. Interfering with signals or stealing line-side copper cable or telegraph wires, are criminal offences in their own right, but the subsequent delays that these acts cause to trains also constitute an additional criminal offence of obstructing the railway by any unlawful act. Even the offence of trespassing upon the railway, which is in itself an unlawful act, can lead to a person being prosecuted for obstructing the railway if a train had to slow down or stop as a consequence of the trespassers being on the track. All nineteenth-century railway companies were obliged to exhibit trespass warning notices upon the railway, especially at railway stations. This still applies today.

Offences of obstructing the railway have unfortunately been an all-too-common occurrence since railways were first introduced in the early nineteenth century. Fortunately, death and serious injuries resulting from these acts have been relatively small.

In the early years of railway construction, railway policemen and watchmen were placed at intervals of a mile or so along a railway line, specifically to ensure that the trains did not encounter obstructions. The rapid expansion of the railway network, combined with improvements in signalling and track safety, soon rendered this practice unnecessary and it ceased after a few years, although to this day it has remained an integral part of a railway policeman's duty to ensure passenger safety which includes dealing with obstructions on the railway lines. Even the introduction of railway policemen and watchmen at regular intervals along the track when the railways were first established did not guarantee that the railway would not be obstructed, as directors of early railway companies soon found out to their dismay.

The first deliberate obstruction of a railway is thought to have occurred on the Liverpool and Manchester Railway in the afternoon of Wednesday, 22 December 1830, just three months after the railway opened.[16] The *Meteor* locomotive left Liverpool for Manchester, with a train consisting of just four passenger carriages. The train was preceded by the *Rocket* locomotive, acting as pilot engine which was a light engine with no coaches or wagons attached, travelling ahead but in sight of a train, to ensure that the track was safe and free from any obstructions.

As the trains approached the bottom of an incline at a location known as Mr Bourne's Colliery, at Sutton, four labourers working near the railway picked up a small stage wagon (intended to be used for the carriage of goods) and waited until the pilot engine had passed before placing it across the rails. They also placed a large iron switcher bar across the track. A watchman, who was stationed to protect that part of the line, remonstrated with the men but they ignored him. He even attempted to remove the obstructions, but the men threatened him and prevented him from doing so. As the train rapidly approached the obstructions, the watchman began waving his arms frantically at the locomotive, in order to make the driver aware of the danger and stop the train. This signal however was either misunderstood or given too late because the train did not slow down and came in contact with the wagon and the iron bar. The collision caused *Meteor* to become detached from the carriages and career down an embankment into a field some six or seven feet below.

The carriages themselves were dragged off the rails but did not career down the embankment and fortunately there was no loss of life. The driver of *Meteor* suffered severe chest injuries after being thrown violently forward into the controls of the locomotive, but the fireman alighted from the locomotive relatively unscathed. Several passengers sustained minor injuries, whilst others suffered the effects of shock and concussion.

In the meantime, the crew of *Rocket*, having lost sight of the train behind them, reversed backwards to ascertain what had happened to it. Upon reaching the scene, the driver and fireman of *Rocket*, together with the fireman from *Meteor* and with the assistance of a number of passengers, managed to get the de-railed carriages back onto the railway lines. The driver and fireman of *Rocket* coupled their engine to the carriages and the train continued its journey to Manchester, where it arrived a little over one hour late. There seems little doubt that the four workmen who carried out this appalling act did so with the intention of causing serious injury or loss of life but their motives for doing so remain a complete mystery. The culprits evaded justice by escaping across some fields, never to be seen again.

In the incident just referred to, the objects which were used to obstruct the railway belonged to the railway company itself. As the years passed, it became fairly common for railway obstructions to consist of railway materials lying close to the track, because they were convenient to use and close to hand. Materials were often delivered to lineside locations in advance of maintenance work being carried out and old materials removed or being replaced were often left alongside the track until it was convenient to collect and dispose of it. As a result, many items deliberately placed on the railway lines had been left there by track maintenance workers. Another such example occurred in 1848.

On the afternoon of 21 June 1848, an express passenger train was approaching Hall's Railway Level Crossing at Ely in Cambridgeshire, when the engine driver noticed something on the railway line which he thought was a large bird. The train was travelling at approximately 25mph. When the train got closer, the driver recognised the object as being a cast iron rail chair (which attaches the metal rail to the wooden sleeper). He immediately blew off steam to reduce boiler pressure and applied the brake. The locomotive slowed down but struck the rail chair whilst still travelling at about 15mph. The flange of the locomotive wheel struck the loose rail chair, which then jammed against a fixed rail chair which was helping to support the railway line, breaking the latter. The locomotive jolted violently but managed to remain on the track until the train came to a halt. There were in excess of 100 passengers on the train at the time of the collision, but no injuries were sustained. Enquiries were made and it was established that a 16-year-old youth by the name of Elijah Creek had been admonished earlier that day by a member of the public after he was seen placing a horseshoe on the line close to where the incident had taken place.

It was known that the land adjoining the railway at that location belonged to the boy's grandfather. Creek was subsequently interviewed by a railway policeman and he admitted placing both the horseshoe and the rail chair on the railway lines. When asked why he had done it, he said; 'I wanted to see how she [meaning the locomotive] would behave as she passed over it.' Creek was charged with obstructing a locomotive and endangering the safety of passengers. He subsequently appeared in court where he pleaded guilty. Mr Justice Maule stated that if any life should be lost in the consequence of obstructions placed on the line of a railway, the person placing the obstructions would be guilty of murder. In the present case, though no life was lost, and the offender was just 16 years of age, it was impossible to award anything but a severe sentence. Creek was sentenced to twelve months penal servitude.[17]

Some young offenders convicted for obstructing the railway in the nineteenth century were subject to what may be considered harsh or even barbaric sentences in today's climate.

A nineteenth-century Great Eastern Railway cast iron rail chair. The two holes are for bolting the chair to a wooden railway sleeper. The steel rail sits in the centre of the chair secured by two wooden wedges (rail keys) hammered into place on either side of the rail.

On Saturday, 10 June 1882, the Salford Stipendiary Magistrate ordered that two brothers, aged 10 and 14, the sons of a boatman, be severely whipped for placing large stones and pieces of timber on the Lancashire and Yorkshire railway line near Pendleton, Clitheroe in Lancashire[18]. The sentence was duly administered. Many people are unaware and surprised to learn that judicial corporal punishment in Britain continued well into the twentieth century and was not abolished until 1948.

Deliberate obstructions are placed on railway lines for various reasons. Children often obstruct the railway out of curiosity, just to see what happens when a train strikes or passes over an object or obstruction. They are often oblivious to the potential dangers involved and the serious nature of their actions. Other people deliberately obstruct the railway with the sole intention of causing an accident and/or endangering the life or safety of people. Former railway staff members themselves have also been known to obstruct the railway out of revenge or as a result of a grudge against their former employer. Such was the case when a man was seen placing objects on the railway line in the Victorian era.

In April 1868, Samuel Jenkins, aged 33, a former railway guard, was seen placing stones and pieces of iron across the railway line on the Great Western Railway line at Kidderminster, shortly before an express passenger excursion train was due. When approached, he ran away but was later apprehended. During an interview with police, he stated that he was seeking revenge against his former employer, the Great Western Railway Company, who had dismissed him from his job as a railway guard a few months earlier.

Jenkins appeared before the Worcester Assizes on 17 July 1868, where he pleaded guilty to obstructing the railway with intent to endanger passengers. The learned judge told him that if he had not been interrupted whilst he was in the act of placing obstructions on the line, there was little doubt that a deplorable catastrophe would have occurred. He went on to say that the offence was a most grievous one and one in which he was bound to press the full penalty of the law. He sentenced Jenkins to penal servitude for life.[19]

Chapter 6

RAILWAY ACCIDENTS AND LIABILITY

Modern railways are considered a safe form of transport and fortunately major railway accidents and fatalities are extremely rare. That has not always been the case and a considerable number of accidents, including fatalities, occurred on Britain's railways during the nineteenth century. They were due to a variety of causes.

Early steam locomotives were basic in design with inefficient braking systems by modern standards and the quality of some of the materials used in the construction of engines and rolling stock often led to malfunctions. A number of locomotive boilers exploded with catastrophic consequences, couplings broke on wagons and many safety devices which we take for granted today were not available to the early railway engineers. In some cases, they took many years to develop.

The first signalling systems introduced onto the railways were hand signals given by the early railway police constables. A constable holding his arm in a horizontal position would indicate to a driver that the railway line was clear and free from obstruction. A constable facing a train, with one arm being held straight up above his head as high as he could, indicated to a driver to slow down. A constable standing with both his arms and hands stretched straight out at right angles to his body, was an indication to stop. Any signal of the arm or anything in the hand waved frantically, or the waving of both arms at a driver, denoted danger and was an indication to stop immediately. Although very basic, these signals were primarily used for safety purposes as it was recognised from the building of the first railways that accidents and safety would always be a cause for concern and as it transpired, railway policemen had to bear the brunt of dealing with and investigating them.

The late 1830s saw railway policemen using flags and lamps instead of just hand signals and constables operated mechanical points and semaphore signals. The mid-nineteenth century saw the introduction of signal boxes which communicated by telegraph and controlled points and signals over the whole railway network. The days of railway policemen controlling train movements came to an end. Locomotives began to travel much faster and both train delays, and more importantly accidents, were considerably reduced.

Despite the safety improvements, accidents were still a major concern for two main reasons. Firstly, the faster that trains travelled meant that any accidents which did occur were likely to be far more serious. Secondly, a facet which often led to accidents was that of human error by railway staff. That was impossible to control.

A considerable number of early accidents were caused by human error or varying degrees of negligence on the part of railway employees. Employees most susceptible to prosecution in such cases, by virtue of their particular jobs, were signalmen, track maintenance workers, locomotive drivers and crossing keepers. As a result, a number of railway employees faced prosecution for a variety of offences, after their actions were deemed to have been instrumental in causing an accident, the most serious offence of which was manslaughter. Serious railway accidents were routinely investigated and dealt with by the railway police. However, in some cases, officers from the local civil police force would become involved, usually if they happened to be the first officers on the scene of an accident, or if called upon to assist the railway police.

As well as routine investigations being carried out by police, railway accidents were closely monitored and regulated by the Board of Trade. In 1840, Her Majesty's Railway Inspectorate was created, in order to oversee the safety of Britain's Railways. All railway companies were obligated to report certain accidents to the inspectorate who would then conduct an independent enquiry, before reporting their findings directly to parliament. In addition, it was their responsibility to inspect all new railway lines being built and report upon their suitability for the carrying of passengers.

In order to demonstrate the sheer volume of accidents which railway policemen encountered during the nineteenth century, set out below is a list of notable accidents[20] which were also investigated by the railway inspectorate in just one single decade between 1880 and 1889:

14 January 1880. Due to human error by a signalman, seven people were killed and thirty injured in a collision near Burscough Junction on the Lancashire and Yorkshire Railway.

10 August 1880. A locomotive hauling the *Flying Scotsman* train ran off the rails at Marshall's Meadows, near Berwick. The driver, fireman and one passenger were killed.

Depiction of a train crash which occurred at Norton Fitzwarren near Taunton on 11 November 1890, when a GWR Plymouth to Paddington boat train collided with a goods train. Ten passengers were killed and a considerable number were injured. Police officers from the Great Western Railway Police attended the accident under the command of Inspector Reeves. They were given the task of recovering bodies from the wreckage and preventing any looting from taking place.

11 August 1880. A Midland Railway train was de-railed whilst rounding a curve at excessive speed at Wennington near Skipton. Seven passengers were killed and twenty injured.

8 September 1880. An express train travelling from Glasgow to Greenock ran into a mineral train near Paisley. The train guard and five passengers were killed. A signalman had placed the mineral train on the wrong track after he had been working excessive hours.

8 August 1881. Two express trains collided on the Lancashire and Yorkshire Railway at Blackburn, which resulted in five persons being killed and forty being injured.

10 December 1881. A series of collisions occurred at Canonbury Junction on the North London Railway when two trains collided in a tunnel. A third train ran into the wreckage, quickly followed by a fourth. Five bodies were recovered from the mangled wreckage and a large number of people were injured.

28 January 1882. Five passengers were killed near Fairfield Road Bridge on the North London Railway when a passenger train collided with some coal wagons.

27 November 1882. Five passengers were killed when a bridge collapsed on the Macduff section of the Great North of Scotland Railway near Auchterless.

14 May 1883. A goods train derailment resulted in trucks blocking the railway line at Lockerbie Junction on the Caledonian Railway. The *Scotch Express*, which was travelling in the opposite direction, came into contact with the trucks whilst travelling at a speed of almost 60mph. Seven people died and many others were injured.

3 June 1884. After the coupling of a passenger train broke near Breamore in Hampshire on the London and South Western Railway, several carriages were derailed and fell down an embankment, resulting in the deaths of five people. Over forty other people suffered injury.

16 July 1884. A serious railway disaster occurred on the Manchester, Sheffield and Lincolnshire Railway at Bullhouse Curve near Penistone. Driver Sam Cawood was in charge of an express train from Manchester which was crowded with passengers. As the train passed through Hazlehead at a speed of approximately 50mph, the crank axle of the leading wheels of the locomotive broke. Driver Cawood applied the brake with all his might, but the impetus of the train forced the carriages off the line. Although the engine and tender remained on the track, the first two carriages were hurled down a steep embankment into a field. The next two carriages were pitched into a country lane, and another five carriages completely overturned with their wheels in the air. No fewer than twenty-four bodies of men, women and children were subsequently recovered from the mangled wreckage. A large number of passengers were injured in the accident, many of them seriously but the exact number of casualties was never accurately established. A Coroner's jury later returned a verdict of accidental death in respect of the passengers fatally injured.

1 January 1885. Following the railway disaster at Bullhouse Curve near Penistone in 1884, passengers began to look upon Penistone as an ill-fated place when another railway accident occurred less than six months later on the same section of line not far from the scene of the first accident. This accident occurred as a result of the axle of a private wagon on a goods train travelling from Ardwick to Kiveton Park breaking just as the goods train was passing an excursion train travelling from Rotherham to Southport on the opposite track.

As the axle broke with a clean fracture, possibly due to extreme frost, the wagon jumped off the rails, struck the locomotive of the excursion train and rebounded before keeling over and striking another carriage with great force, thereby demolishing it. Other carriages on the excursion train which had been travelling at approximately 30mph piled up high in a heap on top of each other. The wreckage was so entangled, that passengers had to be cut free. Four people were killed and some forty-seven injured, but the casualty toll could have been much worse. As in the previous accident, verdicts of accidental deaths were returned for the deceased passengers. In both cases it was decided that the accidents were unavoidable, and the Railway Company escaped having to pay out any compensation. The curse of Bullhouse Curve seems even more bizarre when one considers that both accidents were caused by broken axles.

16 September 1887. Another serious disaster took place, when a Midland excursion train travelling from Sheffield to the Doncaster horse-race meeting came to a halt at a ticket platform at Hexthorpe, as it approached Doncaster station. Two red flags were placed behind the train to protect it from the rear whilst the tickets of passengers in compartments of the non-corridor train were being checked.

A Manchester to Hull express train ignored the red flags and drove into the back of the excursion train whilst travelling at about 25mph. Most of the passengers travelling on the express train were badly shaken, but no serious injuries were reported.

Passengers on the excursion train however did not have such a lucky escape. All the passenger carriages were compressed into each other, creating a mass of broken woodwork, beneath which eight passengers lay dead. Other passengers died as a result of being crushed by the force of the impact. Many lay trapped in the wreckage, some of whom suffered the most appalling injuries. Twenty-five people were killed and over sixty were injured in the disaster. After an investigation into the collision by railway police, an inquest was held and a verdict of unlawful killing was returned by the coroner's jury in respect of all the dead. The jury considered that the driver of the express, Samuel Taylor, and his fireman Robert Davies were guilty of negligence by allowing their train to pass a danger signal. The two men were indicted to stand trial for manslaughter. Both men however were later acquitted at a criminal trial held at the local Assizes. The driver told the court that he was looking ahead and did not see the red flags which had been placed on the railway line.

8 August 1888. A locomotive ran into a stationary passenger train at Hampton Wick on the London and South Western Railway, killing five passengers. Many other passengers suffered injuries. A Coroner's jury subsequently returned a verdict of misadventure in respect of the passengers who lost their lives and the Railway Company were held blameless.

The accidents listed above were the most serious which occurred on the railway during that decade, but they were not the only accidents to have taken place. Many other less serious accidents did take place and railway policemen spent hours dealing with them.

Although railway accident numbers during the nineteenth century were extremely high and unacceptable by modern standards, the railways were deemed at the time to be a relatively safe mode of transport due to the high number of passengers using them. To put the matter into perspective, over the five-year period from 1 January 1885 to 31 December 1889 the total number of passengers (excluding season ticket holders) who travelled upon the railways in Britain (including Northern Ireland), was in excess of three and a half billion. In the same period, 138 passengers were killed and 3,199 passengers injured by accidents.

The numbers of passengers killed and injured in proportion to the numbers who travelled during the above five-year period are set out in the table below:

Year.	Killed.	Injured.
1885	1 in 116,202,171	1 in 1,600,000
1886	1 in 90,698,049	1 in 1,180,000
1887	1 in 29,346,800	1 in 1,363,700
1888	1 in 67,530,000	1 in 1,250,000
1889	1 in 8,808,875*	1 in 763,000*

1889 was a particularly bad year for railway accident statistics as the figures included the railway disaster which occurred at Warren Point in County Armagh, Northern Ireland on the 12 June 1889 in which 80 passengers (many of them children) were killed and 262 injured. This was the worst railway disaster in Europe at the time and was the worst railway disaster in Britain during the whole of the nineteenth century.

During the nineteenth century, railway companies were liable to face legal action and pay compensation when death or personal injury had resulted from an accident on the railway. However, in order to make good the claim, defect, mismanagement or carelessness on the part of the railway company or by employees of the company had to be proved. Where the accident had arisen from the carelessness or misconduct of the injured person, the company was not liable.

In reality, however, pursuing a claim for compensation was not so straightforward. Although large numbers of accidents which occurred during the nineteenth century could have been prevented, the majority of the victims received little or no compensation. Many of the criminal proceedings instituted against individual employees of the railway companies for negligence which caused or contributed towards accidents were dismissed by the courts. This tended to nullify any compensation claims and court orders against a railway company, as awarding restitution against railway companies, where employees had been acquitted and therefore deemed not to be at fault, seldom happened.

It was not only accidents on the railway that were a cause for concern during the nineteenth century. As automation developed, accidents were commonplace within the workforce of factories, coal mining, iron and steel production and other industries. There was no health and safety legislation in those days and accidents were viewed in a different light to those of today. Most accidents were considered by society to be normal day to day events which occurred when an unlucky or unfortunate individual just happened to be in the wrong place at the wrong time. In the most part, people often blamed themselves for not paying enough attention to what they were doing. Pursuit of compensation was almost unheard of and very seldom was it ever contemplated.

There were numerous occasions during the nineteenth century when railway employees did stand trial for criminal offences after being considered responsible for causing a particular accident. A considerable number, after having been convicted, felt aggrieved that they had been used as scapegoats or singled out for prosecution when other people, often of a higher status, who they considered equally blameworthy, did not face criminal charges. A typical example of this occurred when Henry Benge, a railway platelayer foreman, was indicted by a coroner's court to stand trial for manslaughter following an accident which took place in 1865 which he felt was not entirely his fault.

On Friday 9 June 1865, at 3.15pm, a South Eastern Railway passenger boat train travelling from Folkestone to London was derailed whilst crossing the Beult Viaduct near Staplehurst in Kent. The train, which consisted of twelve passenger coaches, was travelling at approximately 20mph. Although the locomotive was derailed, it remained upright on the viaduct together with three coaches. The remaining nine coaches plunged from the viaduct a distance of some ten feet (3 metres) into the bed of the shallow river below. A total of nine passengers on the train were killed and almost fifty were injured, some seriously.

One of the passengers on the train, travelling in a first-class compartment, was Charles Dickens, who was returning home from a visit to France. He was one of the lucky passengers in one of the three coaches which remained upright on the viaduct, and he was unscathed. He climbed out of a carriage window and assisted rescuing other passengers from the train. He later gave assistance to injured passengers before continuing his journey to London on a replacement train. Dickens later wrote his own account of the incident in which he stated that the effects of the accident remained with him forever and following the accident he avoided further journeys by train whenever possible as he felt very nervous and uneasy about travelling on the railway.

Enquiries into the accident showed that an earlier track inspection revealed that a length of railway line on the viaduct near Staplehurst was in need of replacement. As a result, a gang of platelayers attended the location on the 9 June to carry out the work. The person in charge of the workers was a foreman or ganger by the name of Henry Benge. The maintenance gang, including Benge, were under the control of a permanent way inspector, Joseph Gallimore, who had overall responsibility for track maintenance workers and their work, although he was not required to be on site when the actual work was being carried out.

The time allotted to carry out the work was one hour in total which was ample time to complete the job and clear the railway line. It was the duty of Henry Benge, as the foreman of the gang, to check the times of all trains scheduled to run along the track and select a suitable time between trains when there would be a gap in excess of one hour to complete the work.

Mr Benge decided to carry out the work between 3pm and 4pm on Friday 9 June. He worked out that the first train to use the line after 3pm would be the Folkestone to London boat train which departed Folkestone at 4.30pm and was due to cross the viaduct at 5.15pm.

What Benge failed to realise was that whilst checking the train timetable he made a serious error. Instead of checking the column for Friday 9 June, he checked the next column which showed train times for the following day, Saturday 10 June. The Saturday boat train did cross the viaduct at 5.15pm as the timetable showed but, on a weekday (including Friday 9 June), the boat train departed Folkestone two hours earlier at 2.30pm and was due to cross the viaduct at 3.15pm. The scene had been set for a potential disaster.

When the gang started to remove the track, Benge made another fatal error of judgement. It was his duty to appoint two gang members to walk away from the viaduct in opposite directions and place red flags on the track at 500 yards (457m) and 1,000 yards (914m) on either side of the viaduct to act as a warning to any unexpected or unscheduled approaching trains that work was being carried out. Benge was a former railway signalman and fully aware of these regulations.

Benge did instruct two men to carry out the tasks, but they did not fully comply with his orders and only placed flags at 500 yards either side of the viaduct. They did not display the second flags at 1,000 yards as he had instructed and in accordance with regulations.

At 3.15pm, the boat train was spotted in the distance heading towards the viaduct. A section of track on the viaduct had been completely removed ready to be replaced by a new section. Benge immediately ordered a member of his staff to run along the track with a red flag to warn the train driver of the impending danger. This was in vain, as the train was already too close and travelling too fast to stop. The driver later admitted seeing the flag on the track at 500 yards, at which point he shut off the steam and applied the brakes, but he could not stop the train in time. The train speed did reduce from 50mph but was still travelling at about 20mph when the accident took place. Had the 1,000-yard flag been displayed in accordance with regulations, the train would have come to a halt before reaching the viaduct.

Benge and his boss Joseph Gallimore 'the permanent way inspector' were both subsequently arrested by railway police on suspicion of manslaughter. After a coroner's inquest into the nine persons killed in the accident, Benge

Railway Accidents and Liability • 83

Depiction of train accident which occurred at the Beult Viaduct near Staplehurst in Kent on 9 June 1865, in which nine passengers were killed and almost fifty injured when a Folkestone to London passenger boat train was derailed during track maintenance repairs.

and Gallimore were both indicted to stand trial on a specimen charge of manslaughter of Hannah Cunliff. They both stood trial before Mr Baron Piggott at Maidstone Assizes on Wednesday 26 July 1865, charged with the manslaughter of Hannah Cunliff and diverse persons at Staplehurst on 9 June 1865. Joseph Gallimore was acquitted on grounds of insufficient evidence.

Henry Benge, a hardworking man of impeccable character, was found guilty of manslaughter and sentenced to nine months imprisonment. No other charges were preferred against any railway official or the South Eastern Railway Company. Mr Ribton QC, acting on behalf of Henry Benge, had argued that Benge had instructed staff to place flags at 1,000 yards and 500 yards either side of the viaduct and that he was being made a scapegoat in this case. He further stated that Mr Benge alone should not have to shoulder full responsibility for causing the tragic accident. Members of the jury, however, appear to have taken a different view.

Hundreds of railway accidents occurred on Britain's railways during the nineteenth century and the reasons for these accidents were wide ranging and varied. Most accidents to passengers were attributed to passenger trains colliding. The following list shows the various causes of accidents involving passengers in descending order of casualty numbers:

1. Collisions between passenger trains.
2. Collisions between passenger and goods trains.
3. Passenger train derailments (trains leaving the rails).
4. Trains or locomotives travelling in the wrong direction through points.
5. Trains or locomotives travelling too fast.
6. Mechanical faults including failure of axles, couplings, etc.
7. Other miscellaneous causes.

There is no doubt that the railways played a very successful role in nineteenth century Britain, although it was not their finest years when it came to issues involving accidents and safety. Today's railways have far fewer accidents and a vastly superior safety record for passengers. This is mainly due to huge improvements in railway technology, the quality of materials being used and of course, 200 years of experience.

Chapter 7

CRIMES COMMITTED AGAINST PASSENGERS

The building of the railways in the nineteenth century brought about a new era of travel. Within a few short decades, passengers were travelling as never before. The railways were an instant success, with people travelling far and wide to new and exciting places. There was however a darker side to the glamour and speed of travelling on the railways. Wherever decent law-abiding people congregate, a few unsavoury characters will usually appear, nowhere more so than on the railways.

The railways by their very nature attracted criminals and undesirables out to fulfil their own desires. The phrase 'safety in numbers' was a saying worth bearing in mind for passengers contemplating a journey by train in the nineteenth century. Railway police and staff were aware of the dangers involved in travelling by train and their need to protect passengers. Whilst the safety and protection of passengers was paramount, it was not possible to protect everyone, particularly if passengers found themselves travelling alone in a dimly lit railway compartment or standing in the shadows of a subdued gas light on an isolated railway station.

Fortunately, the number of crimes actually committed against the travelling public, in proportion to the number of passengers travelling by train, was very small. This however does not detract from the pain and anguish experienced by the unlucky few who just happened to be in the wrong place at the wrong time. Many perpetrators of crimes against passengers were apprehended in Victorian times and they received little in the way of leniency from the judiciary who did not hesitate to use the full weight of the law to punish offenders and afford protection to the travelling public.

One such person was William Webb, a nasty individual who made an unprovoked attack on Alfred Buckler, a draper's assistant living in Poplar, East London. The motive was one of robbery in order to steal a pocket watch belonging to Buckler by the use of force.

At about eight o'clock on the evening of Thursday, 5 March 1857, Alfred Buckler went to Stepney railway station to catch a train to Hampstead. He purchased a ticket and boarded an empty second-class compartment on the train. Upon arrival at Camden Town Station, William Webb opened the compartment door and got in. Webb sat opposite Buckler and opened a conversation by asking the name of the next station. Buckler informed him it was Hampstead Road. Webb then asked Buckler the time. Buckler took out his watch and said it was almost twenty-five minutes past eight. Buckler put the watch back in his pocket and turned his head to look out of the window. Suddenly, Buckler felt a violent blow on his neck. He sprang to his feet and felt himself struck on the arm in the same manner. He seized hold of Webb and started to grapple with him when he noticed that Webb was holding a knife in his left hand. Buckler felt blood flowing from his neck and arm, but he managed to grab hold of the blade of the knife with his right hand, whilst he used his left hand to grab hold of Webb's right wrist, push it up against his throat and pin him into a corner. Buckler shouted out murder several times. Webb attempted to withdraw the knife from Buckler's hand and although the knife cut deeper into his skin, Buckler held onto it. The train then slowed down and came to a stop at Hampstead Road Station.

Buckler continued shouting, whilst pinning Webb against the carriage and after a short time, the carriage door was opened by William Sandford, a railway porter. Webb immediately let go of the knife and said, 'The knife doesn't belong to me. This man tried to stab me and in self-defence I stabbed him.' Buckler handed the knife to the porter. It later transpired that Webb was a butcher and the knife was a butcher's dressing knife of the type used by Webb in that capacity.

The station master and the guard were quickly on the scene. Police were summoned and Webb was detained. Buckler was taken to the station master's house where his wounds were treated. Stephen Halford, a local doctor, attended the railway station a short time later where he examined Buckler who was covered in blood and suffering from shock. On his neck, approximately two inches beneath the left ear and close to the carotid artery, Dr Halford found a wound about one inch long and one inch deep. There was a similar wound on the outer part of the left arm about two inches deep. It was the opinion of Dr Halford that both these wounds were as a result of stabbings and that a great deal of force must have been used to inflict them. There was also a cut on his forehead and severe lacerations to his right hand where he had grabbed hold of the blade of the knife. Dr Halford administered treatment to the wounds.

William Webb later appeared before Marylebone Magistrates charged with attempted murder and was committed to the Central Criminal Court to stand trial. Accordingly, on Thursday, 9 April 1857, William Webb alias Philip Cohen, alias Philip Neavy, a butcher aged 19, appeared before the Central Criminal Court, charged with the felonious stabbing and wounding of Alfred Buckler with intent to murder him and (second count) with intent to cause grievous bodily harm. Webb pleaded not guilty and was represented by Mr Sleigh. Mr Payne appeared for the prosecution.

The evidence was put before the jury, who, after just a short deliberation, returned a not guilty verdict on the charge of attempted murder, but guilty on the second count of unlawful wounding with intent to commit grievous bodily harm. After the verdict was announced, the learned judge said that in all his experience, the prisoner's offence was one of the very worst he had ever dealt with and he (the judge) would be guilty of a very great dereliction of duty to the public if he did not pass the severest sentence the law permitted, that of transportation beyond the seas for the term of his natural life.[21] The prisoner, who portrayed no surprise at the sentence, was removed from the court.

Unfortunately, a number of offences did take place during the nineteenth century whereby passengers were robbed of their money or personal possessions, usually when they were travelling alone in a compartment. Lone individuals travelling in first class compartments were often the target of thieves as they were more likely to possess such items as gold watches and large amounts of cash. Yet stealing the personal effects of passengers was not the only motive for assaults on passengers travelling by train. Perhaps the most vulnerable passengers are women and children, and it can be a terrifying ordeal when a woman, a child or even both are subject of an ordeal at the hands of a man. That is precisely what happened to Mrs Catherine Costello in 1891.

On Thursday 10 September 1891, Catherine Costello, a housewife of 5 Mark Street, Dublin, travelled to London with her 11-year-old son Lawrence to visit relatives. Mrs Costello and her son boarded the London and North Western Railway paddle steamer *Violet* in Dublin, bound for Holyhead. They disembarked from the ferry at Holyhead and just before midnight they boarded the London and North Western Railway boat train destined for Euston Station in London. They sat in an empty second-class compartment.

A short time later, Robert Dean, a cattle dealer from Manchester, entered the compartment and sat by the door. Another lady and gentleman opened the compartment door to enter but Dean told them that the compartment was full, so they continued to another part of the train. As the train departed the station, Dean pulled down the blinds on the windows next to where he was sitting. Dean asked Mrs Costello where she was going, and he suggested that her son, who was dozing, be stretched out on the seat. He offered her a coat, but she declined.

Dean then stretched himself on the seat and seemingly went to sleep. Mrs Costello followed his example. A short time later, Mrs Costello suddenly awoke to find Dean leaning over her and indecently assaulting her. She pushed him away, jumped to her feet and a struggle ensued. Dean threw her down on at least three occasions, whilst continuing to indecently assault her. Mrs Costello started screaming and pulled down the hat slings in the compartment, in the belief that they were the emergency communication devices. Her son, having been awoken by the screams of his mother, also started to scream and shout but Dean told him to be quiet, threatening to throw him out of the train window. Mrs Costello managed to get to the other side of the compartment, open the window and pull the outside communication cord, even though Dean was trying to prevent her from doing so by hitting her with a stick.

As the train began to slow down, Mrs Costello opened the carriage door. At this point, Dean sat down and told her to close the door or he would have her arrested for trying to steal his watch. Mrs Costello closed the door just as the train was entering Bangor Station. When the train came to a standstill, Mrs Costello leaned out of the window and started screaming to attract attention.

William Jones, the rear brakeman on the train, ran to the compartment and saw Mrs Costello in a very distressed condition. He noticed that her hair was disarranged and she bore marks of having been in a struggle. She pointed to Dean and told the brakeman he had abused her. Walter Fowler, the train guard, who was travelling in the front guard's van of the train, also attended as a result of the communication cord being pulled. Mrs Costello repeated her allegation to guard Fowler.

Police Sergeant Davies of the London and North Western Railway Police, who was on the station platform to meet the arrival of the boat train, was quickly on the scene. Upon seeing him, Mrs Costello jumped from the train and asked that he arrest the man in the compartment for indecently assaulting her. Sergeant Davies spoke to Dean who made an accusation that Mrs Costello had tried to rob him of his watch and chain, and he made disparaging references as to her age and appearance. The officer noticed that Dean's clothing was in disarray and his trouser buttons were undone.

Sergeant Davies spoke to witnesses in the next compartment. A lady said that she had heard screaming coming from the compartment whilst the train was in motion. Another passenger also confirmed this and was also able to state that before departing Holyhead, the man in the compartment (Dean) had prevented other passengers entering the compartment by telling them that it was full.

The boy Lawrence Costello corroborated his mother's version of events and he told Sergeant Davies of the threats made by Dean to throw him out of the window.

Robert Dean was subsequently arrested and when later charged with attempt to ravish and indecent assault, he denied the allegations. Dean was taken before a special court at Bangor later that day and the facts were laid before the magistrates. Whilst Mrs Costello was giving her evidence, she became very distressed and fainted. As a result, she was unable to complete her evidence and was assisted from the courtroom. The magistrates decided, however, that they had heard sufficient for the case against Dean to proceed and remanded him on bail. On Tuesday, 22 September 1891, Robert Dean was committed from Bangor Magistrates' Court, to stand trial at the next County Assizes on a charge of assault with intent to ravish (attempted rape).

On Tuesday, 24 November, Dean appeared before the winter assizes for the counties of Carnarvon and Anglesey. The Honourable Sir Rowland Vaughan Williams presided. The court heard that the London and North Western Railway Company had failed to bring the victim Catherine Costello to court. It appeared that Mrs Costello, who was unable to complete her evidence at a previous court appearance due to distress and feeling faint, was not prepared to leave her home in Ireland and travel all the way to North Wales to face further distress. Her husband, who was employed as a plumber in Dublin, fully supported his wife saying it would be too much of an ordeal for her. He gave notice that he also would not be in attendance at the trial. The judge was left with no alternative other than to dismiss the case against Robert Dean who was pleading not guilty.

Robert Dean was a very lucky man to have evaded justice. The evidence against him was overwhelming and had he been convicted at the County Assize Court, there is little doubt that he would have been severely punished by the judge.[22]

The vulnerability of women travelling alone by train was recognised during the early period of the railways and it has been suggested that discussions were taking place as early as the 1840s regarding the installation of emergency communication devices in railway compartments and setting aside compartments for the exclusive use of ladies only.

Communication devices were first introduced into some new passenger coaches in the 1850s. These early devices sounded a bell in the locomotive cab warning the driver to stop the train. Later, however, communication cords were connected to the passenger guard vans, to warn the train guard, as he was the person officially in charge of the train. Legislation was passed in 1868 making it compulsory for the carriages on all passenger trains to be fitted with emergency communication devices for the use of passengers.

Ladies-only compartments were first officially introduced onto trains in 1874, although it is thought that some companies may have used them prior to this date. Although widely used for many years and still widely used abroad, these compartments were withdrawn by Network Rail in 1977 on the grounds of political correctness. Subsequent lobbying has been made to have them re-introduced, although this appears extremely unlikely.

Public concern about the safety of railway passengers travelling by train during the nineteenth century came to a head in 1864, after the infamous murder of Thomas Briggs, the first ever passenger to be murdered whilst travelling by train in Britain. He was travelling in the first-class compartment of a train on the North London Railway.

The brief circumstances of the case were that on the evening of 9 July 1864, Thomas Briggs was travelling on the 9.50pm train from Fenchurch Street to Chalk Farm in London in a first-class compartment. During the journey he was brutally attacked by a German tailor Franz Muller, who stole his gold pocket watch and chain. Muller then threw Briggs from the moving train and his body was found alongside the track by the driver of a train travelling in the opposite direction. Briggs later died from injuries sustained.

Franz Muller. Hanged for the murder of Thomas Briggs in 1864.

Muller fled to America to escape justice but was later extradited back to Britain where he was put on trial at the Central Criminal Court and found guilty of murder. He was hanged at Newgate Prison in London on 14 November 1864.

Whilst Thomas Briggs was not the first person to have been murdered on the railway in Britain, he was the first railway passenger to be murdered on a train and the events are well documented in history books. This horrendous crime received a huge amount of publicity at the time and was the subject of discussions and reports, many of which appeared in the media which existed at the time.

One such report which appeared in the *Glasgow Morning Journal* on 14 July 1864 raised the question:

> Are the railways to become highways of all the more violent and atrocious crimes? Allusions to Hounslow Heath [considered to be the most dangerous place in England for travellers in the seventeenth and eighteenth century] and highway robberies are out of place, for the Dick Turpins of a former age were gentlemen compared to the scoundrels who go into railway carriages to murder old men and insult and assault young women. It is clear that we have to be on our guard against an infinitely more wicked class of highwaymen than those known to our fore-fathers. Still it would be irrational to give way to any intense alarm. It cannot well be conceived that such a crime as this on the North London Railway is likely to come into fashion....
>
> The only effectual remedy, as seems to us, is the introduction of public saloon carriages as used in the United States of America. The railway companies might still adhere to using first, second and third class compartments, but why should our first and second class passengers not sit together in open saloons instead of private boxes and solitary units, where they may happen to be shut and locked in from the whole world, apart from the ruffian who means to take their life, their purse, or their honour …
>
> The third-class passengers enjoy in this respect a protection from crime of which an absurd exclusiveness and pompous love of isolation deprive the middle and upper ranks of society. A working man, whose duty is sometimes to carry large sums of money for his employers from one place to another, recently told us that whilst he was at liberty to take any class he chose, his invariable rule, when carrying such sums of money, was to travel by third class because he was there among a large number of passengers and felt that he could neither be assaulted nor robbed with impunity. A

little exercise in common sense at once pointed out in this case what was the true and effectual element of security against secret, violent, and audacious crime...

The railway boxes should be discarded except in the few instances in which they might be specially ordered. We believe that this is the proper remedy suggested by this horrible murder on the North London Railway and that as long as passengers are content to seclude and isolate themselves in railway trains and to sit alone with any vagabond who has a good coat upon his back and has paid his fare, a facility will be given for the commission of the worst of crimes which almost no expedient can check.

Some three years later in 1867, it was reported that nearly all railway crimes committed against passengers travelling on trains, occurred in first, or second-class compartments (at a time when there were three classes of travel), once again indicating that isolation of passengers to allow them privacy was a contributory factor in crimes of this nature *(Sheffield Independent,* 14 July 1867*)*.

Although 1874 did see the introduction of American style Pullman Saloon Cars onto the railway network in Britain, the early coaches, which were initially built in America and imported into Britain, were only used by the Midland Railway Company. They operated between Bradford Forster Square and London St. Pancras but were not very successful. It was quite clear that there was no appetite for American type public saloon carriages to be introduced in large numbers onto Britain's railways, even if it did lead to an improvement in passenger safety. The British preferred their traditional private boxes.

The Midland Railway did however persevere with the Pullman Cars and whilst passengers did not use them to ensure safety in numbers, they found them to be ideally suited for use as luxury coaches. As a result, the British Pullman Car Company was founded in 1882 and a different type of Pullman train did make an appearance on our railways in the 1880s and 1890s. These trains, with their famous brown and cream coaches, were the height of luxury and proved popular, particularly amongst the upper classes and business passengers. They consisted of bogie style carriages with first-class and third-class compartments fitted with electric lights and adorned with the finest sycamore panelling, maple moulding and plush cushions fit for a prince. Dining saloon-cars with dainty tables, lace tablecloths and well-appointed fixtures and fittings were provided for passengers and smartly attired waiters

Pullman Saloon Car number eight, built in America in 1876 and imported to Britain for use by the Midland Railway Company.

tended their every need. These luxury Pullman trains were operated by a number of railway companies and continued well into the twentieth century. The amount of crime committed against passengers travelling on these luxury Pullman trains was extremely low.

Railway crime did continue to increase during the latter part of the nineteenth century, in proportion to the increase in the size of the railway network. In 1878, an Extradition Treaty was introduced between Britain and Spain. Railway crime was deemed to have become so significant that 'Malicious Offences on Railways' were specifically referred to and included within the treaty for the first time. Such offences were soon incorporated into other extradition treaties.

In February 1897, another report appeared in *Reynolds's Newspaper,* once again outlining the increases in railway crime caused by the isolation of train passengers, although the mention of men being murdered, women being outraged and drunkards running amok are once again a gross embellishment of happenings, in the true fashion and tradition of the British press:

> The history of railway crimes shows that in every case the evil has been brought about by the rabbit hutch plan of separation. Men have been murdered, women have been outraged, and drunkards have run amuck in carriages divided into compartments. No one is so helpless as a man or woman in the hands of a ruffian in an express train which is flying along at

the rate of fifty miles per hour and which may not stop for an hour and a half. There is little possibility of getting assistance.

There is no remedy for this evil other than to make all railway carriages open to inspection by officials by means of corridors running from one end of the train to another. This is the simple and natural plan and if the railway companies do not voluntarily adopt it, they should be made to do so by a sharp, curt law coming into operation at once.

By 1897, regardless of the above article, corridors were already being introduced onto the railways. The Great Western Railway had introduced side corridor trains on the London Paddington to Birkenhead route as early as 1892, and other companies had conducted experiments with corridors and other forms of gangway connections. These types of trains did meet with the approval of passengers both from a security aspect and also by enabling instant access to toilet facilities for both ladies and gentlemen and access to refreshment and smoking facilities which were introduced into the corridor coaches not long afterwards. As such, corridor trains continued to increase in both popularity and numbers as the railways progressed into the twentieth century.

Despite the many alarming reports which appeared in the Victorian press, passenger safety upon the railway was paramount and scaremongering in the media about passengers being murdered and young women being ravished were both unnecessary and unfounded. Unfortunately, such exaggerated reports did sell newspapers.

In reality, the serious offences of murder and attempted murder of passengers travelling by train were extremely rare, both in Britain and most other European countries during the nineteenth century. During the whole of the nineteenth century, there were just three officially recorded cases of murders against passengers, whilst they were travelling on a train in Britain, the first being the murder of Thomas Briggs by Franz Muller on the North London line in 1864 and the second being the murder of Isaac Frederick Gold by Percy Lefroy Mapleton on the London to Brighton line in 1881. Both these cases were solved and the perpetrators were executed by hanging.

The third murder – which was unsolved – occurred on Thursday, 11 February 1897, when 33-year-old Miss Elizabeth Camp travelled on the London and South Western Railway from Hounslow to London. Miss Camp boarded the 7.42pm train at Hounslow and her bloodstained body was discovered by a carriage cleaner beneath a seat in an empty compartment when the train arrived at Waterloo station some fifty minutes later. There was no sign of any sexual assault having taken place and robbery was deemed to be a likely motive for the attack. Despite an extensive murder investigation conducted jointly between Superintendent Robinson of the London and South Western Railway Police and Chief Inspector Marshall of Scotland Yard, the murder remained unsolved.

There were also two officially recorded cases of attempted murder upon the railway, both of which were attempted assassinations of VIPs travelling by train. One attempt was made during the boarding of a train and the other after the intended victim had alighted from a train. In each case, the offenders were apprehended and dealt with in a court of law.

On 2 March 1882, Roderick MacLean was arrested after attempting to shoot Queen Victoria at Windsor railway station. The queen travelled from Paddington Station to Windsor by royal train. After alighting from the train, she walked to an awaiting horse-drawn carriage to be conveyed to Windsor Castle. As the carriage pulled away from the station, MacLean, who was standing amongst a crowd of public spectators, pulled out a pistol and fired a shot in the direction of the queen before being apprehended. Fortunately, the shot missed its target and the coach drove off at speed towards Windsor Castle, carrying the queen to safety. This had been the eighth and final attempt by different individuals to assassinate Queen Victoria during her reign. Roderick MacLean subsequently appeared before Reading Assizes charged with high treason. He was judged to be insane and after a five-minute deliberation by the jury, he was found not guilty and acquitted. MacLean was detained in Broadmoor Lunatic Asylum during Her Majesty's pleasure and spent the rest of his life confined to the asylum until his death on the 9 June 1921.

The outcome of this case prompted Queen Victoria herself to ask for a change in English Law to be made to enable a verdict of guilty but insane to be handed out in future similar cases as opposed to a not guilty verdict being delivered. A law which enabled this to happen was speedily passed through parliament and the Trial of Lunatics Act 1883 came into force the following year.

The second case of attempted murder of a high-profile passenger travelling by train occurred on 19 November 1889, whilst Samuel Boteler Bristowe, a High Court Judge, was boarding a Great Northern Railway train at Nottingham London Road railway station (closed to passengers in 1944) in order to travel to Derby. A railway porter held open the door of a first-class carriage to allow the judge to board and as Judge Bristowe stepped onto the footboard of the train, a man standing behind him pulled a revolver from his coat pocket and fired a single shot at the judge from point blank range.

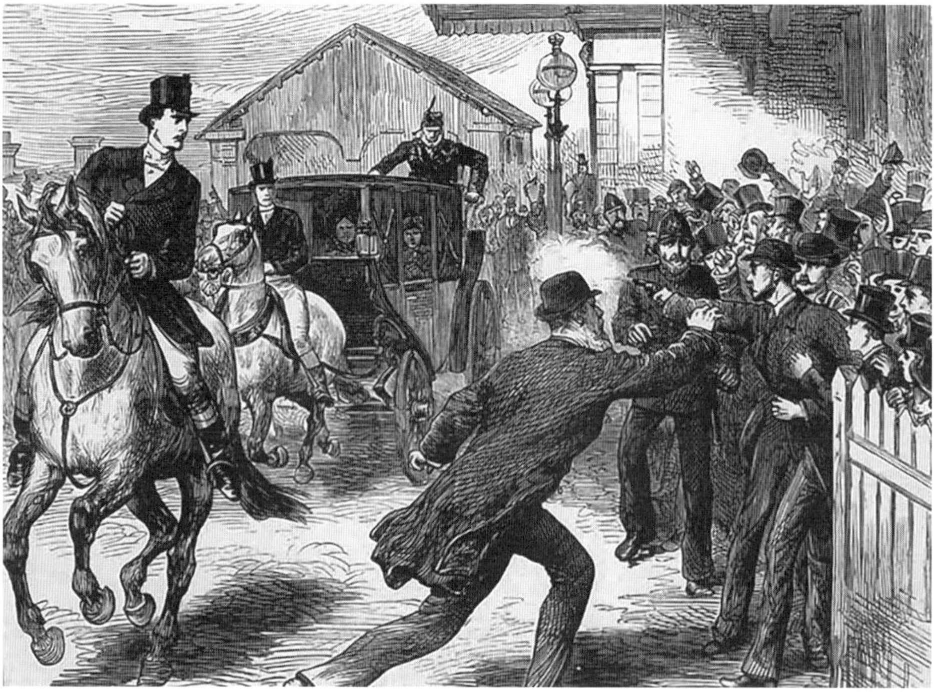

Above: **Depiction of** Roderick MacLean being apprehended whilst attempting to assassinate Queen Victoria at Windsor Railway Station in 1882.

Left: **Judge** Samuel Boteler Bristowe was critically injured but survived a shooting during an assassination attempt whilst boarding a train at Nottingham in 1889.

The bullet pierced the judge between the shoulder blades causing damage to his lung. The judge fell between the train and the platform. He was taken to hospital where he remained in a critical condition for a number of weeks but he did eventually recover from his injuries. A German citizen by the name of Edward Wilhelm Hermann Arnemann was arrested and admitted shooting the judge. He appeared before the Nottingham Assizes on 8 March 1890 where he was sentenced to twenty years penal servitude.

The fact that out of the millions of British passengers who travelled by train during the whole of the nineteenth century, just three officially recorded murders (two of which were solved) and two attempted murders (both solved) took place, does demonstrate just how safe railway travel was in relation to serious violent crime. Statistics in most other European countries over the same period showed a similar trend with regards to the numbers of murders and attempted murders committed as outlined below.

Germany, Belgium, Switzerland and Holland, zero.
Austria, one.
Spain, two.
Britain and Italy, five.
Russia and Turkey, seven.
France, twenty-eight.

Railway travel in France during the nineteenth century was a bit of a risky business it seems, especially at night. France experienced more murders and attempted murders than the combined totals of all the other European countries. Most of these offences took place during evening and night time journeys on express trains and in almost every case, the offences were committed inside first class carriages by passengers travelling alone (rabbit hutch plan of separation). Less than half (thirteen) resulted in convictions, the rest remained unsolved.

This does tend to confirm the old adage that there is indeed Safety in Numbers.

Chapter 8

DANGERS FACING NINETEENTH-CENTURY RAILWAY POLICEMEN

As far as nineteenth-century industrial accidents are concerned, being a railway policeman was a somewhat dangerous job. The railway industry, together with the coal mining industry, were always very high on the agenda with regards to accidents involving staff. The most vulnerable occupations on the railway, when it came to accidents, were platelayers and track maintenance workers, permanent way inspectors, shunters, lineside workers and railway policemen.

Yet whilst many railway policemen have been killed or injured by accidents over the years, relatively few serious acts of violence have been committed against serving police officers during the course of their duty and only a handful of officers are thought to have been murdered. The true figure of officers murdered on duty can never be established. Quite a few dock policemen for example have been found drowned in the dock, sometimes days after the event, with no apparent witnesses. There is no way of telling whether these officers were pushed or thrown into the dock or whether they slipped or fell into the water by accident. Similarly, when a railway policeman is found dead on the railway, having been struck and often badly mutilated by a train, particularly during the hours of darkness, accident is usually the attributed cause, although it is possible that the actual cause could be far more sinister. Having said that, murders have been carried out on railway policemen in the past, where witnesses have been present and evidence has been available.

Perhaps the most infamous murder of a railway policeman on duty during the nineteenth century was that involving Detective Sergeant Robert Kidd. The incident in question occurred in Wigan on the evening of Sunday, 29 September 1895 when Detective Sergeant Robert Kidd of the London and North Western Railway Police was attacked and stabbed to death after disturbing a gang of intruders who were stealing confectionery from goods wagons stabled at Chapel Lane Railway Sidings in Wigan.

The brief circumstances surrounding this case are that Detective Sergeant Kidd, together with Detective Constable Osbourne, had arranged to keep evening and night observations on some wagons, due to them being persistently targeted by thieves whilst stabled overnight in the railway sidings. The two officers arrived at the sidings on foot, just after dark at about eight o'clock in the evening and upon entering the sidings they disturbed some intruders who were already raiding the covered wagons. Both officers apprehended different members of the gang who put up fierce resistance. In a frenzied attack, one of the gang members pulled out a knife and stabbed Sergeant Kidd nine times to the face, neck and chest before making good his escape. Sergeant Kidd collapsed in a pool of blood.

In the meantime, Detective Constable Osbourne was attacked by two other gang members and although he managed to strike one of his assailants a number of times with his truncheon, another gang member intervened until Osbourne was left badly beaten and collapsed on the ground in a state of exhaustion. All the gang members then ran away. Detective Osbourne managed to get to his feet and went to the assistance of Sergeant Kidd who managed to speak a few words before lapsing into unconsciousness.

Osbourne attempted to carry Kidd but after about ten yards he placed him under a wagon and went to summon assistance. Sergeant Kidd later died whilst still under the wagon.

Osbourne did manage to reach a signal box and raise the alarm before he too lapsed into unconsciousness. He was conveyed to hospital and, fortunately, he did eventually make a full recovery from his injuries.

Meanwhile, an immediate investigation was carried out by three separate police forces. The scene of the crime was on the border between the jurisdiction of the Wigan Borough Constabulary and the Lancashire County Constabulary. The first senior police officer on the scene was Superintendent MacIntosh, who, in the absence of Chief Constable Captain Bell, was in overall command of the Wigan Borough Constabulary. He mustered as many available officers as possible and started immediate enquiries at the homes of well-known local thieves and other possible suspects.

Superintendent Brassington of the Lancashire County Police also attended the scene with a large detachment of officers from his Constabulary and although he arrived after it had been established that the railway sidings were within the Borough of Wigan, it was decided that as he was already in attendance, his officers would be deployed to assist in the initial stages of the investigation.

Detective Sergeant Robert Kidd. London and North Western Railway Police. Murdered whilst on duty at Wigan in 1899.

The other police force to have jurisdiction at the crime scene was the London and North Western Railway Police force who had foremost authority regarding jurisdiction. Detectives Davern and Buckingham of the LNWR Police were quickly on the scene and Detective Superintendent Elijah Copping from the LNWR Police headquarters in London was informed and he arrived later to take charge of the investigation.

In the meantime, officers of the Wigan Borough Police, under the command of Superintendent MacIntosh, had achieved some initial success with their house to house enquiries and a total of five men were arrested on suspicion of being involved. The men were all residents of Kay's Houses, a cluster of cottages backing on to the railway sidings where the murder had taken place. The men were coal miners working at local collieries. The five men were subsequently charged with being concerned in the wilful murder of Robert Kidd. Over the next three days, three other men were also arrested in connection with the incident.

This case culminated with three men appearing before Mr Justice Henn Collins at Liverpool Assizes on 26 November 1895. Elijah Winstanley, aged 31, and William Kearsley, aged 43, were both charged with the wilful murder of Robert Kidd. A third defendant, William Halliwell, aged 31, was charged with feloniously wounding William Henry Osbourne. The three men pleaded not guilty. Judge Collins instructed that Halliwell be removed from the dock in order for him to be called as a witness to give Queen's evidence against the other two in the principal trial of wilful murder.

At the conclusion of the trial, the jury deliberated for a mere ten minutes before returning a guilty verdict against Winstanley and Kearsley on the capital charge of the wilful murder of Robert Kidd. They were both sentenced to death by hanging. On the direction of the judge, no evidence was offered against William Halliwell who had turned Queen's evidence at the trial. He was discharged.

After the two men had been found guilty, Elijah Winstanley declared that he himself had stabbed Kidd to death and that Kearsley was not involved in the stabbing. In view of this statement, the death sentence imposed on William Kearsley was later commuted to that of life imprisonment. A letter was sent from the Home Secretary to Mr James Wilson, the solicitor acting for Mr Kearsley, stipulating that the sentence imposed upon his client would be further considered after the prisoner had completed a minimum of ten years penal servitude, although no pledge could be given of the result which may then be arrived at.

William Kearsley served his sentence at Dartmoor Prison. He did not serve the minimum period of ten years as instructed by the Home Secretary. He was released from Dartmoor in February 1903, after serving seven years and three months. Upon his release, he returned home to his wife and family in Wigan.

Elijah Winstanley was hanged at Walton Prison, Liverpool on 17 December 1895. His body was later buried within the precincts of the prison. The executioner was James Billington from Bolton in Lancashire.

The victim in this tragic case was Detective Sergeant Robert Kidd, age thirty-seven. Robert Kidd had originally served as a constable in the Manchester City Police Force, before leaving to join the London and North Western Railway Police in 1885. He performed duties as a uniformed constable before being appointed detective constable at Warrington in 1887. He transferred to Liverpool Edge Hill Station the following year, before being promoted to detective sergeant at Manchester in 1889, where he continued to serve until the day of his death. On that fateful day, he had travelled from Manchester to Wigan by train to assist Detective Constable Osbourne. At the time of his death, he was living at 17, Zebra Street, Salford with his wife Ellen, and their seven children, all under the age of twelve.

As mentioned earlier, James Billington was the executioner of Elijah Winstanley. Under normal circumstances an assistant executioner would also be present at the hanging. On this particular occasion however, his pre-arranged assistant, Thomas Scott, played no part in the event due to a bizarre set of circumstances which took place the previous evening. Thomas

Scott from Huddersfield had been designated to assist James Billington in the execution of Elijah Winstanley and he reported to the prison the previous evening as instructed and had been briefed in his duties for the following morning.

Scott then decided to have a night on the town and started drinking. Later that evening he picked up a local prostitute, 29-year-old Winifred Webb, with whom he had sex. A short time later he discovered that she had stolen his wallet, so he reported the matter to the local police. Webb, who was well known to police, was subsequently arrested and found to be in possession of a wallet and a pair of spectacles belonging to Scott. When the police found out that Scott was due to officiate at the execution of Winstanley, they contacted the Home Office who immediately relieved him of his duties. Scott never again performed duty as either executioner or an assistant executioner in England and Wales. He did however continue to perform his duties in Ireland where he was the chief executioner until 1901. James Billington conducted the execution of Winstanley without an assistant being present.

Another unfortunate nineteenth century railway policeman who became a victim of murder was Police Constable Joseph Byrne who was shot dead whilst diligently carrying out his duties in the typically tranquil village of Plumpton in Cumbria in 1885. At about 8pm on Wednesday 28 October 1885, just after dark, a ruthless gang of professional jewel thieves from London known as the 'ladder gang' committed an audacious burglary at Netherby Hall, the home of Sir Frederick Graham and his wife Lady Hermione Graham. The hall was set in a thirty-six-acre estate at Longtown near Carlisle in Cumbria. The gang gained access to the premises by using a ladder to scale the building before entering an upstairs bedroom window whilst Sir Frederick and his wife were having dinner downstairs.

Having entered the building, the gang stole a quantity of jewellery which included three diamond stars and two diamond earrings from a jewellery case belonging to Lady Hermione. The items were valued at £250 (over £32,000 today).

As the men were about to steal more items of jewellery, they were disturbed by a housemaid banging on the bedroom door which the men had locked from the inside. The maid ran downstairs and sounded the alarm that intruders were on the premises. The men quickly escaped down the ladder and left the estate with the jewellery they had already stolen.

The local police were informed about the burglary and a search for the culprits was quickly under way. Police caught sight of the gang at nearby Kingstown

Netherby Hall, Longtown near Carlisle in Cumbria, scene of the burglary in October 1885.

and Sergeant Roche, accompanied by Constable Johnson of the Cumbria Constabulary, approached the men. A struggle ensued and both officers were beaten with a metal crowbar. Two gang members produced revolvers and shot Sergeant Roche in the arm, before shooting PC Johnson in the chest. Another officer, Police Constable Fortune, later tried to apprehend the men but as he approached them, he was beaten unconscious with the iron bar. No less than nineteen wounds were later found on the skull of Constable Fortune after he was admitted to hospital. The gang members then headed in the direction of Dalston Road railway crossing and were seen walking along the railway track.

Fearing that the men would escape by train, a local railway station master was contacted by police and details of the gang were passed to various railway stations and signal boxes by way of the railway telegraph system and railway staff members were asked to keep an eye out for the three men. In the meantime, the men had made their way to Plumpton Railway Station where at about ten o'clock in the evening they enquired about train times to London. After being told the last train had gone, they started loitering in the area. Police Constable Joseph Byrne of the London and North Western Railway Police was alerted and bravely approached the men but was shot in the head by a revolver before being thrown over a wall where he later died.

The criminals then escaped on a goods train going to Keswick but were spotted boarding the train by a watchful railway guard who then arranged for a telegram to be sent to Tebay Station requesting that police meet the train upon arrival there. When the train arrived in Tebay, the gang was confronted by an angry crowd of railway workers armed with sticks, shovels and other makeshift weapons, who searched the train and found the men hiding under a tarpaulin. One of the men produced a revolver but was disarmed after being struck over the head with a stick by the station master before a vicious struggle ensued. The men were given a sound beating and two of them were tied to telegraph poles until police arrived on the scene. The stolen jewellery, revolvers and other weapons were recovered by police. A fourth member of the gang, William Baker, who was not involved in the assaults and shootings that took place, was later arrested in Lancaster. He did not resist arrest and was subsequently sentenced to penal servitude for his part as an accomplice in the burglary at Netherby Hall.

The three main gang members, who were later named as Anthony Benjamin Rudge, John Martin and James Baker (no relation to William Baker the fourth gang member), were brought before local magistrates and remanded in custody until they appeared before Mr Justice Day at the Cumberland Assizes on 18 January 1886. They were charged with various offences, including the murder of Police Constable Joseph Byrne, other serious assaults and the burglary at Netherby Hall. The men pleaded not guilty. The trial was concluded on Wednesday, 20 January when the jury, after deliberating for just over one hour, returned a guilty verdict against all three defendants. The judge imposed the death sentence on the accused men and on Monday, 8 February 1886, sentence was carried out and the three prisoners were hanged at Carlisle Prison. They showed no remorse.

Being murdered on duty is the ultimate price that a policeman can pay, yet not all cases are as clear cut as the one just referred to due to lack of evidence, as this next example clearly illustrates.

In the nineteenth century, most of the docks and harbours in Britain were owned by railway companies who operated large numbers of ships and ferries. The biggest railway company when it came to shipping, was, without doubt, the Lancashire and Yorkshire Railway, which had the largest shipping fleet of all.

In July 1897, a large-scale industrial dispute over pay and conditions by dock workers employed at the Lancashire and Yorkshire Railway Company Ports of Fleetwood, Barrow and Preston took place. A meeting was held between the workers and management and Mr Ward 'representing the ship brokers' told the workers that unless they returned to work immediately, members of the Shipping Federation who were employed in the large ports of Liverpool, Hull and Grimsby would be sent in to take over their jobs. The workers refused to return to work until their pay dispute was resolved to their satisfaction, so large numbers of Shipping Federation workers were brought in. They were provided with basic sleeping accommodation on vessels berthed within the affected ports. At Fleetwood Docks, a steam trawler, the SS *Ormesby*, was berthed in the Wyre Dock to provide such accommodation for some of these outside workers, two of whom were Peter Carney and Robert Bolton.

On Wednesday 11 August, the strike began to crumble when the dock workers at Preston decided to return to work without having secured any sort of pay deal. They were quickly followed by the dock workers at Barrow. The Fleetwood workers initially refused to go back to work, but without the support of their colleagues at Preston and Barrow, the men slowly returned to their jobs, so the Shipping Federation workers packed their bags and began to return to their native ports. The strike officially ended on Saturday, 21 August, after which the SS *Ormesby* was no longer to be used as sleeping quarters for the dock workers brought in from other ports.

At about eleven o'clock the following evening, the two Shipping Federation workers, Peter Carney and Robert Bolton who had both been drinking, boarded the trawler and were confronted by a night watchman who informed them that the vessel was no longer in use to provide sleeping accommodation and he asked them to leave. They both refused. The night watchman summoned police assistance and Police Constables Marsh and Fisher of the Lancashire and Yorkshire Railway Police attended. After boarding the vessel, the constables approached Robert Bolton and asked him to leave. Bolton refused and started fighting with the two officers. Bolton was eventually restrained and Constable Fisher escorted him from the vessel. In the meantime, Police Constable Alfred Marsh went to another part of the ship where he confronted Peter Carney and requested him to leave the ship. The events which followed are unclear. According to Constable Marsh, Carney refused to leave the vessel and punched him (Marsh) in the face, breaking his jaw. Carney then deliberately threw Marsh some twenty feet into a hold of the ship, causing further severe injuries.

According to Carney, he admitted throwing a punch at PC Marsh, but then ran away. He denied throwing PC Marsh into the hold. At the time of the incident, the hatches on the holds of the vessel were all open. It was pitch dark. There were no lights on the ship and the only available light present was from two oil lamps in the possession of the night watchman who did not witness what happened between Carney and PC Marsh, but heard a thud as Constable Marsh landed in the hold of the ship. Constable Marsh was carried from the hold into the chart-room of the vessel where he was later examined by a doctor before being transferred to Fleetwood Cottage Hospital. Peter Carney and Robert Bolton were both arrested and remanded in custody.

On Tuesday, 24 August, Peter Carney and Robert Bolton appeared before Fleetwood Magistrates Court, charged with the unlawful wounding of Constable Marsh. The court heard Constable Marsh had suffered a broken jaw and a broken rib which had pierced his lung. He had also received a dislocated collar bone as well as being badly bruised and shaken. Although in a serious condition, his injuries were not thought to be life threatening.

Carney, a native of Dundee, and Bolton both stated that they were of no fixed abode and were remanded in custody until the following day. On Wednesday, 25 August, Carney and Bolton again appeared before magistrates. Carney was again remanded in custody. No evidence was offered against Bolton who was not involved in the fracas with Constable Marsh and he was released by the court without charge.

On the afternoon of Tuesday, 28 September, Police Constable Marsh, who was in no fit state to give evidence in court, gave a written deposition before a justice at Fleetwood Cottage Hospital. The accused, Peter Carney who was in police custody, was also present when the deposition was given. The deposition declared that Peter Carney had broken the jaw of PC Marsh with a punch to the face, before throwing him into the hold of the ship, causing the additional injuries.

On Thursday, 21 October, Peter Carney, aged 23, appeared before the Preston Quarter Sessions charged with unlawfully wounding Constable Alfred Marsh. He pleaded not guilty. He was found not guilty due to insufficient evidence, but he was found guilty on a lesser charge of assaulting the officer and sentenced to six months imprisonment.

On the 12 January 1898, Police Constable Alfred Marsh died in Fleetwood Cottage Hospital as a direct result of the injuries which he sustained on the 22 August the previous year. He had been in hospital for over four months. On 27 January, an inquest was held before the Fleetwood Coroner, Mr Parker, into the death of Alfred Marsh. The facts were that Peter Carney was undergoing a sentence of six months imprisonment for assaulting Marsh aboard ship in Fleetwood dock during the dock strike in August the previous year. Constable

Marsh had stated in his deposition that Carney had broken his jaw with a blow and thrown him into the hold of the ship. Carney admitted throwing a punch but denied throwing PC Marsh into the hold of the ship. The doctors confirmed that it was as a result of the injuries sustained when he landed in the hold of the ship that Constable Marsh had died.

The same evidence was given before Mr Parker, the Coroner, as that which had been given before the magistrates and also at the Quarter Sessions, showing the two different versions of the events leading to the death of PC Marsh and the fact that there were no witnesses to corroborate either version of events.

The coroner reviewed the evidence, pointing out that it was almost identical to that which had been presented before the Quarter Sessions jury who had already returned a verdict against Carney. After consulting in private, the foreman of the jury said that the jury agreed that the evidence was not conclusive as to how the deceased Marsh fell into the hold of the vessel, but his death was caused by the injuries sustained as a direct result of that fall. They returned an open verdict. The Coroner then informed Carney that he was at liberty to leave the court.

Many people consider that there was no satisfactory outcome in this tragic case. Was this a case of murder committed by Peter Carney on Constable Marsh? Carney admitted throwing a punch at PC Marsh and a broken jaw is often consistent with receiving a punch to the chin. Recent statistics also show that assaults are a much more common cause of a broken jaw than that of a fall, although in any event the broken jaw itself did not cause the death of Constable Marsh. If Carney did throw Marsh into the hold of the vessel, he would certainly have faced the death penalty. This would give him a strong motive to deny doing so. On the other hand, would PC Marsh have deliberately lied, knowing that he could be sending an innocent man to the gallows?

If Constable Marsh was telling the truth in the deposition, that Carney threw him into the hold of the ship, then Carney would have faced the death penalty. On the other hand, perhaps Carney was telling the truth when he said that he threw a punch at the officer before running away (he may not have known that he had broken the officer's jaw). If that was the case, perhaps Marsh just slipped, tripped or accidentally fell into the hold of the ship in the darkness of the night, then later blamed Carney out of anger, or even out of embarrassment at having fallen into the hold, possibly by not looking where he was going.

There were no independent witnesses as to what happened that night and all the available evidence was studied by three independent bodies, the magistrates, a jury at the Quarter Sessions and by a Coroner's jury. All three came to the same unanimous conclusion. The evidence was not conclusive as to how Marsh came to be in the hold of the ship. Based upon those conclusions and without a confession from Carney there was insufficient evidence to indict Carney on a charge of wilful murder and the verdicts reached at the time were the correct verdicts. One thing is certain, however. Police Constable Alfred Marsh, a family man and a dedicated railway policeman, suffered the ultimate price whilst carrying out his duties. Whether his death was due to an unfortunate accident, or that of murder, nobody will ever know.

Investigations carried out into so-called fatal accidents are not always straightforward and the cause of death is sometimes impossible to establish with any degree of certainty. When the cause of death is thought to be that of drowning, problems often arise if there are no witnesses to show what happened. An example of this occurred at Cardiff Docks in the run up to Christmas in 1869 when a highly experienced Dock Police Sergeant reported for duty for what was to be his last shift. At the time, this busy South Wales shipping port built in the heart of the infamous Tiger Bay was policed by a band of hard yet dedicated officers of the Bute Docks Police Force, a force which later became part of the Great Western Railway Police Force.

On Saturday, 18 December 1869, Sergeant Thomas Howard of the Bute Dock Police was carrying out a routine night patrol on Cardiff Docks, visiting constables who were patrolling their various beats. At about 10.20pm he spoke to Police Constable Gadsby on a bridge over the junction canal between the East and West Bute Docks. They parted company and Sergeant Howard walked away towards the East Dock. A few minutes later, Constable Gadsby heard the sound of a call for assistance on a police whistle (three short sharp blasts) coming from the direction of Sergeant Howard. Constable Gadsby ran towards the East Dock but there was no sign of Sergeant Howard.

In the meantime, Police Constable Higgins, who was patrolling the East Dock, also heard the whistle and hurried towards the junction canal where he heard a cry and saw someone struggling in the dock water. The man, who was not Sergeant Howard, appeared to be drowning and Constable Higgins fished him out of the water with a boat hook. There was still no sign of Sergeant Howard.

After being rescued from the dock by PC Higgins, it transpired that the man was a Russian/Finnish seaman, Johan Halmen, a crew member from the vessel *Hermes*, berthed in the East Dock. PC Higgins sat Halmen on a mooring post and noticed that he was only wearing one boot. When asked about this, Halmen indicated that his other boot was still in the water. Constable Higgins saw something in the water and attempted to pull it out with the boat hook. As he drew the article towards him, he was amazed to find that instead of being a boot, it was a policeman's cape. Higgins asked Halmen if there was a policeman in the water and Halmen nodded his head saying yes. Higgins drew the cape further out of the water and was horrified to find it was attached to the neck of Sergeant Howard.

Up to this point, Halmen had done nothing to assist in rescuing Sergeant Howard and had not given the slightest indication that anyone else was in the water. Whilst Constable Higgins struggled to get Sergeant Howard's body from the water, Halmen started to walk away as if nothing had happened. PC Higgins summoned further assistance with the use of his police whistle and Police Constable Hole arrived at the scene almost immediately. Higgins requested that Hole chase after Halmen and detain him, which he did. A local doctor, Dr Wallace, was called to the scene and after examining the body of Sergeant Howard, formally pronounced life extinct.

Halmen was detained in custody and brought before a Coroner's Inquest, which took place on Monday, 20 December at Cardiff Town Hall, before the Coroner R.L. Rees and a jury. Some difficulty was experienced in getting a clear statement from Halmen, as he was a Russo-Finn and it was necessary to employ two interpreters to communicate with him. In his evidence, Halmen stated he did not know how Sergeant Howard came to be in the water. He further stated that he was approached by Sergeant Howard as he was walking back to his ship. Sergeant Howard grabbed hold of him and wanted to take him somewhere. He did not want to go with the officer, so he resisted and ran away. As he did so, he fell into the water and was later pulled out by the other policeman.

Captain William Wikander of the *Hermes* also gave evidence at the inquest. The captain stated that his vessel was berthed in the East Bute Dock, Cardiff and Johan Halmen was one of his crew members. Having spoken to Halmen about what happened, it was his understanding that Halmen ran away from Sergeant Howard and fell into the water. Sergeant Howard tried to rescue Hallman from the water and whilst doing so, he too fell in. This account was of course different to the account given by Halmen who denied knowing how Sergeant Howard came to be in the water.

The coroner, in addressing the jury, referred to the difficulty they had in obtaining exact evidence owing to the double interpretation of Halmen's evidence. He said that the probability was that both men fell into the water while struggling, but due to there being no evidence of that fact, the jury would have to return an open verdict, which they did.

The coroner pointed out to the jury that Howard was known to be a most experienced officer. There was a bright full moon at the time, but the probabilities were that he accidently fell into the water. A superficial examination of the body had not disclosed any indication of violence having been used towards him. The coroner returned an open verdict and no further action was taken against Halmen.

Whenever a person is killed in the workplace, whatever their occupation, it is a tragic event and there is no doubt that many more lives were lost as a result of accidents during the nineteenth century than are today. It goes without saying that some occupations were far more dangerous than others and whilst there were far more dangerous jobs than that of being a railway policeman, they did suffer their fair share of both fatal and non-fatal accidents whilst on duty.

Appendix C gives an alphabetical list of no less than forty-nine railway and dock policemen who were killed on duty whilst serving between the years 1836 and 1900. The exact numbers of railway and dock police officers killed on duty during the nineteenth century are not known because no known records exist. The list in Appendix C has been compiled primarily as a result of information gleaned from newspaper archives and by carrying out research into railway and dock police history. The true number of officers killed on duty undoubtedly exceeds the list of names which appear in the appendix, but by how many we will never truly know.

Chapter 9

ANALYSIS OF NINETEENTH CENTURY CRIME

By the late 1890s, the railway network had grown so enormously that the passengers carried by the railway companies which existed at the time were counted in hundreds of millions. The Great Northern Railway Company was typical of the many railway companies operating in Britain during the nineteenth century. The company, like most of the other companies, relied on both passenger and freight revenue as its source of income. As with most of the other companies, the Great Northern Railway increased in both size and profitability as the century progressed. By the early 1890s, however, directors of the company had become exceedingly worried about the loss of revenue resulting from fare evasion and ticket frauds committed by passengers. In 1891 alone, there were 44,416 cases of passengers who had to pay excess fare for travelling in superior classes to those for which they had purchased tickets within that one company. Taking into account that well over 100 different railway companies were operating at that particular time, it is difficult to comprehend the massive overall losses in revenue that must have been taking place as a result of fraudulent travel alone.

Sir Henry Oakley, the General Manager of the Great Northern Railway Company, stated that the company had been systematically cheated by fraudulent passengers. Although the railway police officers were dealing with large numbers of ticket fraudsters on a daily basis and prosecutions were being initiated against offenders, it was decided that additional action was required to recoup some of the revenue being lost to fare dodgers.

As a result, a special team of ticket inspectors was introduced into the company and their presence brought immediate success. Excess fare revenue was collected from almost 35,000 passengers found to be travelling fraudulently and 140 passengers were dealt with by police or other means after being found travelling with third class tickets in other carriages and refusing to pay the excess fare. This was a turning point in the fortunes of just one company in greatly reducing revenue losses incurred by dishonest passengers.

In order to demonstrate the sheer volume of passengers travelling on the railways by the 1890s, we can take a look at just one popular national sporting event at the time, the St. Leger horse race meeting held at Doncaster. In September 1892, during the St. Leger race week, the Great Northern Railway Company ran a minimum of fifteen special express trains from London to Doncaster each day for the duration of the meeting. The first class return fare was 12/6d (£80 today).

On St Leger day itself, the busiest day of the meeting, forty trains left the up platform at Doncaster railway station during the late afternoon and evening bound for London and no fewer than forty-three ordinary and special trains departed from the down platform to other destinations. In addition, fifteen special trains departed from the goods shed sidings, seventeen from the Shakespeare sidings, fourteen from St James's bridge sidings and forty from the locomotive sidings. Cherry Tree Station and other sidings were also used. In total there were no fewer than 173 trains packed to the rafters with racegoers. Ladies with their crushed hats and squashed bags struggled to make their way home after watching the French horse La Freche romp home past the winning post to win the St. Leger. Even the train guard's vans were jam-packed with passengers crammed together like sardines in a tin.

By the following year, 1893, the Great Northern Railway Company had amassed a capital of £47 million (equivalent to over £6 billion pounds today) and was carrying over 14 million passengers a year. Their annual receipts from passengers alone amounted to approximately £4 million (equivalent to over £half a billion today). The railways companies at that time were indeed very profitable organisations.[23]

In 1840, the railway department of the Board of Trade was set up, in part to deal with matters relating to railway legislation. An essential part of railway legislation was the Railway Byelaws, which set out a number of minor criminal offences and instructions to both passengers and staff exclusive to the railways and essential to their smooth operation. Byelaws were bespoke and tailor-made to suit each individual railway company, although in practice, the byelaws used by most railway companies were almost identical. They were also intended for the safety and protection of both passengers and staff on the railway. Railway byelaws covered a whole range of issues ranging from the conduct of staff and passengers, to public disorder, ticket offences, damage and a whole range of other issues. Railway byelaws have always been the bread and butter of railway policemen and a huge asset in assisting them in carrying out their day to day duties, from the time they were first introduced, to the present day.

In order to be lawful, a number of certified copies of railway byelaws have to be produced, which bear the signature of the railway company secretary, together with the stamp of the railway company seal. After being approved, they are then signed by the railway secretary of the board of trade. These certified copies are used for legal purposes (such as production in a court of law). The vast majority of printed byelaws, however, were not individually signed and certified as it would have been unfeasible to do so. Many thousands of these 'uncertified' copies were printed in various forms, ranging from large posters to be exhibited at railway stations and depots, to booklets which were (and still are) available for examination by members of the public at various locations, including station booking offices. Copies of the byelaws were also incorporated into railway rule books and regulations issued to all railway staff and of course, railway policemen. Examples of Railway Bye Law Offences are displayed separately in Appendix A.[24]

The early 1840s witnessed a considerable amount of new railway legislation, by the passing of four Acts of Parliament in quick succession. The Railway Regulation Acts of 1840 and 1842, the Railway Act of 1844, and the Railway Clauses Consolidation Act of 1845. These Acts of Parliament set out the manner in which the railways were to be regulated and how they would operate for many years to come. They also created a number of criminal offences which could be committed on the railways. Other similar Acts of Parliament were created as even more railway offences were systematically introduced throughout the nineteenth century and beyond. Some of the acts included legislation which granted certain powers to railway policemen, enabling them to deal with law enforcement more effectively. This included the authority to forcibly eject people from railway premises where necessary and various powers of arrest.

The act of trespassing on private property is normally a civil matter in this country. When the railways were first created however, it was deemed necessary for parliament to make Railway Trespass a criminal offence in order to protect members of the public from the many dangers which existed upon the railway and also to protect railway companies from undesirables entering and roaming on their property. Consequently, legislation was introduced, and the criminal offence of railway trespass was created.

Despite criminal legislation being introduced to prevent it, trespassing upon the railway has always been an everyday occurrence, resulting in the

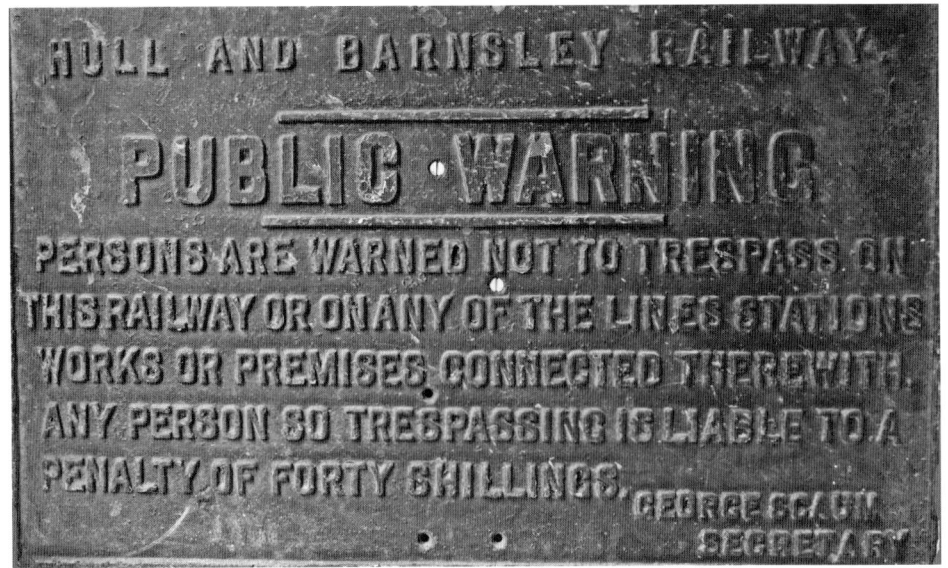

Nineteenth Century, Hull and Barnsley Railway trespass warning notice.

loss of many lives. Dealing with fatalities and handling the human remains of persons being killed by a train were just some of the more unpleasant aspects of a railway policeman's job. Trespass warning notices were (and still are) exhibited at all railway stations and can often be found at the end of station platforms. They can also be found at level crossings, bridges, and many other places on the railway. When railway legislation for trespass was introduced in the 1840s, the maximum penalty for transgressors was £2 (£250 today). The maximum fine today (2022), is £1,000.

Another offence which is all too commonly committed upon the railway is stone-throwing. Whilst stones are traditionally the most common objects to be thrown, the actual offence of stone-throwing not only includes stones as the name suggests, but also includes the throwing or dropping of any missile or object. The offence of stone-throwing is frequently committed by children, who are often unaware of the potential dangers involved. When steam locomotives operated on the railways, children (usually boys) would often drop stones from railway bridges to see if they could land them down the chimneys of passing locomotives. The boys thought this great fun, usually oblivious that this practice frequently caused locomotive cab windows to be shattered, often causing injuries to the drivers and firemen, leading in some cases, to loss of eyesight. Similar injuries were often sustained by passengers sitting alongside windows smashed by missiles being thrown at passing trains.

Stones thrown at signals often shattered the coloured aspects in front of the signal lamps, or the lamps themselves, creating the potential for a serious railway accident. This was in addition to any criminal damage which was caused. Considerable time was spent by railway policemen visiting stone throwing black spots and responding to reports of stone-throwing incidents from the nineteenth century right through to the present day.

Towards the end of the nineteenth century a great deal of concern was being expressed in relation to the unacceptably large numbers of incidents involving the throwing of missiles at and from trains on the networks of all the major railway companies. In 1891, J.H. Nettleship, Goods Superintendent of the Great Eastern Railway, outlined the problem after he announced:

> On this Company's line alone, 199 carriage windows were broken during one month recently, due to stones being thrown at trains in London and the suburbs by gangs of boys in Bethnal Green and Stepney. The folly of throwing stones into trains is only equalled by the criminal thoughtlessness of passengers who fling bottles out of the carriages and send them whisking gaily down the line, utterly regardless of their target. Many a driver has been seriously injured by this pernicious practice and it is also to the terror of the signalman whose box happens to be within the line of fire.
>
> Not long ago, a passenger journeying by the morning express from Liverpool to London threw a bottle out of the window just as the Euston express was passing Berkhampstead. The bottle struck the fireman of the Euston train and nearly cut one of his eyes out. So many cases of injury have occurred through this thoughtless practice of pitching bottles out of railway carriage windows that the London and North Western Railway Company at the commencement of the tourist season now issue a notice, drawing attention to the evil and dangerous habit, making an earnest request that passengers abstain from the practice and stating that empty bottles may be left in the carriages.

Despite the actions of police and railway staff in attempting to curb this type of offence, the incidents continued throughout the nineteenth century and well beyond. Most passenger coaches on our railways today are air conditioned with windows that generally cannot be opened. Due to these modern innovations, the throwing of bottles and other missiles from trains is, thankfully, pretty much a thing of the past.

The Railway Clauses Consolidation Act of 1845 provided early legislation, exclusive to the railways, for railway policemen to deal with acts of wilful and malicious damage. The main provisions of the Act set out details of the various offences, together with powers afforded to railway policemen to deal with these offences. In addition to any fines or punishments issued by the court for people convicted of causing damage to railway property, such offenders were also liable to pay compensation to the railway company concerned who were the victims of such crimes. It also created such offences as omitting to shut or fasten gates on the railway (section 75) and sending dangerous goods by railway (section 105).

Offences like omitting to fasten gates may seem trivial matters at first glance, particularly by townsfolk or city dwellers. Nevertheless, the simple matter of leaving a gate open can lead to a great deal of upheaval on a railway in rural areas. Valuable animals straying onto the railway line are often killed or injured, resulting in hefty compensation payments being paid to farmers by the railway companies. If cattle or sheep are roaming along a railway due to a gate being left open, the railway can quickly become gridlocked leading to train delays which can sometimes result in the cancellation of train services. Owners of animals straying on the railway, often farmers, have to be first identified and then contacted to retrieve their livestock. The tracing of farmers or in some cases private individuals such as dog owners usually falls upon the railway policeman.

Section 154 of the Railway Clauses Consolidation Act 1845 created a power of arrest for railway police officers (not extended to civil police) in respect of offenders of no fixed abode or if their name and address was unknown. This includes the failure or refusal to give a name and address.

Railway policemen were not obligated to use specific railway legislation when dealing with offences committed on the railway. Other non-railway legislation could be used as an alternative if an officer deemed it to be preferable or more appropriate. For example, after the Malicious Damage Act of 1861 was introduced, it was far more commonly used by railway policemen for dealing with persons damaging railway property than using similar railway legislation contained within the 1845 Railway Clauses Consolidation Act, although officers were at liberty to use either.

It is a fact that a substantial increase in railway crime took place during the nineteenth century. This does not mean that as the century progressed the railways became less safe for the travelling public, or that staff and passengers were more likely to be the victims of crime. It was simply due to the increase in size of the railway network, staff and passenger numbers as the years passed by. Between 1830 and 1850, 3,000 miles of track were laid in England, Scotland and Wales but by the end of the century the number had reached over 20,000. Annual passenger numbers also exceeded 1,000 million for the first time in 1899.[25]

The British Transport Police are currently responsible for policing the railways in England, Scotland and Wales and it is their responsibility to compile a record of crime statistics for all offences committed upon the railway network. The figures are then submitted annually to the government to enable the Home Office to publish them, along with the crime statistics of all the other police forces in Britain. This, in theory, gives an accurate reflection of the nation's crime.

During the nineteenth century, things were different. Although railway police forces were responsible for recording all crimes and offences which occurred within their jurisdiction, as they are today, the statistics were submitted along with a report, at regular intervals to the Company Director of the railway company to which they related. The crime figures were later the subject of discussion by management staff and senior railway police personnel at company management meetings, after which the crime statistics were retained by each railway company for inspection by any interested third parties if necessary. Railway crime statistics were not requested by or submitted to any government department or stored in government archives and it is thought that very few, if any, of these records are still in existence.

Likewise, in relation to the reporting and recording of crime by civil police during the nineteenth century, this was also carried out on a local basis until 1898 when all the civil police forces in England and Wales started to submit crime returns to the Home Office. This was the start of collating national crime statistics which were subsequently stored in the Government National Archives. The reporting of all data involving criminal court proceedings and convictions, which are also stored in the government archives, have been routinely submitted by the courts to the Home Office since 1805.

Chapter 10

BEYOND THE NINETEENTH CENTURY

As Britain entered the twentieth century, huge changes were on the horizon. The death of Queen Victoria in 1901 saw the end of an era. The railways continued to operate much as they had done in the late nineteenth century and the railway police maintained their role. In 1908, though, the North Eastern Railway Police made history when they became the first ever police force in Britain to use trained police dogs to track, trace and apprehend suspected criminals, after setting up a dog section. The idea was based upon the successful use of Flemish sheepdogs as police dogs in Belgium. The wide-open spaces and rough isolated terrain often found in railway sidings, goods yards and dock premises seemed ideal for the use of dogs to apprehend offenders and gangs of thieves who frequently operated during the hours of darkness. The dogs also afforded some protection to officers patrolling these isolated and often-fearsome places. Superintendent Dobie (after visiting Belgium) and Inspector Dobson of the NER Police were responsible for setting up the dog section which was run by Inspector Dobson. Airedale Terriers, rather than sheepdogs, were the breed of dogs chosen for use and after undergoing extensive training, they were successfully used to patrol Hull Docks on night shifts during the hours of darkness. By the end of 1908, the successful use of police dogs by the North Eastern Railway Police at Hull, had been extended to other North Eastern Railway Docks at Middlesbrough, Hartlepool and at Tyne Docks in South Shields. Other railway police forces soon followed in the footsteps of the NER Police by setting up their own dog sections.

Over the next few years, storm clouds gathered over Europe, culminating in the Great War of 1914-1918, in which the railways and railway policemen played a vital role. Women Police Officers appeared on the streets of Britain for the first time and also within the ranks of the Railway Police Forces.

The first ever full time Railway Policewoman was Margaret Hood, who was sworn in to join the Great Eastern Railway Police during the First World War

Police Sergeant Number 102 Allinson, of the North Eastern Railway Police with his police dog Jim, pictured at Hull Docks circa 1908. Dog Jim was one of four Airedale Terriers which were the first operational police dogs of any police force to work in Britain. The other three were named Vic, Mick and Ben. They were introduced in 1908 and were primarily used for patrolling Hull Docks during the night-time between 10pm and 5am. The use of police dogs was later extended to other NER Docks at Hartlepool, Middlesbrough and South Shields (Tyne Dock). Alsatians replaced Airedales in railway police forces from 1923.

at Liverpool Street, London in May 1917. The North Eastern Railway Police quickly followed suit by recruiting seventeen Women Constables by the summer of 1918. The London and North Eastern Railway Police also recruited nine women Special Constables during the same period. Recruitment of the first women police was primarily aimed at them dealing with women and children, although their presence also eased the burden of staff shortages, caused by male officers leaving the police service to join the British Armed Forces serving overseas.

The war years, as expected, placed a heavy burden upon the railways. At the end of the war, many railway companies were no longer profitable and the golden days of the railways appeared to be over. It was quickly realised that the railways could no longer survive in their current form, so discussions were held as to the best way forward, which included nationalisation. This idea was considered and rejected but it was decided that the railways did need to be radically re-structured. It was finally decided that future railways would be operated by just four private railway companies. As a result, the Railways Act of 1921 was introduced, which set out the provisions for all the individual railway companies in Britain, of which there were over 120, to be absorbed into four new companies which became known as The Big Four. They were: the London, Midland and Scottish Railway Company; the London and North Eastern Railway Company; the Great Western Railway Company; and the Southern Railway Company. These amalgamations came into effect on 1 January 1923.

It was further decided that the four railway companies would maintain their own police forces, which would be structured the same and standardised wherever possible. Officers from each force would receive the same rates of pay and conditions of service and police uniforms in each of the four police forces would be similar in design.

It was agreed that an existing Railway Police Federation, which was set up in 1920 to look after the interests and welfare of all railway policemen, could continue to serve officers belonging to the four new police forces as it had done in the past. It was further agreed that this federation would be recognised by the new Police Chiefs and Railway Directors as being the official Railway Police Federation for each of the four new Railway Police Forces with effect from 1 January 1923.

A new standardised rank structure was also introduced into the four forces. The police ranks which were adopted, consisted of a Chief of Police (together with an assistant), as being the person in charge of each police force, supported by Superintendents, Chief Inspectors, Inspectors, Sergeants and Constables. The mainstay of each force were the uniformed constables who were employed in large numbers. The new forces also had detachments of plain clothes and detective officers, with the detectives working out of Criminal Investigation Departments. Their role primarily was to investigate serious crimes.

Although the London, Midland and Scottish Railway (LMS) was the largest of the big four Railway Companies, followed (in size order) by the London and North Eastern Railway (LNER), Great Western Railway (GWR) and Southern Railway (SR), the sizes of the Railway Police Forces on the 1 January 1923 was slightly different with the LNER Police having the greatest number of officers.[26] The establishment figures in respect of the four forces were:

LNER Police   1,360 officers.
LMS Police   790 officers.
SR Police   510 officers.
GWR Police   335 officers.

During the 1920s and 1930s, with poverty gripping large parts of the nation, railway policing went through some difficult times. Railway policemen were in the firing line whilst maintaining law and order through the General Strike of 1926. This was quickly followed by the great depression of the 1930s, towards the end of which a number of countries including Britain began to prepare their armed forces for another military conflict which was looming on the horizon. On 1 September 1939, the armed forces of Germany invaded Poland which triggered the start of the Second World War.

In a similar fashion to what happened in 1914, railway policemen were literally thrown into the firing line as they endeavoured to ensure that the railways continued to function through six long years of warfare. Once again, the railways played a vital part in the war effort by transporting troops and munitions on a scale not seen since the Great War. Railway police officers displayed courage and dedication as they served both the railways and their country throughout the conflict. The railways themselves were far more extensively damaged in the Second World War than in the First, due to constant air raids and bombings which took place at the hands of the German Luftwaffe and *Vergeltungswaffen* (V-weapons).

At the end of the Second World War, the railway network was in dire straits once more. After six years of overuse, neglect and lack of maintenance, the railways, which had again been under government control during the war years, were in no fit state to be handed back to the big four companies. This time there was little alternative, other than to nationalise and rebuild the railways.

1 January 1948 saw the railways nationalised, together with the majority of docks, canals, road freight, transport services (including buses and trams) and

a number of other organisations. Nationalisation could not be implemented overnight, so a twelve-month transition period was put in place during which time the British Transport Commission (BTC) was founded as a body designed to oversee the running of these new services as well as introducing a new national police authority to police them.

During the transition period, the big four railway police forces continued to operate as they had done before the war, with the same senior officers in charge. The only difference being that they operated under a new combined title of the British Railways Executive Police and their original area boundaries were changed slightly, to reflect the regions of the newly nationalised railway network, British Railways.

1 January 1949 saw the emergence of the newly formed British Transport Commission Police (BTC Police), which replaced the interim British Railways Executive Police and former LMS, LNER, GWR and SR Police. The New British Transport Commission Police was the first ever national police force in Britain. W.B. Richards MVO was appointed as Chief of Police, the officer in charge of the force. The BTC Police continued to be responsible for policing the railways, but in addition, their jurisdiction was extended to cover the other organisations being administrated by the British Transport Commission, namely ports, docks, harbours, road services and inland waterway. When the inland waterways were absorbed into the British Transport Commission in 1949, police officers who were serving in the private canal police forces were re-sworn in as constables in the new BTC Police Force, but they were allowed to continue policing the canals pretty much as they had done in the past.

In the years that followed, the British Transport Commission Police made a number of changes until in 1957, it was decided to abolish the rank Chief of Police as its highest-ranking officer and replace it with that of Chief Constable in line with Home Office Police Forces. On 7 July 1958, Arthur Charles West OBE, KPM and former Chief Constable of the Portsmouth City Police Force, was officially appointed the first ever Chief Constable of the BTC Police and the first Chief Constable of any Railway Police Force in England and Wales. The rank is still used today by the British Transport Police. The year 1958 also saw the London Transport Police Force, an independent body, absorbed into the British Transport Commission Police. At the end of the 1950s, the BTC Police Force had an establishment exceeding 4,000 regular police officers.

When the inland waterways were taken over by the British Transport Commission in 1949, the canal network alone stretched some 2,500 miles. Canal security had been maintained by a number of private canal police forces, the following of which were absorbed into the new British Transport Commission Police Force, effective from 1 January 1949:-

1. Aire and Calder Navigation Police (founded c.1826).
2. Grand Union Canal Police (founded 1929).
3. Grand Junction Canal Police (founded c.1840).
4. Regents Canal Police (founded c.1840).
5. Lee Conservancy Police (officially founded c.1870, although a police presence had existed on the canal since 1840).
6. Sharpness Docks Police (founded c.1827).
7. Sheffield and South Yorkshire Navigation Police (founded 1895).
8. Shropshire Union Railway and Canal Police (founded 1846).
9. St. Helens Canal and Railway Police (founded 1846).

The first canal to be built in Britain was the Bridgewater Canal near Manchester which opened in 1761 for transporting coal. As Britain's canal network developed, crime emerged, initially with pilfering being carried out from canal barges. This eventually led to the passing of the Canals (Offences) Act of 1840, allowing Navigation Companies to appoint their own police officers. Consequently, after 1840, a number of Canal Police forces were established for the first time.

The canal networks remained under the jurisdiction of the British Transport Commission Police and later the British Transport Police until 1964, when the inland waterways withdrew from their policing arrangements with the force. They formed a new security body called the British Waterways Security Force. This body was replaced in 1977 by the British Waterways Patrol Unit who have continued to enforce security on the canals up to the present day.

The London Passenger Transport Board (LPTB) was established in 1933 to oversee local public transport in London. It traded and operated under the name London Transport. Section 107 of the LPTB Act of 1934 authorised the LPTB to appoint their own police constables. Officers were usually sworn in at Westminster Magistrates Court, before serving in the London Transport Police Force, who were primarily employed to police the underground railway network, together with buses, coaches and trams, within the County of London and adjacent counties within a thirty-mile radius (48 km). The LTPB operated until, on 1 January 1948, it was nationalised (under the provisions of the Transport Act 1947) and renamed the London Transport Executive. It then became a subsidiary organisation of the British Transport

Commission which was formed on the same day. Unlike other transport police forces of the railways, docks, waterways and road freight services, the London Transport Police was not absorbed into the BTC Police in 1949, but for some reason worked independently for almost a decade before finally becoming a part of the BTC Police Force in December 1958. At the end of the 1950s, it had become apparent that the British Transport Commission was far too costly and much too large to be efficient. The writing was on the wall and the British Transport Commission was abolished by the government on 31 December 1962.

On 1 January 1963 the railways entered a new era, under a new governing body called the British Railways Board, which traded under the name British Railways and later British Rail (from 1965). The British Transport Commission Police was renamed the British Transport Police which became operational from 1 January 1963.

The first Chief Constable of the new British Transport Police was Arthur West OBE, KPM, who had been the first Chief Constable of the British Transport Commission Police when he was appointed in 1958 and also the last Chief Constable before the force was renamed in 1963. West, however, did not remain the Chief Constable of the British Transport Police for very long as he retired later that summer and was succeeded by William Owen Gay, commonly known as Bill Gay, who took up office on 1 September 1963 just three weeks after the infamous Great Train Robbery had taken place.

Gay, who had joined the Great Western Railway Police as a constable in 1936 and worked his way through the ranks, was a keen railway police historian and writer. He implemented a number of changes within the British Transport Police Force before his retirement in 1974. After he retired, the British Transport Police went through twenty-five years of changes on its journey into the twenty- first century.

No fewer than eight Chief Constables have been in charge of the force since William Gay sat in the chair in 1974, the latest being Lucy D'Orsi, former Deputy Assistant Commissioner for Special Operations with the Metropolitan Police, who became the first ever female Chief Constable of the British Transport Police when she was appointed in February 2021. A full list of British Transport Police Chief Constables can be found in Appendix D.

As the British Transport Police advances through the twenty-first century, it remains the only national police force in Britain and continues to carry out a specialised role in our society. Although its roots are steeped in history, it is

William Owen Gay OBE, KPM, MA (Oxon). Chief Constable of the British Transport Police from 1963 until 1974.

very much a modern police force. All police officers within the force receive Home Office approved police training alongside officers from Home Office Police Forces. Although the force is no longer responsible for policing docks, ports, canals and other institutions which it has done in the past, it does seem destined for a bright future in the years to come.

Chapter 11

A PICTORIAL HISTORY OF THE TRANSPORT POLICE

This final chapter of the book gives a view through the camera lens of some of the many early transport policemen who afforded protection to the railways, docks and waterways of Britain. It shows in detail the various types of uniforms worn over different decades as the years passed by. Old photographs of early railway policeman are quite rare and difficult to come by, so whilst the quality of some of the photographs in this chapter leave a lot to be desired by today's standards, they are of great interest and do capture glimpses of the past which words alone cannot describe. Whilst each of the photographs in this chapter has its own caption, additional information is included where appropriate.

Brilliantly captured on camera is this group of Manchester, Sheffield and Lincolnshire Railway Policemen, taken at Grimsby Docks in 1895. The officer in charge of the men exaggerates his status as he sits proudly on a chair in the centre, at the front of the photograph, whilst the constable on the extreme left of the picture is slouched against the wall.

The Manchester, Sheffield and Lincolnshire Railway was founded in 1847, after the Sheffield, Ashton-under-Lyne and Manchester Railway was authorised to expand their existing railway to reach Grimsby by merging with the Sheffield and Lincolnshire Junction Railway, the Great Grimsby Railway and the Sheffield Junction Railway.

The Manchester, Sheffield and Lincolnshire Railway, with its headquarters in Manchester, operated under that name until 1897, just two years after this photograph was taken. In 1897, the name of the company was changed to the Great Central Railway in anticipation of the opening of the GCR London extension between London Marylebone and Rugby. Upon completion of the extension, the newly created Great Central main line ran from London Marylebone to Manchester London Road Station (renamed Manchester Piccadilly in 1960).

Uniformed policemen who served in the Manchester, Sheffield and Lincolnshire Railway Police (and later the GCR Police) were not issued with the new type of reinforced police helmets adopted by many forces when they were introduced in the 1860s but continued to wear caps throughout the nineteenth century and into the early twentieth century as can be seen in the photograph.

The vast majority of Grimsby Docks was built and developed from the 1840s by the Manchester, Sheffield and Lincolnshire Railway Company and was policed by that company until 1897, then by the Great Central Railway Police, until it was absorbed into the London and North Eastern Railway Police in 1923. In more recent times, the port was policed by the British Transport Police until 1985, when Associated British Ports introduced private security staff to replace police in all twenty-one of their ports which they had acquired from the British Transport Docks Board, after the docks were privatised under the provisions of the Transport Act 1981.

In its heyday in the early twentieth century, Grimsby Docks was considered to be the largest fishing port in the world. Although world famous as a fishing port, both timber and coal were also shipped through the port in large quantities.

The London, Brighton and South Coast Railway Company was founded in 1846 by the amalgamation of five railway companies, namely the London and Brighton Railway, the London and Croydon Railway, the Brighton and Chichester Railway, the Brighton, Lewes and Hastings Railway and the Croydon and Epsom Railway. The company was famed for its main line between London and Brighton, and was commonly referred to as The Brighton Line.

Police Constable John Holman, of the London, Brighton and South Coast Railway Police, is in the centre/right of this picture wearing a top hat, surrounded by members of the station staff at Portsmouth Railway Station in the 1890s. This may well be one of the last pictures of any British policeman wearing a top hat whilst on duty, as they were gradually phased out after helmets were introduced in the 1860s.

The London, Brighton and South Coast Railway also developed Newhaven as a Channel Ferry Port to rival Dover and they built three paddle steamers to operate ferry services between Newhaven and Dieppe. Whilst the port of Newhaven stood the test of time and is still in operation today, it never did rival Dover as the Dover to Calais route was the quickest, cheapest and most popular ferry crossing between Britain and France.

The London, Brighton and South Coast Railway employed a considerable number of railway policemen throughout its history and a total of 145 officers belonging to the London, Brighton and South Coast Railway Police Force were absorbed into the Southern Railway Police Force when the railway groupings took place in 1923.

The building of Clapham Junction Station was a joint venture between the London and South Western Railway Company, the London, Brighton and South Coast Railway Company and the West London Extension Railway Company (a

Members of the London, Brighton and South Coast Railway Company Station Staff pose for a photograph at Clapham Junction Railway Station in London, circa 1900. In the centre of the picture in the back row, wearing a helmet, is an LBSCR Policeman who would have been on duty there at the time the photograph was taken.

Over a decade before the previous photograph was taken, members of the London and South Western Railway Station Staff posed for a photograph at Clapham Junction Railway Station in 1889. Two London and South Western Railway Policemen can be seen in the centre of the picture on the back row.

railway connecting Clapham Junction in SW London to Willesden Junction in NW London). Despite the names, the railway junction itself and the railway station are not actually located in Clapham, but in the heart of neighbouring Battersea. When the station was opened in March 1860, it was thought that the name Clapham, which was a more affluent area of London than Battersea, sounded more appealing, so it was used, in order to attract passengers from the upper and middle classes in the surrounding areas. Each of the three railway companies employed staff to deal with their respective trains, two of which (LSWR & LBSCR) had police constables based there during the nineteenth century.

Railway porters navigate a luggage barrow along the station platform at Ascot Station, Berkshire in June 1908. The boxes on the barrow contain three trophies, one of which is the Ascot Gold Cup, destined for the Royal Ascot Race meeting. Security is tight (although not by modern day standards) as an LSWR Railway Constable keeps a close eye on proceedings. These measures were put in place after the original Gold Cup was stolen whilst at the Royal Race Meeting the previous year and never recovered.

The London and South Western Railway Company started life as the London and Southampton Railway Company which was founded in 1834. In 1839, the name was changed to the London and South Western Railway when the company decided to extend its railway network to Plymouth. Like all the large railway companies, the company employed a police force, the London and South Western Railway Police, soon after it was inaugurated.

The London and South Western Railway Police Force was the largest railway police force operating in Southern Britain during the nineteenth century and over 220 officers were absorbed into the Southern Railway Police in 1923.

The original London and South Western Railway Workshops opened at Nine Elms, London in 1843 and operated until its closure in 1909. It was replaced by Eastleigh Works which officially opened in 1910, although construction started with the building of the carriage and wagon works in 1899 followed by a motive power depot in 1903. The works were policed by the London & South Western Railway Police from 1910 until 1923.

A small group of London and South Western Railway Policemen pose for a photograph at Eastleigh Works, Hampshire 1910. This was to commemorate the official opening of the works, although large parts of it had already been in use for a number of years.

Possibly the last photograph ever taken of a group of Southampton Harbour Force Policemen at Southampton Docks in 1890. Just two years after this picture was taken, the force was absorbed into the London and South Western Railway Police, who took over the policing of Southampton Docks.

The present-day Southampton Docks first opened in 1843, administered by the Southampton Docks Pier and Harbour Board who established the Southampton Harbour Board Police Force in 1847.

The above photograph, taken in 1890, shows Inspector Henry Rowthorn in the front row wearing a cap with his hand across his tunic; he had been the officer in charge of the force since 1877. The total number of officers in the force in 1890 when the photograph was taken, including Inspector Rowthorn, was just seventeen officers.

The force was absorbed into the London and South Western Railway Police in 1892, shortly after the above photograph was taken. Inspector Rowthorn and all his officers were re-sworn as LSWR Police officers and continued policing the docks.

The Bristol and Exeter Railway Company was founded in 1836, to enable the Great Western Railway to extend its London to Bristol line into Devon and Cornwall. Isambard Kingdom Brunel was appointed Chief Engineer of

This early photograph, taken in 1859, shows (L-R), a lad porter/messenger, shunter, railway policeman, ticket collector and a station porter at Bridgwater Railway Station in Somerset, which was part of the Bristol and Exeter Railway. The policeman wearing a top hat was a constable in the Bristol and Exeter Railway Police.

the project and proceeded to build the line to a seven foot (213.4cm) broad gauge specification, compatible with his GWR design. The B&E Railway opened in stages between 1841 and 1844 and employed its own police force in the form of the Bristol and Exeter Railway Police. The Bristol and Exeter Railway Police Force was absorbed into the GWR Police Force in 1876 after the Bristol and Exeter Railway Company became a part of the GWR Company.

A Great Eastern Railway Policeman poses for a photograph with station staff at Southend c.1910.

The Great Eastern Railway was founded in 1862 by the amalgamation of the Eastern Counties Railway, the Eastern Union Railway and several other railway companies. The Company Headquarters was in Liverpool Street in London and the main railway line ran from Liverpool Street to Norwich. The railway served places which included Cambridge, Chelmsford, Colchester, Great Yarmouth, King's Lynn, Ipswich, Southend-on-Sea and the East London Docklands. The GER Company employed one of the largest railway police forces in Britain and over 300 officers were absorbed into the LNER Police when the railway groupings took place in 1923.

The Great Eastern Railway Police was also responsible for much of the security surrounding the royal family and other VIPs due to Wolferton Railway Station being within their jurisdiction. The railway station served the royal residence of Sandringham House

The Lyn and Hunstanton Railway merged with the West Norfolk Junction Railway in 1874 and became the Hunstanton and West Norfolk Railway, until it was sold to the Great Eastern Railway Company in 1890. The Great Eastern Railway Company completely rebuilt Wolferton Station in 1898 and connected the single track from King's Lynn with a double track. The new station consisted of two platforms adorned with Tudor-style buildings and two luxurious royal waiting rooms. A new signal box was built, together with seven railway sidings, mainly to accommodate royal trains and locomotives which frequently used the station. Sadly, the railway line closed in 1969, although the station itself was bought by a private buyer and has since been preserved.

The photograph which appears at the top of the next page, which was taken in Norwich in 1911, shows why such large numbers of policemen were employed by companies such as the GER. Over fifty officers in this photograph were in Norwich for five days to cover just one event, the Royal Agricultural Show. It is likely that additional officers who do not appear in the photograph were also used to police the show.

For this one event, two special railway stations were purpose-built to cope with the passenger numbers. Each station had two platforms, 700 feet (213 metres) long and 75 feet (23 metres) wide, with a connecting footbridge. To facilitate passengers, toilets, refreshment rooms, cloakrooms and other facilities were provided. Although security of the king was paramount, the event itself was well organised and very successful.

The Great Eastern Railway and the GER Police Force were both founded in 1862. To commemorate fifty golden years of the GER Police, smart new uniforms were issued to all officers in 1912. These uniforms were based on

A large gathering of Great Eastern Railway Police Officers pictured at Norwich, ready to perform duties at the Royal Agricultural Show, a five-day event which took place from 26 to 30 June 1911, visited by George V on 28 June.

Marking an occasion. A group of GER Policemen pictured in 1912 to commemorate the fiftieth anniversary of the creation of the Great Eastern Railway Police Force. They are kitted out in a new style uniform, wearing striped armbands for the first time and new cockscomb design helmets. A comparison with the previous photograph (taken a year earlier) clearly shows the difference in two styles of uniforms being worn.

An unknown Great Eastern Railway Police Constable poses for a studio photograph circa 1912. He is wearing his new style GER Police uniform (issued in 1912) with a striped armband and a helmet with a distinct cockscomb top, similar to the City of London Police uniforms.

those worn by the City of London Police with cockscomb or cockscomb top helmets (as opposed to rose top helmets worn by the Metropolitan Police and other railway police forces) and striped armbands. The City of London Police serves an area of just one square mile which incorporates the former GER railway stations of both Liverpool Street (HQ of the GER) and Fenchurch Street.

An unknown Great Eastern Railway Police Sergeant circa 1913. Although wearing the new GER Police style uniform issued in 1912, he is not wearing the striped armband on his left arm. This may be because he was off duty when he posed for this studio photograph.

Police Constable Number 86 (name unknown), of the North Staffordshire Railway Police, poses for a studio photograph circa 1900. This rare picture may be the only surviving photograph of a North Staffordshire Railway Policeman in existence. It is believed that Constable Number 86 was stationed at Newcastle-Under-Lyme.

The North Staffordshire Railway Company, which became affectionately known as 'Knotty' after its Staffordshire knot logo, was founded in 1845 to promote the Staffordshire Potteries and surrounding areas. The railway opened in stages from June 1846 onwards. The section from Stoke-on-Trent to Newcastle-Under-Lyme opened to both goods and passenger services in 1852.

The North Staffordshire Railway was a relatively small company, surrounded by other larger companies and as the nineteenth century progressed several attempts were made to buy it out, or amalgamate it with one or more of the neighbouring railway companies. The London and North Western Railway in particular made repeated take-over bids which were rejected. The North Staffordshire Company continued to prosper as an independent company for over seventy-six years, before being forcibly absorbed into the London, Midland and Scottish Railway Company, when the railway groupings took place in 1923. The North Staffordshire Railway Police then became part of the LMS Railway Police.

In the previous photograph, Constable Number 86 (name unknown) is wearing the type of cap which replaced the top hat in some police forces in the late 1850s, early 1860s. Most police forces were wearing helmets by the time this picture was taken but the North Staffordshire Railway Police was one of the few forces that continued wearing caps until the early twentieth century.

The Staffordshire Knot symbol appears on the policeman's cap, above the word Police and in between the letters N and S, although it is almost illegible in the photograph. The origin of the knot itself is not really known but it is a distinctive three looped knot which became a symbol of the Staffordshire Potteries and Staffordshire itself. It was also displayed on the coat of arms adopted by the North Staffordshire Railway Company and of course on police uniforms.

The London and North Western Railway Company was founded in July 1846 by the amalgamation of the London and Birmingham Railway, the Manchester and Birmingham Railway and the Grand Junction Railway. All three companies employed their own railway policemen who then merged to create the new LNWR Police Force. The London and North Western Railway continued to join forces with other railway companies until it became the largest railway company operating in Britain by the end of the nineteenth century, having absorbed over 100 different railway companies.

The first national strike by British coal miners occurred in 1912, in which rioting occurred after over one million men walked out for thirty-seven days until the government passed a minimum wage law. Between 1917

This very early photograph shows an unknown London and North Western Railway Policeman at Rugby Station, standing alongside locomotive No. 35, which is working a Rugby to Market Harborough passenger service circa 1860. The locomotive was built by Sharp, Stewart and Company of Manchester in 1848. The railway policeman, who is wearing a tailcoat and top hat, is carrying what is presumed to be a green flag, which he will use to inform the engine driver of line clear, so he may depart with his train.

and 1921, the coal mines had been taken under government control and it was expected that the coal industry would be nationalised. Instead, in 1921 the industry was handed back to the private mine owners, who in many cases refused to pay the miners the salary which they were receiving when the pits were under government control. This led to a three-month strike. Rail Unions and Transport Unions, who normally supported miners in a triple alliance with each other during strike actions, refused to support the mineworkers. Their actions were seen as a betrayal of the miners and breach of solidarity.

Two London and North Western Railway Uniformed Policemen pictured at Wigan with an unknown person, possibly an LNWR Detective, in April 1921, during the coal miners' strike. Wigan has a rich history of coal mining with many hundreds of mine shafts being sunk in the surrounding area which was part of the Lancashire Coalfield. Coal mining production in Lancashire peaked in 1907.

Police Constable James Jackson of the Taff Vale Railway Police, pictured at Cardiff c.1899.

The Taff Vale Railway opened in 1840 to connect Merthyr Tydfil in South Wales to Bute Dock in Cardiff which had opened the previous year. This enabled the coal and iron which was being produced by collieries and foundries in and around Merthyr to be exported from Cardiff Docks. The railway also carried passenger traffic between Cardiff and Merthyr.

In order to use the port facilities in Cardiff, the TVR leased the whole of the west side of the Bute Dock and agreed to police it with their own police force which had been formed to police the Taff Vale Railway.

The Taff Vale Railway Police continued policing the docks until 1858 when a new police force, the Bute Dock Police, was created to police the whole of Cardiff Docks as a result of a second Bute Dock having been built and due to open the following year. All Taff Vale Railway police officers were then withdrawn from Cardiff Docks and transferred to duties policing the TVR railway network.

In 1850, after rich coal deposits were discovered in the Rhondda Valley, the TVR built a twelve miles long branch line the length of the valley from their line at Pontypridd to Treherbert to serve the new collieries. The line was completed in 1856 for coal traffic and passenger traffic was introduced into the valley in 1863.

In 1865, the railway was further extended from Cardiff to nearby Penarth Dock which the Taff Vale Railway then leased in order to export coal more cheaply than using the Cardiff Bute Docks where tariff charges had been introduced.

When the Taff Vale Railway Police Force was created in 1840, George Fisher, Assistant Chief Civil Engineer of the railway, was also appointed Superintendent/Chief of Police in charge of the Force. In effect, he had two completely different jobs within the railway company. Although this appears to be a very unsatisfactory arrangement and is without doubt unique in the history of railway policing, it obviously suited the Board of Directors of the Taff Vale Railway Company, as Mr Fisher continued performing both jobs for thirty years.

In 1870, at the age of 60, Fisher retired as Chief of Police, but continued working as a civil engineer for a number of years on a part time basis. He eventually died at his home in Cardiff in 1891 at the age of eighty-one. The Taff Vale Railway Police Force was absorbed into the Great Western Railway Police in 1923; thereafter, GWR police officers had jurisdiction on the former Taff Vale Railway and Cardiff Docks.

The South Wales Railway Company was originally formed in 1845 after being sponsored by the Great Western Railway, who wanted a broad-gauge

This early photograph shows Police Constable Runnicles, of the South Wales Railway Police, taken circa 1860. Although the photograph is rather poor quality, mainly due to age, it may well be the only photograph of a South Wales Railway Policeman in existence, as the railway which was built between 1850 and 1859 survived for just thirteen years before being absorbed into the Great Western Railway in 1863. All SWR Police Officers were then sworn in as GWR Policemen.

railway built to connect the Great Western Railway, at Gloucester, to South Wales and the West Wales ports of Fishguard Harbour, Pembroke Dock and Milford Haven. The engineer for the project was Isambard Kingdom Brunel.

The first section of the line opened in June 1850. It consisted of seventy-five miles of broad-gauge track from Chepstow to Swansea. A missing link between Gloucester and Chepstow was delayed due to the building of Chepstow Bridge and did not fully open until 1853.

The line from Swansea to Carmarthen was completed by October 1852, after which it was decided that, due to escalating costs, the proposed line would not extend to Fishguard and Pembroke but would terminate at Neyland Point in the Milford Haven Waterway. The GWR did eventually extend the line from Haverfordwest to Fishguard Harbour, but not until 1906.

Prior to that, a new railway line was built by the Pembroke and Tenby Railway Company, which was formed to connect the Royal Naval Dockyard at Pembroke to Tenby. The line, financed by local support, was completed in 1863. The line was then further extended to connect to the South Wales Railway at Whitland and completed in 1866. It is still in regular use today.

The South Wales Railway had been promoted by the Great Western Railway from the day it was founded and the two companies were closely allied thereafter. It came as little surprise when the companies amalgamated in 1863.

During its short lifespan, the South Wales Railway employed a number of railway policemen. Little is known or has been written about the South Wales Railway police force, but it is known that their constables were issued with elaborately painted truncheons, one of which can be seen in a photograph in Chapter 2.

A group of Bute Dock Police Officers, pictured outside Cardiff Docks Police Station in the mid 1890s. Superintendent John O'Gorman, officer in charge of the force, is sitting in the middle of the front row. Note that the constables in the picture are wearing helmets, whilst the sergeants are wearing caps. Although this photograph is black and white, the uniforms worn by Bute Dock Policemen were green in colour.

The first modern dock in Cardiff was called the Bute Dock which was opened in 1839. The Bute Dock Company initially did not employ a police force, instead, from 1840, the dock was policed by the Taff Vale Railway Police. The TVR Company agreed to this after they leased part of the dock when they became the main dock user in 1841.

Bute Dock was soon working to full capacity so a new dock was built which opened in 1859. The new dock was called East Bute Dock, so the original Bute Dock was re-named the West Bute Dock. In 1858, just prior to the opening of the East Bute Dock, the Bute Dock Company created its own police force called the Bute Dock Police, which assumed policing for both the East and West Docks. The Taff Vale Railway Police officers who had worked the docks since 1840 were withdrawn from the dock and transferred to Taff Vale Railway duties. Two further docks, the Roath Dock (opened 1887) and the Queen Alexandra Dock (opened 1907), were later built at Cardiff and both were policed by the Bute Dock Police Force.

Bute Dock Bobbies were instantly recognisable by their green uniforms which they were proud to wear. They were renowned as being tough, hard, no-nonsense policemen, yet they commanded respect and were held in high esteem by the local populace who relied on them for protection in the rough community of Tiger Bay. Bute Dock Constables were routinely issued with cutlasses for use on night patrol duties from 1860 until 1887. A photograph of an original Bute Dock Police cutlass appears in Chapter 2.

At its peak, Cardiff Docks was one of the largest and busiest docks in the world, exporting vast amounts of coal and iron ore. A total of almost 11 million tons of coal was shipped out of Cardiff Docks in 1913 alone and well over 100 shipping companies operated from the port. More than 250 tramp steamers which carried minerals and other products were owned by companies based in Cardiff.

The Bute Dock Police Force continued to police Cardiff Docks during and after the First World War, retaining their green uniforms until they reluctantly became a part of the Great Western Railway Police Force from January 1923. The GWR Police then took over the policing of Cardiff Docks until the railways were nationalised in 1948. The docks came under the jurisdiction of the British Transport Commission Police from 1949 until 1962, followed by the British Transport Police in 1963. The BTP continued policing Cardiff Docks until 1985 when their services were withdrawn in favour of private security measures following the privatisation of the British Transport Docks Board by the Thatcher government in the 1980s.

Above left: **Police Constable** No.10, William Morgan of the Cardiff Bute Docks Police force, circa 1910.

Above right: **Police Constable** No.12, James Gadsby joined the Bute Dock Police in 1865, when constables were still being issued with cutlasses for their protection whilst patrolling Cardiff Docks during the evenings and night-time. Photograph taken in the early 1900s.

Officers of the Regent's Canal and Dock Police pose for a group photograph in London, circa 1921.

Construction of the Regent's Canal started in 1812 to link the then Grand Junction Canal at Paddington in West London, to the River Thames at Limehouse in East London, a distance of some 8.6 miles (14 km). Although proposed in 1802, construction of the canal did not start until a decade later in 1812. The first section of the canal from Paddington to Camden Town opened in 1816 and the remaining section, which was completed in 1820, terminated at the Regent's Canal Dock which today is known as the Limehouse Basin.

The Regent's Canal Dock built at Limehouse was used to transfer cargo between the seafaring vessels and canal barges. Various other basins were constructed along the canal which soon became an important transport hub for the distribution of cargo in the capital. Unfortunately, the canal had been built too late and the construction of the railways which had started in earnest by the late 1830s was already becoming a threat. The canal networks could not compete with the railways and their trade rapidly declined. Several attempts were made over the years to convert the Regent's Canal into a railway, but without success. However, like most other canals, it did survive and continued transporting cargo until the middle of the twentieth century.

Throughout their working lives, the Regent's Canal and the Regent's Canal Docks were an important part of the inland waterways network, protected for much of the nineteenth and twentieth centuries by the Regent's Canal and Dock Police Force which is believed to have been formed in the mid-1840s.

The Regent's Canal merged with the Grand Union Canal in January 1929 and the police officers who had served in the Regent's Canal Police Force became part of the Grand Union Canal Police. In January 1949, police officers serving in the Grand Union Canal Police (including former Regent's Canal and Dock Police Officers) were absorbed into the British Transport Commission Police which became the British Transport Police in 1963.

The canal has survived to the present day and like many other canals in Britain it is used by private sailing vessels and is very popular with pedestrians walking its towpaths to visit attractions such as Little Venice. It is indeed a popular part of the leisure industry in London and has been protected by private security services since 1964, when the inland waterways severed policing arrangements with the British Transport Police.

The photograph which appears overleaf, shows Superintendent David Johnson (middle of the second row, wearing a trilby hat), who was the officer in charge of the Swansea Harbour Trust Police Force. In 1923, he retained his

Over fifty officers of the former Swansea Harbour Trust Police Force proudly pose for one final photograph in July 1923, wearing their original Swansea Harbour Trust Police uniforms. All the men in this photograph had been re-sworn in as Great Western Railway Policemen after the GWR Police took over the Force in January of that year.

rank with the GWR Police after the Swansea Harbour Police Force became a part of it. He remained at Swansea Docks until 1925, when he was transferred to Cardiff Docks where he worked as a Divisional Police Superintendent for sixteen years until his retirement in May 1941. Sadly, he did not enjoy a long and happy retirement as he died in February the following year.

The Swansea Harbour Trust itself was established in 1791 to build a modern port to replace the many wharves which were operating on the River Tawe in Swansea. The wharves were unable to cope with the huge amounts of minerals being exported from Swansea at a time when the town was exporting almost sixty per cent of the world's copper which was being produced in the lower Swansea Valley. The town of Swansea, now a city, was even nicknamed Copperopolis. In addition to exporting copper, vast amounts of coal were also being shipped out of Swansea from surrounding collieries.

The first modern dock to be built in Swansea was the North Dock which opened in 1852. Also in 1852, the Swansea Dock Company, a private company, started to build a second new dock, Swansea South Dock. The Swansea Dock Company was later bought out by the Swansea Harbour Trust who completed and opened the South Dock in 1859. The Harbour Trust continued expanding Swansea Docks by building the Prince of Wales Dock in 1881 (extended in 1889), the Kings Dock in 1909 and the Queens Dock in 1920.

When the North and South Docks were built in the 1850s, the Swansea Harbour Trust employed a number of dock-gate keepers to prevent unauthorised persons entering the docks. However, the trust did not consider it necessary to create its own police force like most other dock companies had done, as the local Swansea Borough Police (established 1836) seemed quite happy to police the docks and they continued to do so for almost forty years.

In 1889, the population of Swansea was in the region of 78,000 and the total establishment for the Swansea Borough Police was just 99 police officers, which included 11 officers who were classified as Docks Policemen by the then Chief Constable of the Swansea Borough Police, Captain Colquhoun. The eleven Swansea Borough Dock Policemen patrolled beats which had been created on Swansea Docks over a period of time by extending the area of the town beats as the docks developed.

Throughout the 1880s, the Swansea Borough Police 'Watch Committee' voiced concerns about policing the docks and expressed their views that local taxpayers should not be funding policing of the docks which was private property. Pressure was brought to bear on the SHT who eventually capitulated and founded their own SHT Police Force in 1893. Officers were sworn in before local magistrates and given the powers to act as Borough Constables in the Swansea Harbour Trust Police (known locally as the Swansea Harbour Police), with jurisdiction upon the whole of Swansea Docks and within a half mile perimeter of the dock estate.

The Swansea Harbour Police Force continued to police the whole of Swansea Docks until they were absorbed into the GWR Police, who took over the policing of the docks in January 1923. By 1925, the GWR Police had been divided into divisions, sub-divisions and police stations or police posts. Swansea Docks was designated a sub-division of a GWR Police Division in Cardiff. Routinely, all GWR Police Divisions were under the command of a Police Superintendent and Sub-Divisions under the command of a Police Inspector. Consequently, a Police Inspector was appointed in charge of Swansea Docks and Superintendent Johnson was transferred to Cardiff Docks where he worked as a Divisional Police Superintendent until his retirement in May 1941.

The GWR Police Force policed Swansea Docks until the railways were nationalised in 1948. In January 1949, the docks came under the jurisdiction of the British Transport Commission Police, followed by British Transport Police in 1963. The British Transport Police severed all ties with Swansea Docks in 1985 after the docks were privatised under the ownership of Associated British Ports who decided to engage private security officers in all the South Wales Ports, instead of maintaining a full time police presence.

The Midland Railway Company was founded in 1844 by the amalgamation of the Midland Counties Railway, the North Midland Railway and the Birmingham and Derby Junction Railway. The company headquarters were located in Derby. The railway was extended to Gloucester in 1846, after it merged with the Birmingham and Gloucester Railway Company. The Midland Railway continued to expand during the nineteenth century by acquiring over thirty additional railway companies, making it one of the largest railway companies in Britain by the turn of the century. The railway extended from London, Bristol and Bath in the south to Manchester, York and Carlisle in the north. The company also built a

A group of Midland Railway Policemen pose for a photograph at Birmingham in 1902. Superintendent Harry Carr, who was the senior officer at Birmingham, can be seen sitting in the front row of the picture wearing civilian clothes.

A small group of Midland Railway Policemen at Derby just after the First World War, circa 1919.

large harbour at Heysham in Lancashire which opened in 1904. When the railway groupings took place in 1923, a total of 332 Midland Railway policemen were absorbed into the London, Midland and Scottish Railway Police.

The first ever National Strike by railway workers in Britain took place in 1911 and the Midland Railway Police along with all the other railway and dock policemen in the country were very much in the firing line. The dispute began in July of that year when unofficial action started to be taken by some railway workers at various locations, over the length of time being taken to improve the low pay and conditions of railway workers. The issues had been under discussion for over four years, after a Conciliation Board was set up by the government in 1907 to look into the matter. In the opinion of the workers, little or no progress had been made.

The first ever railway union had been established as early as 1872 and by 1911, four trade unions represented the workers. The Amalgamated Society of Railway Servants, the Associated Society of Locomotive Engineers and Firemen, the General Railway Workers Union and the Signalmen and Pointsmen's Society. As a result of the unofficial action being taken by some

Ambergate Station Junction Signal Box in Derbyshire was located at one of the most important railway junctions in the Midlands at the beginning of the twentieth century. This photograph shows the importance afforded to its protection during the railway strike of 1911. A Midland Railway Policeman, standing guard, is flanked on either side by four armed guards from the Royal Dublin Fusiliers. A railway porter is present to attend to their needs. The signalman standing inside the signal box is one of many railwaymen who worked through the strike to keep the railways running. *This image also appears on the back cover.*

workers, the four unions held an emergency meeting in Liverpool, after which they issued an ultimatum to the Railway Companies (and the government), that company delegates must discuss all future negotiations directly with representatives of the unions or they would exert their authority and call a national railway strike.

The prime minister of the Liberal government of the day, the Right Honourable Herbert Asquith, refused the ultimatum and instructed the Railway Companies to keep their trains running, stating that troops and police would be deployed where necessary to assist in doing so. On 17 August, the trade unions called for a National Railway Strike to take place with effect from 19 August 1911.

The Home Secretary, Winston Churchill, ordered troops to march into over thirty towns and cities throughout Britain, as well as assisting police to protect vulnerable railway targets such as busy railway junctions and signal boxes. Although most Railway Companies did manage to keep the railways running with many members of staff not wishing to go on strike, over 200,000 railway workers heeded the unions' call and turned out to bring the railways to a standstill.

The events that followed led to serious public disorder and rioting in many parts of the UK. In Liverpool, troops opened fire on striking workers during a riot and several men were wounded, one fatally. At Scarborough on the North Eastern Railway an attempt was made to derail a passenger train by jamming a large piece of coal into some points as the train approached a river bridge.

The worst riot of all occurred in Llanelli, South Wales where mass picketing took place. Railway trucks were set on fire at Llanelli Station, resulting in an explosion which killed four people and as the riots continued, two men were shot dead by soldiers. Fortunately, the strike was quickly called off by the evening of Saturday 19 August 1911 after just two days and the dispute came to an abrupt end. George V sent a special message to representatives of both the Railway Companies and Railway Workers for the successful termination of the strike which no doubt prevented further loss of life.

Tyne Dock in South Shields was just one of the docks policed by the former North Eastern Railway Police. Other docks owned and policed by the North Eastern Railway Company during the nineteenth century were at Hull, Middlesbrough and Hartlepool. Coal was also shipped out of Blyth and Gateshead from staithes (quays) which were also owned by the NER Company and policed by the North Eastern Railway Police.

The Midland Railway Police employed a number of Special Constables to assist regular constables in their day to day duties. This photograph, taken at Derby in August 1911, shows some Midland Railway Specials taking time to pose for the camera during the National Rail Strike in August 1911. Midland Railway Special Constables wore flat caps as can be seen in the photograph as opposed to the helmets worn by regular constables at the time.

A group photograph of North Eastern Railway Police Officers taken at Tyne Dock, South Shields c.1910. *This photograph also appears on the front cover of the book.*

The NER Company itself was founded in 1854 by the amalgamation of the York, Newcastle and Berwick Railway, the York and North Midland Railway, the Malton and Driffield Railway and the Leeds Northern Railway. The railway headquarters were at York.

As the nineteenth century progressed, the North Eastern Railway expanded by absorbing numerous other railway companies which included the Newcastle and Carlisle Railway (merged 1862) and the Stockton and Darlington Railway (merged 1863). They continued to expand into the twentieth century and, as late as April 1922, they amalgamated with the Hull and Barnsley Railway Company, less than one year before the main railway groupings took place.

Police Constable Number 55, George Pettinger of the North Eastern Railway Police, pictured at Middlesbrough in 1903.

Two unknown North Eastern Railway Dock Constables pictured at Hartlepool Docks, c.1898.

Seventeen North Eastern Railway Policewomen pictured at York in the summer of 1918.
  L-R Standing; E.J. Timmings (York & Leeds), A.H. Hall (Middlesbrough), M.A. Weatherall (Newcastle), A. Speading (Newcastle), M.M. Collins (Middlesbrough), M. Stephenson (Newcastle), A.M. Duffit (Hull), M.M. Dickenson (Hull), M.H. Whitwell (York & Leeds), S. Cooper (Darlington), L-R Seated; A. Smith (Newcastle), F. Potter (York), K.F. Morgan (York), Sergeant M. Roberts (York), M. Smailes (Newcastle), A. Storey (Newcastle), C. Davison (Newcastle).

All the ladies in the above picture are wearing armbands above their left wrists on their tunics, with the exception of Sergeant Roberts who is wearing her armband above her right wrist (centre of the front row). Sergeant Roberts was the first Woman Police Sergeant to be appointed in any British Police Force.

Woman Constable F. Potter, sitting second from the left in the front row of the photograph, is thought to be of Asian origin and is likely to have been the first non-white woman police constable, or indeed the first ethnic minority police officer, to serve anywhere in Britain.

Women Police Officers first appeared in Britain during the twentieth century, although as early as the 1890s some officers' wives and relatives did assist the police by acting as volunteer matrons to look after woman who were in custody after being arrested by police. A few years later, the concept of employing policewoman began to emerge with discussions and campaigns by women's pressure groups, pointing out that the lack of women being present to deal with searching female prisoners and attending to their needs was wrong. As a result, a Voluntary Women's Force was set up at Bath in 1912, followed by unpaid women volunteers being allowed to organise police patrols which later became known as the Women's Police Service.

After the outbreak of the First World War in 1914, large numbers of male officers left the service to join the armed forces. A number of police forces decided to recruit women police officers to be sworn in with the full police powers. This was due in part to enable them to deal with women and children, but also to increase the police numbers in order to compensate for the shortfall caused by male officers leaving the service to join the military.

The first ever policewoman in Britain was Edith Smith who joined the Lincolnshire Constabulary at Grantham in August 1915. Other forces followed suit. In May 1917, Margaret Hood was the first ever policewoman to join a railway police force when she was sworn in as a constable with the Great Eastern Railway Police at Liverpool Street in London, with the same powers as her male counterparts. The North Eastern Railway Police wasted little time and four policewomen were sworn in during December of that year. By the summer of 1918, the North Eastern Railway Police had a total of seventeen female officers working in uniform. The Metropolitan Police started recruiting female officers in 1919.

In April 2017, exactly 100 years after the first British policewomen, Cressida Dick DBE QPM, was appointed the first ever woman Commissioner of the Metropolitan Police. Less than four years later, Lucy D'Orsi, Deputy Assistant Commissioner (Special Operations) with the Metropolitan Police, was appointed Chief Constable of the British Transport Police from February 2021. She is the first ever woman to take command of a Transport Police Force in Britain.

The North Eastern Railway Police, like many other police forces, experienced a very busy year in 1911 when the photograph on the next page was taken. The country was in the grip of industrial turmoil due to discontent amongst the working classes. The summer months saw nationwide strikes from seamen, dock workers, railway workers, firemen and all manner of both skilled and unskilled workers. Docks were brought to a standstill as far afield as Aberdeen, and Glasgow in the north, to London, Southampton and Bristol in the south. The North Eastern Railway Docks at Hull were in the thick of things as riots took place, which necessitated over 500 extra police officers being drafted into the city from elsewhere to manage the troubles.

A Group of North Eastern Railway Policemen pictured at Hull Docks during the 1911 Dock Strike.

Even the nation's schools saw strike action from pupils who imitated the actions of their fathers. Pupils refused to obey teachers and took to the streets with banners requesting shorter hours, free pencils and no cane, supposedly in support of striking workers. The school strikes spread to over sixty towns and cities around Britain, including Hull.

Front line officers in all the railway and dock police forces experienced animosity and ill feeling from both members of the public and workers during times of industrial civil unrest, as did civil police officers nationwide. The work being carried out by uniformed officers in all forces in quelling riots and controlling masses of demonstrators was difficult and one of the more unpleasant aspects of being a policeman, yet it was an important role which had to be carried out.

Although trade union membership increased in the 1914-1918 war years, industrial unrest declined after strikes were prohibited under the Munitions of War Act which was introduced in 1915.

After the war, the railway groupings took place which dramatically changed the face of Britain's railways and 1923 saw the Big Four Railway Companies emerge, together with four new railway police forces which worked in unison to police the national railway network, together with a number of Docks, Ports and Harbours. The North Eastern Railway Company became a major part of the new London and North Eastern Railway Company and its serving police officers were absorbed into the LNER Police force.

The Furness Railway Company was one of the smaller railway companies which operated in the former counties of Cumberland, Westmorland and North Lancashire in North West England. The company started operating in 1846 and extended from Whitehaven in the north, down the coast to Barrow-in-Furness then eastwards to Carnforth and Windermere. The Company also built four massive docks at Barrow which opened between 1867 and 1881, before developing local iron and steel works in the area. By the end of the nineteenth century, Barrow had the largest steelworks in the world and one of the biggest shipbuilding centres in Britain. The Furness Railway also had a complete monopoly over the busy docks.

The Furness Company enjoyed rich pickings by transporting both iron-ore and slate from local quarries to the docks at Barrow for export, as well as

This rare photograph shows a small group of Furness Railway Policemen posing for a photograph at Barrow-in-Furness in 1920, not long before being absorbed into the LMS Railway Police in January 1923.

conveying passengers on company owned ships which sailed to and from Barrow to local beach holiday resorts and destinations further afield. In addition, the Furness Railway transported many thousands of passengers in the summer months to Windermere and other parts of the Lake District for their annual summer holidays.

Little has been written about the Furness Railway Police, but no doubt they would have operated on similar lines to other railway and dock police forces. One interesting fact that is known, is that the Furness Railway Company, unlike most, if not all, of the other railway companies, employed a considerable number of women in the 1840s and 1850s, to perform point duties and gate duties on the railway, instead of using railway policemen, although uniformed railway policemen were still responsible for overseeing the actual running of the trains by using hand signals, lamps and flags in a similar fashion to railway policemen working for other railway companies.

The Furness Railway Company and the Furness Railway Police Force successfully operated for over seventy-six years from 1846 until 1923 when they were absorbed into the LMS Railway Company and LMS Railway Police respectively.

The Hull and Barnsley Railway Company started life in 1885 as the Hull, Barnsley and West Riding Junction Railway and Dock Company. The railway stretched some seventy miles from Hull Docks to Cudworth near Barnsley in South Yorkshire with branches to Denaby and Wath-upon-Dearne. The purpose of the railway was to access the busy South Yorkshire Coalfields and transport the coal to Hull Docks for export.

The North Eastern Railway Company already had a monopoly for the railways and docks in the north east of England, so in order to break the monopoly, the Hull and Barnsley Railway, after obtaining authorisation to build their railway, also built a large dock, the Alexandra Dock at Hull, for exporting coal which opened in 1885.

In 1905, the railway company changed its name by shortening it to the Hull and Barnsley Railway Company. Although it was primarily built for transporting coal, it did operate a passenger service between Hull and Cudworth. There, the service linked with a Midland Railway push and pull auto-train which regularly ran into Barnsley just three miles away.

The Hull and Barnsley Railway became a very successful company, so much so that the company decided to expand further by building another dock at Hull to handle larger coal ships and new steam fishing trawlers. Discussions were held between the North Eastern Railway Company and the

Two Harrys from Hull. Police Constable number 21, Harry Waite, and number 24, Harry Smith, of the Hull and Barnsley Railway Police pictured at the King George Dock in Hull circa 1920. Both are well turned out with shiny boots and carrying capes over their left shoulders.

Hull and Barnsley Railway Company and an agreement was reached to build the new dock jointly. As a result, the King George Dock was duly constructed and opened in June 1914.

The company employed a substantial number of railway policemen who operated on similar lines to their neighbours in the North Eastern Railway Police. The two forces worked closely together. Most of the work undertaken by the Hull and Barnsley Railway Policemen related to working on the busy docks at Hull, rather than the railway, which ran predominantly through lightly populated rural countryside in Yorkshire.

The North Eastern Railway Police became the first police force in Britain to introduce trained police dogs onto Hull Docks in 1908. After introducing police dogs onto other North Eastern Railway Docks at Hartlepool, Middlesbrough and Tyne Docks, the North Eastern Railway Police dog section then offered to introduce police dogs to their neighbours, the Hull and Barnsley Railway Police, which they gratefully accepted.

In November 1908, the Hull and Barnsley Railway Police became the second police force in Britain to use police dogs when a dog named Charlie, which had been given by the North Eastern Railway Police, became operational. Charlie became the first of several police dogs to join the Hull and Barnsley Railway Police. Their use was confined to the docks area of the force and they were not used along the seventy mile stretch of railway line to Cudworth.

The four officers pictured in the photograph below, which was taken in 1905, are sporting a new insignia on the helmet plates of the constables and the cap badge of the sergeant. The emblems were introduced earlier that year when the name of the railway company was changed from the Hull, Barnsley and West

A rather portly sergeant with a snow-white beard and three rotund constables of the Hull and Barnsley Railway Police take time to pose for a photograph between duties at the Alexandra Dock, Hull in 1905. L-R; Police Constable Charles Ladagos, PC William Ireland, PC George H. Brown and Police Sergeant Blythe Kemp.

Riding Junction Railway and Dock Company to the Hull and Barnsley Railway Company. The new badges were worn until the Hull and Barnsley Railway Police force was absorbed into the North Eastern Railway Police force in 1922 as a prelude to the railway groupings which took place the following year.

A combined total of 428 serving police officers from the former North Eastern Railway and Hull and Barnsley Railway police forces became a part of the new London and North Eastern Railway Police force when it became operational on 1 January 1923.

The Great Western Railway was an early railway founded in 1833 and commencing operation in 1838. It was designed and built by the famous railway engineer Isambard Kingdom Brunel as a broad gauge railway (7 foot, 2133.6mm) to connect London to the sea port of Bristol. It later expanded into the counties of Devon and Cornwall, most of Wales and other places such as Shrewsbury, Birmingham, Wolverhampton and Birkenhead.

The Railway Regulation (Gauge) Act was introduced in 1846 which stated that all railways in Britain (excluding Ireland) built for the conveyance of passengers, must have a gauge of 4ft. 8 ½ inches (standard-gauge). Consequently, the GWR started introducing standard gauge onto their railways in the 1850s, yet it took some forty years before the last of the broad gauge lines were phased out in 1892.

The Great Western Railway Police was founded in 1835 and the first railway policemen worked out of the GWR London Terminus Station at Paddington. Initially, thirty-three constables were recruited to work under the command of an Inspector and four Sergeants. In 1838, 37-year-old Joseph Collard, a serving officer in the Metropolitan Police Force, was head-hunted for the position of Chief of Police for the GWR Police force. He accepted the position and was installed in the capacity of Superintendent (Chief of Police), Great Western Railway, based at Paddington Station. Superintendent Collard remained in charge of the GWR Police for some twenty years until his retirement in 1858. He then continued working on a part time basis until 1860 when he finally left the force. He spent his retirement years living in Reading until his death in 1873.

After taking command of the force, Superintendent Collard continued to recruit officers as the railway expanded (the GWR Act of 1835 authorised the GWR to appoint its own constables to be sworn in by local magistrates). As the nineteenth century progressed, the Great Western Railway force soon exceeded 200 men. The major railway stations on the network were London Paddington, Bristol Temple Meads, Birmingham Snow Hill and Cardiff. All four stations

A group of four (pre-grouping) Great Western Railway Uniform Constables and two detectives, pictured at West Bromwich in 1922, posing for one last photograph before being absorbed into the new Great Western Railway Police Force on 1 January 1923.

were bases for numerous railway policemen, as was Swindon where the company's locomotive construction and engineering works were located.

When the 1921 Railways (Grouping) Act came into effect, the Great Western Railway Police had an establishment of 335 serving police officers who were absorbed into a new police force on 1 January 1923, the name of the new police force continuing to be Great Western Railway Police.

Likewise, the original Great Western Railway Company, which since its formation in 1833 had amalgamated with a number of other railway companies, saw its name also being retained for use by one of the new big four railway companies which emerged in 1923.

Two smart young Great Western Railway Police Constables pictured in a rural setting at an unknown location circa 1935.

Two British Transport Commission Police officers carrying out a routine check on a magnificent looking old motor car leaving Southampton Docks via Dock Gate number eight in 1951.

The British Transport Commission Police (BTC Police) became operational on 1 January 1949. It was the first ever National Police Force in Britain and was created to police a number of British Transport Undertakings which were nationalised by the government in 1948, namely, the British Railways Board, British Transport Docks Board, Inland Waterways, Road Haulage, Road Transport (buses and trams) and other subsidiary companies.

The British Transport Commission Police comprised of police officers who had served in police forces of the former 'big four' railway companies which made up the national railway network, as well as officers who had served in many of the former dock, harbours, river and canal police forces which had existed in Britain prior to 1949. The BTC Police operated for just fourteen years until 31 December 1962.

Considered by many to be the world's first supermodel, Lisa Fonssagrives, a Swedish fashion model, glances over her shoulder for a quick peek at a London Bobby as she strolls along a deserted railway platform at Paddington Station whilst on a surprise visit to the capital in 1951. The well turned out British Transport Commission Police Constable proudly upholds the traditions of an old fashioned British policeman by demonstrating a military bearing and stiff upper lip as he no doubt resists the urge to stand and stare or even take a fleeting glimpse of the stylish young lady as she passes by.

During the post war years most villains would say that they could spot a copper a mile away. That was true to a large extent as the picture on the next page clearly demonstrates. Detectives were expected (and in some cases, instructed) to wear a collar and tie, along with a traditional Macintosh raincoat and trilby hat whilst on duty.

Spot the detectives. Four British Transport Commission Police Detectives find a quiet spot to furtively pose for a photograph in London during the 1950s. Basil Nichols, the detective on the extreme left of the picture, eventually aspired to become a Detective Superintendent in charge of the B. T. Police CID.

At a time when very few households had a television, large sections of the population would regularly attend cinemas, often to watch crime dramas where detectives would typically be seen surreptitiously standing on street corners, sometimes purporting to be reading a newspaper. They stood out like a sore thumb, much to the amusement of the cinema audiences.

Their actions often became the butt of jokes until fortunately, by the end of the nineteen fifties, their outlook was beginning to change and did indeed change in the swinging sixties, along with their attire.

The Police Training Centre at St Cross, Walton-on-the Hill, Tadworth in Surrey, a former school, was officially opened in December 1948, as a Training Centre for

A passing out parade for new recruits at the British Transport Commission Police training centre at Tadworth, Surrey in March 1959.

railway police officers. It served as a police training school for both the BTC Police and the British Transport Police until its closure in 2010. It was later demolished, but a blue plaque now stands at the entrance to the site to commemorate the BTP Training School which formerly occupied the site for over sixty years.

The above photograph shows a constables' recruit training course being inspected after successfully completing three gruelling months of initial police training to become probationary police constables. An achievement to be proud of.

The officers would then have returned to their respective police divisions, nationwide, to work alongside more experienced officers as part of their continued training, before returning to Tadworth for a first and second year refresher course. Officers would then be finally evaluated regarding their suitability to continue working as fulltime police officers, having completed a two year probationary period.

Police uniforms in the 1950s and 1960s were manufactured by J. Compton Sons & Webb Ltd of London and every police officer was individually

A British Transport Police constable pictured in the mid-1960s wearing a typical police uniform of that era. The officer is in fact Malcolm Clegg, author of this book.

measured, to enable their uniform tunics and trousers to be tailor made. This resulted in well-fitting uniforms, although officers often had to wait a couple of weeks for them to arrive.

Unfortunately, uniform trousers had old fashioned buttons at the front instead of a zip fastener and the shirts were also old fashioned with detachable starched collars secured by a front and back stud. All shirts had long sleeves with no provisions for fitting epaulettes in summer months as tunics were worn all year round.

Fast forward to the 1970s and uniforms were issued from a clothing store 'off the peg' in the same manner that modern clothes are purchased from stores. Long or short sleeved shirts with fitted collars were issued for winter use and short sleeved shirts with detachable epaulettes were available for use in the hot summer months when officers were allowed to discard their tunics to work in shirt sleeve order when appropriate. Trousers had zip fasteners instead of the old-fashioned buttons.

Photograph of a Police Cadet training course nearing completion at the British Transport Police training centre at Tadworth, Surrey in May 1964. Class instructors are sitting in the front row.

The first Transport Police Cadets were recruited into the British Transport Commission Police in the 1950s and recruiting continued into the British Transport Police era after the force was renamed in 1963. Cadets were also recruited into most home office police forces at that time. The minimum age to join was sixteen, although in some home office forces it was seventeen.

Their initial training course of ten weeks (as shown in the previous photograph) was similar to that of a probationary constable's recruit course. Police Cadets who were successful in passing their training were automatically appointed as probationary constables on their nineteenth birthday without the need for a further medical or entrance examination which they had been required to undergo before becoming a police cadet. A number of former police cadets were later promoted through the ranks.

British Transport Police Constables Steve Beamon and Valerie Smiles caught on camera at Euston Station in London in the mid-1970s.

Police Constables Sarah Burfoot and Kevin Gordon, both immaculately turned out, pose for this photograph after having been selected as the first British Transport Police Officers to attend the Remembrance Day Parade held at the Cenotaph in Whitehall in November 2004.

'**Out with** the old, in with the new.' March 2012 saw changes within the British Transport Police. The traditional dark blue uniforms with silver buttons and helmets which had been the trademark of British Bobbies since the nineteenth century were replaced with a completely new design high visibility twenty-first century uniform.

A British Transport Policeman wearing his new style police uniform as he strolls along a station platform in 2012.

British Transport Police, Armed Counter Terrorism Unit Officers pictured in London 2012.

Police in Britain have never routinely carried firearms, although they have always been available for use where necessary. During the Second World War, some railway and dock police officers were issued with firearms. Officers on the London Underground engaged in carrying out routine checks of passengers were armed. LNER police dog handlers working at Hull Docks carried Webley pistols during the conflict and GWR policeman working the South Wales Ports were issued with Webley revolvers. After the war, these GWR police revolvers were stored in a locked police cell at the old Cardiff Docks Police Station where they remained until the early 1960s, before being taken to Llanwern Steelworks in Newport and disposed of by melting them down in a furnace. In more recent times, some British Transport Police officers performing duties on the royal train also carried firearms.

The year 2012 saw BTP counter terrorism armed patrol units being introduced in London (see previous photograph) and they have since continued to operate, due to the constant threat of terrorism activities in Britain.

Two BTP Constables pictured outside Cardiff Central Station, with a rugby mascot in readiness for the 2015 Rugby Union World Cup which later took place in the nation's capital. It will be noted that the word HEDDU can be seen on the shirt sleeves of both officer above the word POLICE. *Heddu* is a Welsh language word meaning police and appears on the uniforms of all officers based in Wales.

British Transport Police Superintendent Gill Murray in conversation with Sadiq Khan, the Mayor of London, during routine operations being carried out at Liverpool Street Station in May 2017.

British Transport Police Officers take time to pose for this photograph at Windsor, before receiving the crowds of spectators which turned out to witness the marriage of Prince Harry and Meghan Markle on 19 May 2018. Note that each of the officers is wearing a bodycam over their right shoulder.

The years 2020 and 2021 will be remembered as the years when Britain and the rest of the world was in the grip of Coronavirus. This photograph, taken in November 2020, shows British Transport Police Constable No. 2582 wearing a face mask whilst performing duty at an almost deserted Victoria Railway Station in London during the second national coronavirus lockdown.

Appendix A

RAILWAY BYELAWS[27]

In 1840, the railway department of the Board of Trade was set up, in part to deal with matters relating to railway legislation.

By the mid-1840s, most railway companies had introduced their own railway byelaws which had been authorised by Acts of Parliament appertaining to each specific railway company. The byelaws of all railway companies set out offences which could be committed upon the railway of the company to which the byelaws referred, together with the penalties for transgressors. Although each company possessed their own byelaws, in practice, the wording of the byelaws (and penalties) for each company were identical or similar in almost every respect.

In order to become law, the byelaws drawn up by each company had to bear the railway company seal, and be signed by the company secretary, before being approved and signed by the railway departmental secretary of the board of trade, or a person acting on his behalf. A number of these certified copies of the byelaws were drawn up for legal purposes (such as production in a court of law). In addition, many hundreds or thousands of uncertified copies of the byelaws were printed in various forms, ranging from large posters to be exhibited on railway stations and depots, to booklets which were made available for examination by members of the public at various locations, including all railway station booking offices. Copies of the byelaws were also incorporated into railway rule books and regulations issued to all railway staff including railway policemen.

A typical example of railway byelaws from the eighteen forties was introduced by the North Staffordshire Railway Company in 1848 and reads as follows:

North Staffordshire Railway Bye-laws 1848.

1. No passenger will be allowed to take his seat in or upon any carriage used on the railway, without having first booked his place and paid his fare. Each passenger booking his place, will be furnished with a ticket, which he

is to show when required by the guard in charge of the train and to deliver up before leaving the premises, upon demand, to the guard, or other servant of the company, duly authorised to collect tickets. Each passenger not producing or delivering up his ticket, will be required to pay the fare from the place whence the train originally started, or in default of payment thereof, shall forfeit and pay a sum not exceeding Forty Shillings.

2. Passengers at the road [railway] stations will only be booked conditionally; that is to say, in case there shall be room in the train for which they are booked. In case there shall not be room for all the passengers booked, those booked for the longest distance shall have the preference, and those booked for the same distance shall have priority according to the order in which they are booked.
3. Smoking is strictly prohibited, both in and upon the carriages and in the Company's Stations. Every person smoking in a carriage, is hereby subjected to a penalty not exceeding Forty Shillings; and every person persisting in smoking in a carriage or station after being warned to desist, shall in addition to incurring a penalty not exceeding Forty Shillings, be immediately, or if travelling, at the first opportunity, removed from the Company's premises, and forfeit his fare. Note: - Persons wilfully obstructing the Company's Officers in the execution of their duty, are liable, to be apprehended and fined Five Pounds, with two months' imprisonment in default of payment.
4. Any person found in a carriage or station in a state of Intoxication, or committing any nuisance, or otherwise wilfully interfering with the comfort of other passengers; and any person obstructing any of the Company's Officers in the discharge of their duty, is hereby subjected to a penalty not exceeding Forty Shillings, and shall immediately, or if travelling, at the first opportunity, be removed from the Company's premises, and forfeit his fare.
5. Any passenger cutting the linings, removing or defacing the number-plates, breaking the windows, or otherwise wilfully damaging or injuring any carriage on the railway, shall forfeit and pay a sum not exceeding five pounds, in addition to the damage done.

Note:- Under the provision of the Company's Acts and the Railway Clauses Consolidation Act 1845, - Any person who shall travel or attempt to travel in any carriage on the railway, without having previously paid his fare, and with intent to avoid payment thereof, or who having paid his fare for a certain distance, shall knowingly and wilfully proceed in any such carriage beyond such distance, without previously paying the additional fare for the additional distance, and with intent to avoid payment thereof; or who shall knowingly and wilfully refuse or neglect, on arriving at the point to which he has paid his fare, quit such carriage, is, for every such offence, liable to a penalty of Forty Shillings.

6. Passengers are forbidden to get into or upon, or to quit any carriage, after the train has been put in motion; and any person doing so, or attempting to do so, is hereby made liable to a penalty not exceeding Forty Shillings.
7. Dogs will be charged for according to distance, but they will not be allowed to accompany passengers in carriages.

Bye Laws Certified under the Common Seal of the Company, This Twelfth day of February 1848. Signed, J. SAMUDA, Secretary/ (Seal).

Allowed by the Commissioners of Railways, this Fifteenth day of February 1848, Signed, EDWARD STRUTT GRANVILLE, EDWARD RYAN & H. R. BRANDRETH (Seal).

*Forty shillings (£2) in 1848 = approximately £250 today.

As the years from the 1840s progressed, new byelaws were introduced as and when they were deemed necessary. Each of the Railway Companies regularly submitted new byelaws to the Board of Trade for approval. The North London Railway Company issued a new set of byelaws in 1875 which once again were typical of the byelaws of other railway companies during that time. It will be noted that these byelaws as set out below were more comprehensive in their nature than the much earlier North Staffordshire Railway Bye-laws of 1848 outlined above. The number of byelaws listed in 1848 was seven which had increased to seventeen by 1875.

North London Railway Company Bye-Laws and Regulations 1875.

1. *(Obtaining ticket and delivering up the same).* No passenger will be allowed to enter any carriage used on the railway, or to travel therein upon the railway, unless furnished by the company with a ticket specifying the class of carriage and the stations for conveyance between which such ticket is issued. Every passenger shall show and deliver up his ticket (whether a

contract or season ticket or otherwise) to any duly authorised servant of the Company, whenever required to do so for any purpose. Any passenger travelling without a ticket, or failing or refusing to show or deliver up his ticket, as aforesaid, shall be required to pay the fare from the station whence the train originally started to the end of his journey.

2. *(Using ticket for any other day).* Any passenger using or attempting to use a ticket on any day for which such ticket is not available, or using a ticket which has been already used on a previous journey, is hereby subjected to a penalty not exceeding Forty Shillings.

3. *(Using ticket for any other station).* Any passenger using or attempting to use a ticket for any other station than that for which it is available will be required to pay the difference between the sum actually paid and the fare between the stations from and to which the passenger has travelled, or at the option of the Company the fare from the station to which he was booked to the end of his journey.

4. *(Defacing tickets).* Any passenger wilfully altering or defacing his ticket, so as to render the date, number, or any material portion thereof illegible, is hereby subjected to a penalty not exceeding Forty Shillings.

5. *(Sale and purchase of return tickets).* A return ticket is granted solely for the purpose of enabling the person for whom the same is issued, to travel therewith to and from the stations marked thereon, and is not transferable. Any person who sells or attempts to sell, or parts or attempts to part with the possession of the return half of any return ticket in order to enable any other person to travel therewith, is hereby subjected to a penalty not exceeding Forty Shillings; and any person purchasing such half of a return ticket, or travelling or attempting to travel therewith, shall be liable to pay the fare which he would have been liable to pay for the single journey, and shall in addition thereto be subjected to a penalty not exceeding Forty Shillings.

6. *(Tickets issued when there is room).* At the intermediate stations the fares will only be accepted, and the tickets issued, conditionally; that is to say, in case there shall be room in the train for which the tickets are issued. In case there shall not be room for all the passengers to whom tickets have been issued, those to whom tickets have been issued for the longest distance shall (if reasonably practicable) have the preference, and those to whom tickets have been issued for the same distance shall (if reasonably practicable) have priority in accordance with the order in which the tickets have been issued, as denoted by the consecutive numbers stamped upon

them. The Company will not, however, hold itself responsible for such order of preference or priority being adhered to, but the fare or difference of fare, if the passenger travel by an ordinary train in a class of carriage inferior to that for which he has a ticket, shall be immediately returned, on application, to any passenger for whom there is not room as aforesaid, if the application be made before the departure of the train.

7. (*Smoking*). Every person smoking in any shed or covered platform of a station, or in any building of the Company, or in any carriage or compartment of a carriage not specially provided for that purpose, is hereby subjected to a penalty not exceeding Forty Shillings. The Company's officers and servants are required to take the necessary steps to enforce obedience to this bye-law, and any person offending against it is liable, in addition to incurring the penalty above mentioned, to be summarily removed, at the first opportunity, from the carriage, or from the Company's premises.

8. (*Using ticket for superior class*). Any person travelling without the special permission of some duly authorised servant of the Company, in a carriage or by a train of a superior class to that for which his ticket was issued, is hereby subjected to a penalty not exceeding Forty Shillings; and shall, in addition, be liable to pay the fare, according to the class of carriage in which he is travelling, from the station whence the train originally started, unless he shows he had no intent to defraud.

9. (*Being intoxicated or using obscene or abusive language, etc.*) Any person found in a carriage, or elsewhere upon the Company's premises, in a state of intoxication, or using obscene or abusive language, or writing obscene or offensive words on any part of the Company's stations or carriages, or committing any nuisance, or otherwise wilfully interfering with the comfort of other passengers, is hereby subjected to a penalty not exceeding Forty Shillings, and shall immediately, or, if a passenger, at the first opportunity, be removed from the Company's premises.

10. (*Damaging property*). Any person who wilfully cuts or tears any lining, or window strap, or curtain, removes or defaces any number plates, or breaks or scratches any window of a carriage used on the railway, or who otherwise, except by unavoidable accident, damages, defaces, or injures any such carriage, or any station, or other property of the Company, is hereby subjected to a penalty not exceeding Five Pounds, in addition to the amount of any damage for which he may be liable.

11. (*Travelling on roof, steps, etc.*) No passenger shall be permitted to travel on the roof, steps, or footboard of any carriage, or on the engine, or in

the guard's van, or any portion of any carriage not intended for the conveyance of passengers; and any passenger persisting in doing so after being warned to desist by the guard in charge of the train, or any duly authorised servant of the Company, is hereby subjected to a penalty not exceeding Forty Shillings, and shall be liable to be summarily removed from the Company's premises.

12. *(Entering or leaving carriage when in motion).* Any passenger entering or leaving, or attempting to enter or leave, any carriage while the train is in motion, or elsewhere than at the side of the carriage adjoining the platform, or other place appointed by the Company, for passengers to enter or leave the carriages, is hereby subjected to a penalty not exceeding Forty Shillings.

13. *(Entering full carriage).* Any passenger persisting in entering a carriage or compartment of a carriage containing the full number of persons which it is constructed to convey, when any such person objects to his so entering the carriage or compartment, is hereby subjected to a penalty not exceeding Forty Shillings.

14. *(Conveyance of dogs in carriages).* Dogs and other animals will not be allowed to accompany passengers in the carriages, but will be conveyed separately and charged for, and any person taking a dog or other animal with him into any passenger carriage used on the railway is hereby subjected to a penalty not exceeding Forty Shillings.

15. *(Taking loaded firearms).* Loaded firearms are on no account to be taken into or placed upon any carriage, wagon, truck, or other vehicle forming, or intended to form a train or any portion of a train on the railway, or to be brought to the station, or on the premises of the Company, and every person so offending is hereby subjected to a penalty not exceeding five pounds.

16. *(Travelling with infectious disorder).* The Company may refuse to carry any person who has any infectious disorder. If any person who has any such disorder is found upon the premises of the Company, or travels, or attempts to travel, on the railway of the Company, without the special permission of the Company, he shall be liable to a penalty not exceeding Forty Shillings, in addition to the forfeiture of any fare which he may have paid, and may be removed at the first opportunity from the Company's premises. Any person who has charge of any person suffering from an infectious disorder while upon the premises of the Company, or travelling or attempting to travel on the railway, or who aids or assists any person

suffering from such disorder in being upon the premises of the Company, or travelling or attempting to travel on the railway, shall be liable to a penalty not exceeding Forty Shillings, unless the person suffering from such disorder be travelling with the special permission of the Company.

17. *(Omnibuses, etc., drivers obeying servants of Company).* Every driver or conductor of an omnibus, cab, carriage, or other vehicle, shall while in or upon any station, yard, or other premises of the Company, obey the reasonable directions of the Company's officers and servants duly authorised in that behalf, and every person offending against this regulation is hereby subjected to a penalty not exceeding Forty Shillings.

(Seal of the North London Railway Company) Given under the common seal of the North London Railway Company, the Fourth day of August 1875.

Signed, G. BOLLAND NEWTON, Secretary of the Company. The Board of Trade hereby signify their allowance and approval of the above Bye-Laws and Regulations. Signed, by order of the Board of Trade, the Eleventh day of August, 1875. Signed, HENRY G. CALCRAFT, An Assistant-Secretary to the Board of Trade.

As can be seen, the number of byelaws more than doubled in numbers from the 1840s to the 1870s. This was as a result of normal day to day events which unfolded during the early railway years which necessitated new legislation to protect passengers, staff and other members of the public and try to ensure their comfort and safety, as well as affording adequate protection to railway property itself. It will be noted that additional byelaws were introduced in relation to the use surrounding 'railway tickets', as a means of protecting railway revenue from potential fraudsters. Additional powers were also granted to railway staff (including railway policemen) to eject persons from the railway when they were found committing or having committed various bye-law offences. Railway policeman (and other staff members or persons assisting) were allowed to use sufficient force as was necessary to eject persons from railway premises where necessary.

During the latter half of the nineteenth century the number of byelaws used by each of the railway companies continued to increase to keep pace with new problems being encountered by railway policemen and other staff members during the course of their duties. Set out below are extracts of some of the additional railway byelaws which were introduced during the eighteen eighties and eighteen nineties.

Additional Railway Bye-Laws (1880s/1890s).

1. Except by express permission of the guard of the train, no male person above or apparently above the age of eight shall travel or attempt to travel in a compartment marked as being reserved for the exclusive use of members of the female sex. (This bye-law came into effect following the introduction of ladies only compartments to the railways in the latter part of the nineteenth century.)
2. No person shall take into, or place or cause to be placed, or have in or upon any carriage or vehicle using the railway, or in or upon the Company's premises, or approach to any station, any cylinder, tube, receptacle, containing any inflammable, explosive, or corrosive gas, spirit, liquid or substance.
3. Except with permission of the company, no person shall hawk, sell, or offer for sale any articles or goods of any description whatsoever in or upon any railway station, yard, approach or any premises of the company, and no person shall tout, ply for hire, solicit custom or employment of any description.
4. No person shall enter or remain in, or use any railway carriage or any part of the Company's premises, or any approach to any station of the Company, for the purpose of bookmaking, or betting or wagering, or agreeing to bet or wager with any other person.
5. Any person who shall enter, loiter or remain in or upon any railway station, station-yard or approach to any station of the Company, or in or upon any vehicle upon the railway, when requested not to do so, will be liable to a maximum penalty of Forty Shillings. In addition to the maximum penalty of Forty Shillings, a person having received one warning, may be removed from the railway.
6. A person upon the railway, whose dress or clothing (in the opinion of the train guard) might soil or injure the linings or cushions of any carriage will be liable to a maximum penalty of Forty Shillings. In addition to a maximum penalty of Forty Shillings, any person may be refused admission or removed from any carriage or any part of the Company's premises, including any approach to any station.

(The above bye-law was primarily used to prevent men such as coal miners travelling to and from works in dirty clothes which were likely to soil the seats of carriages and cushions which would later be used by other passengers. This was in the days before pit head baths and other washing facilities were introduced into the workplace.)

7. No person shall wantonly, maliciously or negligently, throw or drop from any carriage or vehicle upon the railway, a bottle of any kind, or any article or thing whatsoever capable of injuring, damaging or endangering any person or property.
8. No person shall spit upon the floor or upon any part of any carriage using or being on the railway, or upon the platform at any station of the Company, or upon the floor, side or wall of any hall, office, waiting-room, refreshment-room or public passage at any station of the Company.

(Spitting was quite common by men in the nineteenth century.)

9. The Company's porters will render every facility to passengers in loading and unloading luggage at different stations. No Fee or Gratuity is permitted to be taken by any of the Company's servants under any circumstances whatever, under pain of instant dismissal.

This was an interesting byelaw that was seldom, if ever, used and was one of the few byelaws that did not stand the test of time. As the railway era progressed into the twentieth century, the tipping of porters for assisting with luggage soon became common practice. This led to this particular byelaw being withdrawn and subsequently forgotten.

By the end of the nineteenth century a substantial number of railway byelaws had been introduced and they made an invaluable contribution to the control of law and order upon the railways. These byelaws were without doubt a railway policeman's friend and they, together with the associated powers and authority which accompanied them, were an invaluable asset whilst carrying out his daily duties.

Nineteenth Century. Bye-Law Penalties.

A rough estimate of what the nineteenth century penalties for contravening railway byelaws would cost today:

Forty Shillings (£2) in 1840 = £210.   1875 = £236.   1899 = £264.
Five Pounds in   1840 = £525.   1875 = £590.   1899 = £660.
-

The above North Staffordshire Railway Byelaws of 1848 and the North London Railway Company Byelaws and Regulations are supplied courtesy of the National Railway Museum, York, research facilities.

Appendix B

BRITISH TRANSPORT POLICE - CONSTITUENT FORCES[28]

Constituent Forces are former police forces, founded over the past 200 years, which either amalgamated with, or were absorbed into other police forces, eventually leading to the creation of the British Transport Police which exists today.

A two part list of constituent forces is set out below in alphabetical order. Part one consists of railway police forces and part two comprises of dock, port, harbour and canal police forces. Both lists cover the geographical areas of England, Scotland and Wales.

The first railway policemen in the world were employed on the Stockton and Darlington Railway which opened in 1825. Initially, the company employed a superintendent and four uniformed constables. As the railway expanded, the police numbers increased accordingly. This later applied to most other railway companies.

Many of the early railway companies were extremely small companies and whilst most did employ railway policemen, some companies, particularly the early companies, initially only employed a handful of policemen and in some cases, just one or two. In locations where just one or two policemen were based, they were often considered to be a part of the station staff by some railway companies and as such they were primarily under the control of the local station master.

A number of early railway companies only operated for a short period of time before being bought by, or absorbed into, larger companies. Although these companies did play a role in railway history, it was, overall, quite inconsequential. For this reason, railways which were in operation for less than five years have generally not been included in the list below, regardless as to whether or not they employed railway police personnel, although there are some exceptions which are mentioned.

Constituent Forces (Part One) Railway Police Forces.

The dates shown in brackets after the name of the police force are the dates the railway company was in operation. Whilst all the companies listed below did employ railway policemen at some stage, a few companies did not employ railway policemen for the entire duration of their existence, whilst others engaged them during the construction phase of their railway as well as after railway became operational.

Aberdare Railway Police (1845-1902). Absorbed into the Taff Vale Railway Police in 1902.

Aberdeen Railway Police (1847-56). Absorbed into the Scottish North Eastern Railway Police in 1856.

Ardrossan Railway Police (1831-54). Absorbed into the Glasgow & South Western Railway Police in 1854.

Banff, Portsoy & Strathisla Railway Police (Banffshire Railway Police) (1859-67). Merged with the Great North of Scotland Railway Police in 1867.

Barry Railway Police (1889-1922). Absorbed into the Great Western Railway Police in 1923.

Berwickshire Railway Police (1863-76). Absorbed into the North British Railway Police in 1876.

Birkenhead, Lancashire & Cheshire Junction Railway Police (1847-59) - Renamed the Birkenhead Railway Police (1859-60). In 1860, the force was absorbed into the GWR Police, after the Railway Company was bought out jointly by the Great Western Railway Company and London & North Western Railway Company.

Birmingham & Derby Junction Railway Police (1839-44). Absorbed into the Midland Railway Police in 1844. (The Birmingham & Derby Junction Railway Company, merged with the Midland Counties Railway Company and the North Midlands Railway Company in 1844, to form the new Midland Railway Company.)

Birmingham & Gloucester Railway Police (1840-45). Absorbed into the Birmingham & Bristol Railway Police in 1845. The Birmingham & Bristol Railway Police (1845-46) only operated for twelve months from 1845 until 1846 before being absorbed into the Midland Railway Police in 1846. The

Bristol & Gloucester Railway Police also only operated for twelve months (1844-45) before being absorbed into the Midland Railway Police in 1845.

Birmingham, Wolverhampton & Stour Valley Railway Police (1852-67). Absorbed into the London & North Western Railway Police in 1867.

Blyth, Seghill & Percy Main Railway Police (1847-74). Renamed Blyth & Tyne Railway Police in 1853 before being absorbed into the North Eastern Railway Police in 1874.

Brecon & Merthyr Railway Police (1863-1923). Absorbed into the Great Western Railway Police in 1923.

Bristol & Exeter Railway Police (1841-76). Absorbed into the original (pre-1923) Great Western Railway Police in 1876.

British Transport Police (formed in 1963 and still in operation). (See BTC Police below.)

British Transport Commission Police (BTC Police Force) - (1949-62). This was the first National Police Force in Britain when it was founded on 1 January 1949. It was comprised of the former 'Big Four' Railway Police Forces, namely the LMS Railway Police, LNER Railway Police, GWR Police and the SR Police. It also incorporated numerous Dock, Port, Harbour and Canal Police Forces as well as being responsible for policing other transport and road haulage companies. When formed, the British Transport Commission Police was the second largest Police Force in Britain, after the Metropolitan Police Force in London. The London Transport Police Force was also absorbed into the BTC Police, but not until 1958. The BTC Police Force was renamed the British Transport Police from 1 January 1963.

Buckinghamshire Railway Police (1847-79). Absorbed into the London & North Western Railway Police in 1879.

Caledonian & Dunbartonshire Junction Railway Police (1850-62). Absorbed into the Edinburgh & Glasgow Railway Police in 1862.

Callander & Oban Railway Police (1865-1923). Absorbed into the London, Midland & Scottish Railway Police in 1923.

Cambrian Railways Police (1864-1921). Absorbed into the old pre-1923 Great Western Railway Police on 1 January 1922.

Canterbury & Whitstable Railway Police (1830-44). Absorbed into the South Eastern Railway Police in 1844.

Carlisle & Silloth Bay Railway & Dock Police (1856-64). Absorbed into the North British Railway Police in 1864.

Caernarvonshire Railway Police (1862-70). Absorbed into the London & North Western Railway Police in 1870.

Central London Railway Police (London Underground Central Line) (1900-13). Absorbed into the Underground Electric Company of London in 1913.

Charing Cross Railway Police (1859-64). Absorbed into the South Eastern Railway Police in 1864.

Chester & Birkenhead Railway Police (1840-47). Absorbed into the Birkenhead, Lancashire & Cheshire Junction Railway Police in 1847.

Chester & Holyhead Railway Police (1848-59). Absorbed into the London & North Western Railway Police in 1859.

Clarence Railway Police (1833-53). Merged with other companies to form the West Hartlepool Harbour & Railway Company Police in 1853.

Cornwall Railway Police (1859-89). Absorbed into the Great Western Railway Police in 1889.

Cornwall Minerals Railway Police (1874-96). Absorbed into the Great Western Railway Police in 1896.

Crieff Junction Railway Police (1856-65). Absorbed into the Scottish Central Railway Police in 1865.

Deeside Railway Police (1853-67). Absorbed into the Great North of Scotland Railway Police in 1867.

District Line Railway Police. – See Metropolitan District Line Railway Police.

Dundee & Arbroath Railway Police (1838-12). Absorbed into the Scottish North Eastern Railway Police in 1862.

Dundee & Newtyle Railway Police (1831-63). Absorbed into the Scottish Central Railway Police in 1863.

Dundee & Perth Railway Police (1847-63). Absorbed into the Scottish Central Railway Police in 1863. (Renamed Dundee, Perth & Aberdeen Railway Police in 1849.)

East Lancashire Railway Police (1844-59). Absorbed into the Lancashire and Yorkshire Railway Police in 1859.

Eastern Counties Railway Police (1839-62). Absorbed into the Great Eastern Railway Police in 1862.

Eastern Union Railway Police (1846-56). Absorbed into the Eastern Counties Railway Police c.1855.

Edinburgh & Dalkeith Railway Police (1831-45). Absorbed into North British Railway Police in 1845.

Edinburgh & Glasgow Railway Police (1842-65). Absorbed into the North British Railway Police in 1865.

Edinburgh & Northern Railway Police (1845-62). Absorbed into the North British Railway Police in 1862.

Furness Railway Police (1846-1922). Absorbed into the London, Midland & Scottish Railway Police in 1923.

General Terminus & Glasgow Harbour Railway Police (1848-65). Absorbed into Caledonian Railway Police in 1865.

Garnkirk & Glasgow Railway Police (1831-44). The Garnkirk & Glasgow Railway started life as a mineral railway for carrying coal. In 1838, the railway expanded and was re-named the Glasgow, Garnkirk & Coatbridge Railway in 1844 before being leased to and worked by the Caledonian Railway from 1846. The Glasgow, Garnkirk & Coatbridge Railway was officially absorbed into the Caledonian Railway in 1865 along with the railway police.

Glasgow & North Western Railway Police (1850-1923). Absorbed into the London, Midland & Scottish Railway Police in 1923.

Glasgow, Barrhead & Kilmarnock Joint Railway Police (1869-80). Absorbed into Glasgow & South Western Railway Police in 1880.

Glasgow Harbour Railway Police (1848-65). See General Terminus & Glasgow Harbour Railway Police.

Glasgow, Paisley and Greenock Railway Police (1841-47). Absorbed into the Caledonian Railway Police in 1847.

Glasgow, Paisley, Kilmarnock & Ayr Railway Police (1838-50). Absorbed into the Glasgow & South Western Railway Police in 1850.

Grand Junction Railway Police (1837-46). Absorbed into the London & North Western Railway Police in 1846.

Great Central Railway Police (1897-1922). Absorbed into the London & North Eastern Railway Police in 1923.

Great Eastern Railway Police (1862-1922). Absorbed into the London & North Eastern Railway Police in 1923.

Great North of England Railway Police (1841-46). The Great North of England Railway ran between York & Darlington. Absorbed into the Newcastle & Darlington Junction Railway in 1846 (renamed the York &

Darlington Railway), followed by a merger with the Newcastle & Berwick Railway in 1847. Together with other companies, formed the North Eastern Railway Company in 1854 and all serving police officers were absorbed into the NER Railway Police.

Great North of Scotland Railway Police (1854-1922). Absorbed into the London & North Eastern Railway Police in 1923.

Great Northern Railway Police (1850-1922). Absorbed into the London & North Eastern Railway Police in 1923.

Great Western Railway Police (1838-1922). Absorbed to form the new GWR Police in 1923.

Great Western Railway Police (1923-48). Absorbed into the British Transport Commission Police from 1 January 1949.

Greenock & Wemyss Bay Railway Police (1862-93). Absorbed into the Caledonian Railway Police in 1893.

Hayle Railway Police (1837-52). Absorbed into the West Cornwall Railway Police in 1852.

Hereford, Ross & Gloucester Railway Police (1855-62). Absorbed into the Great Western Railway Police in 1862. The company was also known as the Gloucester & Dean Forest Railway Company.

Highland Railway Police (1865-1923). Absorbed into the London, Midland & Scottish Railway Police in 1923.

Hull & Holderness Railway Police (1854-62). Absorbed into North Eastern Railway Police in 1862.

Hull, Barnsley & West Riding Junction Railway and Dock Company Police (1885-1905). The name of the railway company was shortened in 1905 to that of the Hull & Barnsley Railway. The railway company then operated as the Hull & Barnsley Railway (together with the Hull & Barnsley Railway Police Force) until 1922. In April 1922, the H&B Railway became a part of the North Eastern Railway Company, before being absorbed into the new London & North Eastern Railway Company in January 1923. All serving police officers then became a part of the London & North Eastern Railway Police Force.

Hull & Selby Railway Police (1840-72). The railway was leased jointly to the York & North Midland Railway and the Manchester & Leeds Railway from 1845 until 1854 when the lease was taken over by the North Eastern Railway who acquired the railway outright in 1872. Serving police officers were absorbed into the NER Police in 1872.

Inverness & Aberdeen Junction Railway Police (1856-65). Absorbed into the Highland Railway Police in 1865.

Inverness & Nairn Railway Police (1855-61). Absorbed into the Inverness and Aberdeen Junction Railway in 1861 (see above), followed by the Highland Railway in 1865.

Kendal & Windermere Railway Police (1847-59). The railway was leased to the Lancaster & Carlisle Railway in 1850 on a 999-year lease but both companies were absorbed into the LNWR the following year, 1859. Serving police officers were absorbed into the LNWR Police.

Lancashire & Yorkshire Railway Police (1847-1922). Merged with the London & North Western Railway on 1 January 1922 before being absorbed into the new London, Midland & Scottish Railway on 1 January 1923. Serving police officers from both the Lancashire & Yorkshire Railway and the London & North Western Railway were absorbed into the new London, Midland & Scottish Railway Police Force in 1923.

Lancashire, Derbyshire & East Coast Railway Police (1896-1907). Absorbed into the Great Central Railway in 1907.

Lancaster & Carlisle Railway Police (1846-79). The L & C Railway Company was leased to the London & North Western Railway from 1859 until 1879 when it was fully absorbed into the LNWR. All serving police officers were absorbed into the London & North Western Railway Police in 1879.

Lancaster & Preston Junction Railway Police (1840-48). Absorbed into the Lancaster & Carlisle Railway Police in 1848.

Leeds & Bradford Railway Police (1846-53). Absorbed into the Midland Railway Police in 1853.

Leeds & Selby Railway Police (1834-44). Absorbed into the York & North Midland Railway Police in 1844.

Leeds & Thirsk Railway Police (1848-54). The railway was renamed Leeds Northern Railway in 1851 and merged with other companies in 1854 to form the North Eastern Railway Company. All serving police officers were absorbed into the NER Police in 1854.

Leicester & Swannington Railway Police (1832-45). Absorbed into the Midland Railway Police in 1845.

Liskeard & Caradon Railway Police (1844-1909). Absorbed into the Great Western Railway Police in 1909. The railway closed completely in 1917.

Liverpool & Manchester Railway Police (1830-45). Absorbed into the Grand Junction Railway in 1845 and together with the London & Birmingham and the Manchester & Birmingham Railways, they formed the London & North Western Railway the following year (1846). Serving police officers from each of the railway companies became part of the new London & North Western Railway Police in 1846.

Liverpool, St Helens & South Lancashire Railway Police (1895-1906). The railway was founded in 1889 but did operate until 1895. Absorbed into the Great Central Railway Police in 1906.

Llanelli Railway & Dock Police (1835-89). Railway operated by the Great Western Railway from 1873 until 1889 when they purchased it and absorbed it into the GWR. The serving police officers were absorbed into the GWR Police.

Llynfi & Ogmore Railway Police (1866-83). The railway was operated by the Great Western Railway from 1873 until it was fully absorbed into the GWR in 1883. Serving Police Officers were absorbed into the GWR Police.

London & Birmingham Railway Police (1833-46). Absorbed into the London & North Western Railway Police in 1846.

London & Blackwall Railway Police (1840-1923). The railway was leased by the Great Eastern Railway from 1866 until 1922 before being absorbed into the London & North Eastern Railway in 1923. Serving police officers were absorbed into the LNER Police Force.

London & Brighton Railway Police (1839-46). The railway company amalgamated with the London & Croydon Railway, the Brighton & Chichester Railway and the Brighton, Lewes & Hastings Railway to form the London, Brighton & South Coast Railway in 1846. Serving Police Officers from each of the railway companies were absorbed into the newly created London, Brighton & South Coast Railway Police Force.

London, Brighton & South Coast Railway Police (1846-1922). Absorbed into the Southern Railway Police in 1923.

London, Chatham & Dover Railway Police (1859-1922). Absorbed into the Southern Railway Police in 1923. In 1898, the London, Chatham & Dover Railway Company and the South Eastern Railway Company came to an agreement to operate both railways under one umbrella. The two railways for operational purposes were collectively named the South Eastern & Chatham Railway, although this was never a railway company. Both the LCDR and the SER remained separate companies until they were absorbed into the Southern Railway Company in 1923.

London & Croydon Railway Police (1838-46). Merged with other companies to form the London, Brighton & South Coast Railway Police in 1846.

London Electric Railway Police (1910-33). Absorbed into the London Passenger Transport Board in 1933. Policed by the newly created London Transport Police. The LER Railway was formed and owned by the Underground Electric Railways Company of London to manage three underground railway companies, namely, the Baker Street & Waterloo Railway, the Charing Cross, Euston and Hampstead Railway and the Great Northern, Piccadilly and Brompton Railway. These railways are now part of the Bakerloo Line, Northern Line and Piccadilly Line in Central London.

London & Greenwich Railway Police (1836-1922). Absorbed into the South Eastern Railway Police in 1845. From 1845 until 1923, the L & GR was leased to the South Eastern Railway Company for which they received just an annual rent that was distributed amongst the shareholders. The railway was totally operated and policed by the SER Company until 1922. It was then absorbed into the new Southern Railway Company in 1923 and serving police officers were absorbed into the Southern Railway Police.

London, Midland & Scottish Railway Police (1923-48). Absorbed into the British Transport Commission Police in 1949.

London & North Eastern Railway Police (1923-48). Absorbed into the British Transport Commission Police in 1949.

London & North Western Railway Police (1846-1922). Absorbed into the London, Midland & Scottish Railway Police in 1923.

London & South Western Railway Police (1839-1922). Absorbed into the Southern Railway Police in 1923.

London, Tilbury & Southend Railway Police (1854-1912). Absorbed into the Midland Railway Police in 1912.

Manchester & Birmingham Railway Police (1840-46). Absorbed into the London & North Western Railway Police in 1846.

Manchester & Bolton Railway Police (1831-46). Absorbed into the Manchester & Leeds Railway Police in 1846.

Manchester & Leeds Railway Police (1836-47). Absorbed into the Lancashire & Yorkshire Railway Police in 1847.

Manchester, Sheffield & Lincolnshire Railway Police (1847-97). Renamed the Great Central Railway Police in 1897. Absorbed into the London & North Eastern Railway Police in 1923.

Maryport & Carlisle Railway Police (1840-1922). Absorbed into the London, Midland & Scottish Railway Police in 1923.

Metropolitan District Line Railway Police (1868-1933). Absorbed into the Underground Electric Company of London in 1905 and merged with the Metropolitan Railway and together with tramway and bus companies, formed the London Passenger Transport Board in 1933, policed by the newly created London Transport Police.

Metropolitan Railway Police (1863-1933). Absorbed into the London Transport Police in 1933. (London Passenger Transport Board was the name of the transport authority.)

Midland Counties Railway Police (1839-44). Absorbed into the Midland Railway Police in 1844.

Midland Railway Police (1844-1922). Absorbed into the London, Midland & Scottish Railway Police in 1923.

Monkland & Kirkintilloch Railway Police (1826-48). Merged with two small adjoining railways and renamed the Monkland Railway (and Monkland Railway Police) in 1848.

Monkland Railway Police (1848-65). Absorbed into the Edinburgh & Glasgow Railway Police in 1865 then that company was absorbed into the North British Railway the following day. Serving police officers from both the Monkland Railway and the Edinburgh & Glasgow Railway were both absorbed into the North British Railway Police in 1865.

Morayshire Railway Police (1852-80). Absorbed into the Great North of Scotland Railway Police in 1881.

Newcastle & Berwick Railway Police (1845-54). Name changed to the York, Newcastle & Berwick Railway Police in July 1847. Absorbed into the North Eastern Railway Police in 1854.

Newcastle & North Shields Railway Police (1839-45). Absorbed into the Newcastle & Berwick Railway Police in 1845.

Newcastle & Carlisle Railway Police (1837-62). Absorbed into the North Eastern Railway Police in 1862.

Newport, Abergavenny & Hereford Railway (1853-60). Merged with the Worcester & Hereford Railway and the Oxford, Worcester and Wolverhampton Railway in 1860 to form the West Midland Railway Company, who in turn was operated by the Great Western Railway from 1863, before being officially absorbed into the GWR in 1872. Serving police officers were absorbed into the GWR Police between 1863 and 1872.

North British Railway Police (1844-1922). Absorbed into the London & North Eastern Railway Police in 1923.

North Eastern Railway Police (1854-1922). Absorbed into the London & North Eastern Railway Police in 1923.

North London Railway Police (1850-1922). The NLR Company was operated by the London & North Western Railway Company from 1909 until 1922 when the NLR Company was formally absorbed into the LNWR Company. The NLR Police Force was absorbed into the LNWR Police Force when they took over the running of the railway in 1909.

North Midland Railway Police (1839-44). Absorbed into the Midland Railway Police in 1844.

North Staffordshire Railway Police (1848-1922). Absorbed into the London, Midland & Scottish Railway Police in 1923.

North Union Railway Police (1834-89). Serving Police Officers absorbed either into the London & North Western Railway Police or the Lancashire & Yorkshire Railway Police in 1889. (North Union Railway (located in Lancashire) was taken over jointly by the LNWR and the L&YR.)

North Western Railway Police (1849-74). This railway was located in north west England and commonly known as the Little North Western Railway to distinguish it from the London & North Western Railway which became the largest pre-grouping railway in Britain. The Little North Western Railway Company together with the (little) North Western Railway Police were absorbed into the Midland Railway (and Midland Railway Police) in 1874.

Northern & Eastern Railway (1840-1902). Absorbed into the Great Eastern Railway in 1902. The Northern & Eastern Railway Company was originally intended as a railway from London to York but was only constructed from Stratford (East London) to Hertford when it ran into severe financial problems. Consequently, from 1844, the railway was leased to the neighbouring Eastern Counties Railway Company before being absorbed into the Great Eastern Railway in 1902. It was policed by officers from the Eastern Counties and Great Eastern Railway Police.

Oxford, Worcester & Wolverhampton Railway Police (1853-60). Absorbed into the West Midlands Railway Police in 1860 who in turn was absorbed into the Great Western Railway Police in 1863. All the serving Police Officers were absorbed into the GWR Police in 1863.

Peebles Railway Police (1855-76). The railway was leased to the North British Railway from 1861, until being officially absorbed into the North British Railway Company in 1876.

Pembroke & Tenby Railway Police (1863-97). Absorbed into the Great Western Railway Police in 1897.

Port Talbot Railway & Docks Police (1897-1922). Absorbed into the original pre 1923 Great Western Railway Police in January 1922, followed by absorption into post grouping GWR Police in 1923.

Rhymney Railway Police (1858-1922). Absorbed into the original pre 1923 Great Western Railway Police in March 1922, followed by absorption into post grouping GWR Police in 1923.

Scottish Central Railway Police (1848-65). Absorbed into the Caledonian Railway Police in 1865.

Scottish Midland Junction Railway Police (1848-56). Merged with the Aberdeen Railway to become the Scottish North Eastern Railway Police in 1856 (see below).

Scottish North Eastern Railway Police (1856-66). Absorbed into the Caledonian Railway Police in 1866.

Sheffield & Rotherham Railway Police (1838-45). Absorbed into the Midland Railway Police in 1845.

Sheffield, Ashton-under-Lyne & Manchester Railway Police (1841-47). Absorbed into the Manchester, Sheffield & Lincolnshire Railway Police in 1847.

Shrewsbury & Hereford Railway Police (1853-71). The railway was leased jointly by the London & North Western Railway and the Great Western Railway from 1862 until 1871 when ownership of the railway was acquired jointly by both companies who continued to police it.

South Devon Railway Police (1846-76). Absorbed into the Great Western Railway Police in 1876.

South Eastern Railway Police (1836-1922). Absorbed into the Southern Railway Police in 1923.

South Leicestershire Railway Police (1860-67). Absorbed into the London & North Western Railway Police in 1867.

South Wales Railway Police (1850-63). Absorbed into the Great Western Railway Police in 1863.

South Yorkshire Railway Police (1849-64). Absorbed into the Manchester, Sheffield & Lincolnshire Railway Police in 1864. The South Yorkshire Railway was also known as the South Yorkshire Coal Railway and the South Yorkshire, Doncaster & Goole Railway Company.

Sutherland & Caithness Railway Police (1874-84). Absorbed into the Highland Railway Police in 1884.

Southern Railway Police (1923-48). Absorbed into the British Transport Commission Police in 1949.

St Helens & Runcorn Gap Railway Police (1833-64). Absorbed into the London & North Western Railway Police in 1864. In 1845, the St Helens & Runcorn Gap Railway Company amalgamated with the Sankey Brook Navigation Company to become the St Helens Canal & Railway Company and in 1854 it was renamed The St Helens Railway Company.

Stockton & Darlington Railway Police (1825-63). Absorbed into the North Eastern Railway Police in 1863.

Taff Vale Railway Police (1840-1921). Absorbed into the Great Western Railway Police in 1922.

Underground Electric Railways Company of London (1902-33). This company was not a traditional railway company but was in fact a railway administrative company. It was the parent company of the District Railway Company (Metropolitan District Line) and owners of the London Electric Railway Company, both of whom operated and policed underground railways in London. The UERL Company was absorbed into the London Passenger Transport Board in 1933 along with the aforementioned companies who were all then policed by the newly created London Transport Police.

Vale of Neath Railway Police (1851-65). Absorbed into the Great Western Railway Police in 1865.

West Cornwall Railway Police (1852-66). Absorbed into the Great Western Railway Police in 1866. The West Cornwall Railway Company experienced financial difficulties and was bought by a group of companies, namely the Great Western Railway, the Bristol & Exeter Railway and the South Devon Railway who took over the railway in 1866.

West Hartlepool Harbour & Railway Company Police (1853-65). Absorbed into the North Eastern Railway Police in 1865.

Wishaw & Coltness Railway Police (1833-49). Absorbed into the Caledonian Railway Police in 1849.

Wye Valley Railway Police (1876-1905). Absorbed into the Great Western Railway Police in 1905.

York & North Midland Railway Police (1839-54). Absorbed into the North Eastern Railway Police in 1854. In 1854, the York & North Midland Railway Company merged with the Leeds Northern Railway Company, the York, Newcastle & Berwick Railway Company and the Malton & Driffield Railway

Company to form the new North Eastern Railway Company, policed by the NER Police.

York, Newcastle & Berwick Railway Police (1847-54). Between 1845 and 1847 the company was named the Newcastle & Berwick Railway. Absorbed into the North Eastern Railway Police in 1854.

CONSTITUENT FORCES (Part Two).

DOCKS, PORTS, HARBOURS AND CANAL POLICE FORCES.
Set out below (in alphabetical order) is a list of former Dock, Port, Harbour and Canal Companies in England, Scotland and Wales who are known or believed to have been policed by the British Transport Police or its Constituent Forces at various times during their history.

Aberdare Canal Police (1812-1900). Canal closed in 1900. Police Force disbanded.
Aire and Calder Navigation, Yorkshire.
Alexander Dock, Newport, South Wales.
Angerstein Wharf, London.
Ardrossan Harbour, Ayrshire, Scotland.
Avonmouth Docks (Bristol).
Ayre Harbour, Scotland.
Barrow Docks.
Barry Docks, South Wales.
Battersea Wharf, London.
Birmingham Canal Navigations.
Bristol Harbour.
British Transport Commission
Bute Docks, Cardiff.
Calder and Hebble Navigation.
Canada Dock, Liverpool.
Coventry Canal Navigation.
Deptford Wharf, London.
Dover Western Docks.
Fleetwood Wrye Dock.
Fishguard Harbour, West Wales.

Folkestone Harbour, Kent.
Forth and Clyde Canal, Scotland.
Garston Dock, Liverpool.
General Terminus and Glasgow Harbour.
Glamorgan Canal, South Wales.
Gloucester Docks.
Goole Docks. (BTC Police took over policing of the port from local police on 1 August 1954.)
Grand Union Canal.
Grangemouth Docks, Scotland.
Grimsby Docks.
Hartlepool Docks (West Hartlepool Docks).
Harwich Port (Parkeston Quay), Essex.
Hereford and Gloucester Canal.
Heysham Harbour, Lancashire. Police at Heysham Harbour also covered the Lake Windermere Steamers, the three piers at Lakeside, Bowness and Ambleside.
Holyhead Port, Anglesey.
Huddersfield and Manchester Canal (Huddersfield Narrow Canal - formerly owned by the London & North Western Railway Company).
Hull Docks.
Huskisson Dock, Liverpool.
Immingham Docks, Lincolnshire.
King's Lynn Docks, Norfolk.
Lee (Lea) Navigation (A Canal System from Hertford into the heart of London). Policed by the Lee Conservancy Police Force from 1870 until they were absorbed into the British Transport Commission Police in 1948.
Leeds and Liverpool Canal.
Llanelli Docks, South West Wales.
Lydney Docks, Gloucestershire. (Policed from Newport Docks in the 1960s and 1970s.)
Newhaven Harbour, East Sussex.
Methil Docks, Fife, Scotland.
Monmouthshire Canal.
Morpeth Dock, Birkenhead.
Newport Docks, South Wales.
North Dock, Liverpool.
Parkeston Quay, Harwich, Essex.

Penarth Dock, Vale of Glamorgan.
Plymouth Docks.
Poplar Dock. A railway dock in East London.
Port Talbot Docks, South Wales.
Regent's Canal and Dock Company, London.
Rothesay Dock, Clydebank, Glasgow.
Sandon Dock, Liverpool.
Seaham Harbour, County Durham.
Sharpness Docks, Gloucestershire.
Sheffield & South Yorkshire Navigation. Canal and navigable river network in South Yorkshire and Lincolnshire.
Sheffield Canal.
Silloth Docks, Cumbria.
Southampton Docks.
Southampton Harbour Board.
Stranraer Harbour, Dumfries and Galloway, Scotland.
Swansea Docks, South West Wales.
Swansea Harbour Trust.
Trent & Mersey Canal.
Troon Harbour, South Ayrshire, Scotland.
Tweed Dock, Berwick-upon-Tweed, Northumberland.
Tyne Docks, South Shields, Tyne and Wear (Formerly County Durham).
Victoria Dock, Hull.
Victoria and Albert Docks, London.
Worcester and Birmingham Canal.
Waterloo Dock, Liverpool.
Wyre Docks, Fleetwood.

Many of the above Dock, Ports, Harbour and Canal Companies came under the jurisdiction of the British Transport Commission Police for the first time after the companies were nationalised in 1948, although a considerable number of dock and harbours, which had been previously built and owned by various railway companies, had been policed by railway policemen, particularly during the nineteenth century.

After the government abolished the British Transport Commission in 1962, the BTC Police Force was renamed the British Transport Police. In the immediate years that followed, the British Waterways Board, the new body created to administer the river and canal networks in Britain, severed their ties with the British Transport Police and introduced their own private security measures to police the inland waterways.

During the 1980s, the Thatcher government introduced privatisation for many docks, ports and harbours in Britain. As a result, by the end of the 1980s the British Transport Police no longer policed the Docks, Ports and Harbours in Britain, which like the waterways network, had introduced private security firms to replace the British Transport Police, primarily as a cost cutting measure.

The British Transport Police still operates as a modern, successful police force, although its jurisdiction is now mainly confined to the railways, like that of its predecessors almost two hundred years ago.

Appendix C

NINETEENTH CENTURY RAILWAY AND DOCK POLICEMEN KILLED ON DUTY[29]

Below is a list of forty-nine serving police officers who were killed whilst performing their duties during the nineteenth century, in former British Transport Police constituent police forces. (Ireland not included).

It is not known how many officers were killed on duty during this period as no official figures are thought to exist. The names and details which appear on this list have been obtained from various sources during research carried out by myself and others into the history of railway policing. There is little doubt that considerably more officers were killed on duty than the unfortunate officers who are mentioned below. The surnames of individual officers concerned are listed in alphabetical order.

ATKINSON John. ACCIDENT.
John Atkinson, aged about 40, had been a constable with the North Eastern Railway Police at Manors Station (Newcastle) on the East Coast Main Line for a number of years. On 17 March 1886 he was struck by a northbound train whilst walking through a railway tunnel on the Tynemouth Line. His left leg was severed below the knee. He was conveyed to the local infirmary but died very soon afterwards. He left a widow and a number of children.

BEALES George. ACCIDENT.
George Beales, aged 33, was a constable in the Great Eastern Railway. On 27 June 1896, he suffered severe head injuries and internal injuries when he was accidentally knocked down and run over by a GER locomotive at Leyton in Essex. He survived for almost four months, until 21 October when he died of his injuries. An inquest was held two days later, and a verdict of 'accidental death' was returned. He was buried near his home in Kessingland, Suffolk. The inscription on his gravestone reads, 'George Beales, eldest and dearly beloved son of Isaac and Rose Beales who lost his life from injuries received whilst doing his duty as constable on the Great Eastern Railway'.

BISHOP George. ACCIDENT.
George BISHOP, aged 54, was employed as a Special Constable in the Bristol and Exeter Railway Police at Dunball near Bridgwater in Somerset. He was killed on 9 February 1853 after being struck by a train when crossing the railway line. He had been a special constable for four years. A Coroner's Inquest later returned a verdict of 'accidental death'.

CARTER George. ACCIDENT.
On Tuesday 3 July 1883, an inquest was held at Great Bridge near Wednesbury in Staffordshire, into the death of George Carter, a railway policeman with the London and North Western Railway who was stationed at Walsall. The inquest heard that the deceased was on the lineside watching a luggage train when he was knocked down and killed by a passing passenger train. A verdict of accidental death was recorded.

CARVER John. ACCIDENT.
John Carver was a constable with the Great Western Railway Police, stationed at Pangbourne near Reading. On Saturday, 19 January 1856, whilst on night duty, he was apparently struck by the up-mail train at 2.45am that morning. He was badly injured and lay beside the line until found by a railway porter 'Elijah Higgs' over two hours later. He told the porter he had been hit by a train. After being taken to the Royal Berkshire Hospital, his condition worsened and he died at 3pm that afternoon. Constable Carver was 45 years of age and described as a steady and sober man. He had twelve years' service. An inquest was held at the hospital the following morning and a verdict of 'accidental death' was recorded.

COOK Daniel. ACCIDENT.
Daniel Cook was a Detective Constable with the Great Eastern Railway Police, stationed at Hackney Downs Junction Station (renamed Hackney Downs Station from 1896). On 22 September 1894, whilst making enquiries into a robbery, he was crushed by a train at Hackney. He was an experienced officer who had previously served in the Metropolitan Police. An inquest later returned a verdict of 'accidental death'.

CROCKER Augustus. ACCIDENT.
A fatal accident happened on the evening of 8 June 1874 when Great Western Railway Policeman Augustus Crocker was knocked down by trucks during shunting operations near the entrance to the west yard of

Swindon Locomotive Works. Realising that some points needed to be changed to allow the trucks to be shunted into the yard, he ran across the lines but before he could clear the rails, he was struck and run over by the trucks. The wheels of the trucks cut his body completely in two and he died instantly. He had been stationed at Rodbourne Lane level crossing, Swindon for nearly thirty years. A Coroner's Inquest subsequently returned a verdict of 'accidental death'.

DANIEL James. ACCIDENT.
On Friday, 28 September 1838, at about 10pm, Police Constable James Daniel, aged 48, of the London and Birmingham Railway Police stationed at Watford, was struck by a train whilst inside a railway tunnel at Watford. His body was found a short time later by two of his colleagues, Inspector Howe and Constable Wharton. A Coroner's Inquest later recorded a verdict of 'accidental death'.

DEAVILLE Samuel. ACCIDENT.
Samuel Deaville was a Railway Policeman with the Leicester and Swannington Railway Company. During the evening of Thursday, 22 November 1838, Constable Deaville entered the locomotive shed near West Bridge Railway Station, Leicester, in order to clean his lantern. Whilst inside the shed, a locomotive entered tender first without him seeing or hearing it. Constable Deaville was crushed against a wall and died shortly afterwards. He had only been employed as a railway policeman for just four days, having transferred from the Leicester Borough Constabulary. A Coroner's Inquest later returned a verdict of 'accidental death'.

ELLIOT John. ACCIDENT.
On Tuesday, 8 September 1896, Detective Constable John Elliot of the North Eastern Railway Police jumped from a train at Tweedmouth, Northumberland and fell onto the track. He was run over and killed by a pilot engine. He left a wife and family. A Coroner's Inquest later returned a verdict of 'accidental death'.

FAZAKERLEY James. ACCIDENT.
At 7pm on Saturday, 30 September 1838, a goods train travelling from Liverpool to Manchester was passing through Newton Junction near Warrington, where

Police Constable Fazakerley of the Liverpool and Manchester Railway Police was standing, whilst waiting to cross the railway line.

At the precise moment that the train approached him, a coupling towards the rear of the train broke and several wagons became detached from the rest of the train. A gap appeared as the detached wagons started to slow down. After the front section of the train had passed, Constable Fazakerley, believing the whole train had passed, started to cross the line and was run over by the detached wagons which were by then free-wheeling a short distance behind the train. He was killed instantly. James Fazakerley had seven years' service. A Coroner's Inquest later recorded a verdict of accidental death.

FELLOWS Henry. ACCIDENT.
Henry Fellows, born circa 1823, joined the Southampton Docks Police Force in his early thirties and worked his way up through the ranks until he became a Superintendent and officer in charge of the force in 1875.

On Saturday, 13 October 1877, he was returning home by train, from a visit to London with his wife, when he alighted from the moving train as it was arriving at Basingstoke Station. As he stepped down from a first-class carriage, he slipped and his legs became trapped between the running board of the train and the station platform. He was dragged along and suffered appalling injuries. He was conveyed to hospital but died the following day. His funeral was well attended by local dignitaries and a large number of police officers, both from Southampton Docks Police and the local Constabulary.

Although Henry Fellows was not killed whilst he was on duty, his name has been included in this list due to his high-ranking status as officer in charge of the Southampton Docks Police Force and the circumstances surrounding his death. Henry Fellows was not immune from accidents and he, more than most people, would have been fully aware that alighting from a moving train was dangerous, as well as being unlawful by virtue of the Railway Byelaws.

These Byelaws were created in part, for the safety of passengers, yet instead of setting an example to others, Superintendent Fellows contravened two separate railway byelaws by opening the door of a train in motion (1) and by alighting from a moving train (2), blatantly disregarding both the law and the consequences of his actions. Sadly, he paid the ultimate price for doing so.

FLAVELL Thomas. FOUND DROWNED IN DOCK.
On Monday, 27 December 1869, Police Constable Flavell worked a night shift at Gloucester Docks. Police Constable Solomon Fudge, another officer on duty that night, spoke to Constable Flavell at 2.15am and that was the last time he saw him. Constable Flavell should have opened the dock gates at 5.40am but failed to do so.

Police Constable Fudge later told an inquest that Thomas Flavell had been talking that night about taking time off work for a holiday. When he did not open the dock gates, Constable Fudge opened them himself, assuming PC Flavell had gone home early. He did not report Constable Flavell missing.

On Thursday, 30 December, it was realised that Constable Flavell not been seen for two days. Suspecting that he may have fallen into the dock and drowned, the dock was dragged but a search for his body was unsuccessful. Two days later it came to light that a young boy had found a bowler hat floating in the Victoria Dock. The hat was recovered from the boys home and identified as having belonged to the missing officer. The boy indicated where he had found the hat and after a nearby boat was moved, Flavell's body was recovered, having been trapped underneath.

An inquest was held at the Albion Hotel on Monday 3 January 1870. The coroner expressed his concern as to how an officer who knew every step of the docks had entered the water and why his disappearance had not been reported sooner. The Coroner also criticised Dock Policemen Solomon Fudge for not reporting his missing colleague sooner. The jury returned a verdict of 'death by drowning'.

FOULKES John. FOUND DROWNED IN DOCK.
PC John Foulkes of the Midland Railway Police resided near Wrexham in North Wales but was lodging at Swansea and serving at Swansea Docks during the latter part of 1890. He had been on night duty when, on the morning of the 25 September 1890, his body was found in the New Cut Channel by a fellow officer. A Coroner's Inquest later returned a verdict of 'death by drowning'.

GOATMAN William. ACCIDENT.
On Saturday, 18 February 1860, William Goatman of the Midland Railway Police was performing point duty near Gloucester Railway Station when he was struck by a guard's van during shunting operations. He suffered severe

injuries from which he died a short time later. A Coroner's Inquest later returned a verdict of 'accidental death'. He left a wife and three children.

GORRINGE George. ACCIDENT.
George Gorringe was a Constable in the London, Brighton and South Coast Railway Police. On Tuesday, 13 September 1842, he was performing duties at Clayton Tunnel near Brighton. Police Constable Gorringe went inside the tunnel to sprinkle sand on the rails after drivers reported them wet and slippery. Whilst inside the tunnel he was struck by a train which amputated his hand and broke his arm. He also suffered head injuries.

Gorringe spent several weeks in hospital and was expected to make a full recovery but suffered a relapse and died on 3 November 1842. His death was attributed to the injuries sustained in the accident and a verdict of 'accidental death' was recorded by Mr Gill, the district coroner.

GOSS. First name not known. ACCIDENT.
On Tuesday, 15 November 1836, Police Constable Goss, of the Warrington Grand Junction Railway Police, was on point duty at Watery Lane near Warrington. After changing a set of points and setting a signal lamp to the line clear position, he is believed to have sat down alongside the railway line and fallen asleep. Guard Grindly, who was in charge of a passing passenger train, felt a bump in the guard's van as the train passed the junction. He reported the matter when his train stopped at Warrington Station and a worker was sent to the location to examine the track. Upon his arrival, he found PC Goss lying across the track. One of his legs had been badly lacerated by the train and his foot on the other leg had been completely severed. Constable Goss was still alive but died at 6am the following morning. A Coroner's Inquest later returned a verdict of 'accidental death'. It is thought that this may be the first ever recorded fatality of a railway policeman whilst on duty.

HASSALL Henry. ACCIDENT.
Henry Hassall, a Constable with the London & North Western Railway Police, was on night duty at Longsight Sidings, Manchester on 18 December 1880 when he was knocked down and killed during a shunting operation. A shunter named Thomas Godfrey saw that the officer was in danger and shouted out to him but he did not respond. The officer was killed instantly. An inquest was later held by the Coroner Mr. F. Price and the jury returned a verdict of 'accidental death'.

HILLIER William. ACCIDENT.
William Hillier was a Constable with the Great Western Railway Police stationed at Steventon, about four miles west of Didcot. He had just six months service when on Friday, 16 October 1868, he was struck by a goods train and killed instantly. His body was badly mutilated. The inquest took place the following day at the Red Lion public house, Milton before the Coroner Mr. Bartlett. A verdict of 'accidental death' was returned.

HOLLAND George. ACCIDENT.
George Holland, aged 42, was a Detective Constable with the Lancashire & Yorkshire Railway Police. On Wednesday, 26 April 1882, whilst crossing the goods yard near the East Lancashire Railway Warehouse at Preston, he was struck by five wagons during shunting operations. The wagons passed over his head and body, killing him instantly. A Coroner's Inquest later returned a verdict of 'accidental death'. He left a widow and seven children.

HOWARD Thomas. OPEN VERDICT.
Thomas Howard of the Bute Docks Police in Cardiff was found drowned in suspicious circumstances at Cardiff Docks on 18 December 1869. Full details of the circumstances surrounding the death of Sergeant Howard can be found in Chapter 8.

HURDLE Albert. ACCIDENT.
On Friday, 24 January 1896, just after 6pm, 58-year-old Constable Albert Hurdle of the London, Brighton and South Coast Railway Police was on duty at Brighton Railway Station when he accidentally tripped over some telegraph cables in the darkness. This caused him to fall into the path of a London-bound passenger train. He was run over and killed instantly. An inquest later returned a verdict of 'accidental death'.

KIDD Robert. MURDER.
Detective Sergeant Robert Kidd of the London and North Western Railway Police was brutally murdered after being repeatedly stabbed in a frenzied attack at Wigan on 29 September 1895. Full details of the circumstances surrounding the death of Detective Sergeant Kidd can be found in Chapter 8.

LEGGE Hezekiah. ACCIDENT.
On Thursday, 14 August 1873, Police Constable Hezekiah Legge of the Bristol and Exeter Railway Police was on duty at Bristol Station. Whilst standing

on the platform edge, he turned to warn passengers to keep clear, when he himself was struck by a train and knocked onto the railway line. Several trucks then passed over his legs. He was conveyed to hospital where he later died. Although only having three years' service with the B&E Railway Police, he had previously served as a Constable for thirteen years in the Bristol Borough Police Force.

LOXTON Aaron. ACCIDENT.
Aaron Loxton was a Police Constable with the South Wales Railway Police, stationed at Cardiff Riverside Station (re-named Cardiff General, then Cardiff Central Station). On Tuesday, 22 February 1859, at about 10pm, Constable Loxton was walking along the railway from Cardiff Riverside Station to Cardiff Canton level crossing when he was struck by a passing train. It is thought that he died instantly. His body was found at 5.30am the following morning. A Coroner's jury later returned a verdict of accidental death.

MAGUIRE (Forename unknown). ACCIDENT.
On 29 December 1845, Police Constable Number 61 Maguire, of the London and South Western Railway police, was on main gate duty at the Nine Elms Terminus Railway Station (the station closed in 1848). Whilst opening the great gates at the terminus to allow a post-chaise to enter, he was struck on the head by a pole, fell to the ground and was run over by the carriage. He was conveyed to St Thomas Hospital where he died the following evening. A Coroner's Inquest held two days later returned a verdict of accidental death.

MANNING Richard. ACCIDENT.
At about 11pm, on Saturday 19 January 1861, Constable Richard Manning of the Bristol & Exeter Railway Police was on duty at Taunton when he picked up a night lamp and went to meet the up-mail train travelling towards Bristol to give it the all-clear to proceed. A few moments later, a down-train passed though the station travelling in the opposite direction. After a short time lapse, Constable Manning failed to emerge so another constable, fearing for his safety, went to look for him. The officer's fears were well founded when he found Richard Manning's body on the railway line, some fifteen feet from where he would have been standing when he gave the up train the all-clear. It seemed apparent that he had been struck by the down-train as it was passing in the opposite direction and killed outright. A Coroner's Inquest later returned a verdict of 'accidental death'.

MARSH Alfred. OPEN VERDICT.
On 23 August 1897, Police Constable Alfred Marsh of the Lancashire & Yorkshire Railway Police was found lying in the hold of a ship at Fleetwood Docks after boarding the vessel to deal with an incident. He was examined by a doctor and admitted to hospital where he remained for some four months before he eventually died as a direct result of his injuries. Full details of the circumstances surrounding the death of Constable Marsh can be found in Chapter 8.

MAULE John Clement. FOUND DROWNED IN DOCK.
On Saturday, 7 November 1868, Police Constable John Maule, aged just 23, of the Newport Harbour Commission Police Force, performed a night patrol duty on the Old Town Docks in Newport, Monmouthshire. At 5am the following morning after the tide receded, the body of Constable Maule was found lying in the mud near Tredegar Wharf. It had been a windy, stormy night and it was believed that his cape had been blown into the water and he drowned whilst trying to retrieve it. He was a married man who left a young widow. A Coroner's Inquest later returned a verdict of 'accidental death'.

McCLURE James. FOUND DROWNED IN DOCK.
On Saturday, 20 August 1859, Police Constable James McClure, aged 45, of the Bute Dock Police Force, carried out a night duty patrol on Cardiff West Dock. He had been employed as a Dock Policeman for less than two weeks. PC McClure was visited on his beat at about 12.30am by his patrol sergeant and he spoke to a dock night-watchman shortly before 2am. That was the last time he was seen alive. It was a clear moonlit night.

Later that morning, another constable on patrol, PC Woodhouse, heard a splash in the water but failed to see anything so he noted the matter and later reported it. When Constable McClure failed to arrive back at the Docks Police Station to book off duty, a search was carried out. Close to where PC Woodhouse had earlier heard the splash, the body of James McClure was found in the water. There were no signs of a struggle but a small mark above his right eye suggested that he had fallen into the water and struck some rafts of timber which were floating next to his body.

McNAMARA John. ACCIDENT.
Shortly after 6am on Saturday, 29 December 1861, Police Constable John McNamara of the London and North Western Railway Police was walking

along the railway line from Sudbury Station near Wembley in North West London to the Brent Railway Branch signal post to relieve a signalman who had been working there all night. Whilst walking along the track, he was struck by the morning down-mail train which departed Euston Station at 6.15am. The train passed over Constable McNamara and severed both his legs from his body. He died instantly. A Coroner's inquest later recorded a verdict of 'accidental death'.

MURRAY Donald. ACCIDENT.
Shortly after 6am on Friday, 10 October 1873, Police Constable Donald Murray of the London and North Western Railway Police was on duty at Euston Station in London when, for some reason, he decided to cross the railway lines from one platform to another. As he did so, a two-coach passenger train was reversing into the platform, coaches first, due to it being a terminus station. Unfortunately, Constable Murray failed to allow himself sufficient time to clear the railway lines and was run over by the rear passenger coach of the train. He was killed instantly. A Coroner's Inquest later returned a verdict of 'accidental death'.

NASH William. FOUND DROWNED IN DOCK.
On Saturday, 11 August 1855, Police Constable William Nash, aged 31 of the Newport Harbour Commission Police, was found drowned near Cinderhill Wharf after carrying out a routine patrol of the Old Town Docks. There were no known witnesses to the incident. A Coroner's Inquest later returned a verdict of 'found drowned'.

NEWSHAM John. ACCIDENT.
On 21 December 1846 John Newsham, a constable on the Manchester, Sheffield and Lincolnshire Railway, was engaged in signalling duties near the entrance to Woodhead Tunnel on the Sheffield to Manchester line. It was a cold winter's day with snow on the ground. Whilst performing his duties, he attempted to board a pilot engine to go a few yards to change some signal points. The step of the engine was covered in snow and ice causing Constable Newsham to slip and fall under the wheels of the engine which amputated his right foot. He died in hospital a week later. A Coroner's inquest later returned a verdict of 'accidental death'.

RALPH George. ACCIDENT.

On Saturday, 13 October 1882, Police Constable George Ralph, of the Great Western Railway Police, worked a night shift at Paddington Station. He was performing gate duties at the Harrow Road Gates. At about 3.30am, Sergeant George Allot, a night duty sergeant, went to visit Constable Ralph at the gates but there was no sign of him. Sergeant Allot made a search of the surrounding area and came across the body of Constable Ralph on the railway track near Westbourne Bridge. He had been run over by a train which had cut the body in half. A Coroner's inquest later returned a verdict of 'accidental death'.

RODAWAY Alfred Biggs. FOUND DROWNED IN DOCK.
On Thursday, 7 January 1864, Police Constable Rodaway of the Newport Harbour Commission Police performed night duty patrolling the Old Town Docks in Newport, Monmouthshire. He failed to return to the police station after finishing his shift at 6am the following morning. A search was carried out and fellow officers found his body floating in the dock at about 8am. His watch had stopped at four o'clock. It was assumed that he had fallen into the dock and drowned at that time. He left a widow and ten children. The youngest, a two-month-old baby, became ill and died very shortly afterwards.

ROSS William. ACCIDENT.
On Wednesday, 15 January 1868, Police Constable William Ross of the Lancashire and Yorkshire Railway Police was checking goods wagons near Bolton Trinity Street Railway Station when he accidentally stepped into the path of an oncoming train and was killed instantly. The accident was witnessed by the night duty goods inspector. He left a wife and three young children. A Coroner's inquest later returned a verdict of 'accidental death'.

SCUDAMORE John. FOUND DROWNED IN DOCK.
At about 5am on Thursday, 4 November 1858, Police Constable John Scudamore of the Bute Dock Police force was patrolling near the junction feeder canal at Cardiff Docks when he accidently fell into the water and drowned. An inquest was held later the same day. Evidence was presented to the jury by Police Constable Frewin of the Bute Docks Police that Constable Scudamore had been seen very shortly before he fell into the dock. He appeared in good health, he was sober and alert. Frewin went on to say that Scudamore had recently considered leaving the job because it was too dark and dangerous to patrol during the night. He also stated that the whole area where the accident took place was very poorly lit and unfenced, which failed to prevent people stepping off the quayside into the water.

After hearing other evidence, the jury deliberated to consider their verdict. They later informed the Coroner Mr Lewis Reece that by a majority of 8-3, they wished to deliver a verdict of manslaughter against the Dock Company. This was rejected by the Coroner who then adjourned the inquest. On Friday, 12 November 1858, a second jury was sworn in and delivered a verdict of 'accidental death'.

SHOPLAND Robert. ACCIDENT.
At 4.45pm on Saturday, 29 September 1863, Police Constable Robert Shopland of the Bristol and Exeter Railway was performing crossing and signalling duties at the junction of the main Bristol to Exeter line and the Watchet branch line when he was struck on the head and killed instantly by the buffer beam of a passing locomotive. At a Coroner's Inquest held on Tuesday, 29 September, the jury returned a verdict of 'accidental death'.

SMITH Frank. ACCIDENT.
On the evening of Sunday, 20 December 1885, Police Constable Frank Smith of the North Staffordshire Railway Police was on duty at Stoke on Trent railway station when he attempted to board a moving passenger train as it pulled into the station platform. He lost his footing and fell between the running board of a carriage and the station platform. He suffered severe injuries and died instantly. The platform was crowded with passengers at the time. A Coroner's inquest later returned a verdict of 'accidental death'.

STAGG Edwin. ACCIDENT
On Saturday, 2 August 1873, Police Constable Edwin Stagg of the Great Western Railway Police was standing on the platform at Wootton Bassett Station in Wiltshire, speaking to a railway porter. After the conversation, Stagg decided to cross the railway lines to the opposite platform. At this juncture, a London to Bristol passenger train came into view and approached the station at about 35-40mph. It was not due to stop at the station.

As the train got nearer, Constable Stagg seemed undecided whether to cross the railway lines or let the train pass. After Stagg hesitated, the porter shouted, 'Stop, Stagg, stop,' but Constable Stagg jumped from the platform and proceeded to cross the track in front of the oncoming train. In doing so, he was struck by the front buffer beam of the locomotive and rendered unconscious. He died shortly afterwards from multiple internal injuries. A subsequent Coroner's Inquest returned a verdict of 'accidental death'.

STEBBINGS John Thomas. FOUND DROWNED IN DOCK
On Saturday, 21 October 1899, the body of Police Constable John Stebbings of the Regent's Canal Police Force was found drowned in the Limehouse Basin whilst on a routine patrol of the Regent's Canal Dock. It was believed that Stebbings had lost his way in the fog before falling into the water. At the time of the incident, thick fog had been hovering over the metropolis for several days leading to at least three workers falling into nearby docks and drowning. A Coroner's Inquest held 23 October returned a verdict of 'accidental death'.

TALLEY Thomas. ACCIDENT
At about 10am, on Friday, 9 January 1863, Police Constable Thomas Talley of the London and North Western Railway Police was performing duties at Bletchley Railway Station. Part of his duties included the operation of signal points at Bletchley Junction just outside the station. It was common practice for a constable performing these duties to hitch a ride on an engine from the station to the junction which Constable Talley decided to do. There was a goods train standing in the station taking on water at the time, so Talley decided to jump onto the footplate of the engine. In doing so, he slipped, causing him to fall heavily into the gap between the locomotive footplate and the platform edge. His right leg was broken and his left leg was badly shattered with severe injuries to the left foot. After being conveyed to hospital, his injuries were treated, which necessitated his left foot being amputated. The operation appeared to go well until the following day when his condition took a turn for the worse. His condition deteriorated even further on the Sunday and he died on Monday, 12 January 1863. A Coroner's Inquest later returned a verdict of 'accidental death'.

TEMPLAR William. ACCIDENT
On Tuesday 8 January 1867, 22-year-old William Templar, a Police Constable in the Great Western Railway Police at Cardiff, worked a night shift controlling a railway level crossing at Newtown in Cardiff. He had been employed as a railway policeman for just three months. At 8.40 that evening, a goods train from Swansea passed over the crossing and the driver of the train, Mr Dixon, saw Constable Templar standing on the crossing at his usual place. The constable waved to driver Dixon. That was the last time Constable Templar was seen alive.

Shortly after ten o'clock that evening, complaints began to emerge that there was no policeman on duty at Newtown crossing. The police lodge was locked and unoccupied. The fire inside the police lodge was very low on coal and had obviously not been attended to for some time.

A search was made of the area and eventually, Mr Thomas, a railway switchman, who had been sent to man the crossing in the absence of a policeman, found the body of Constable Templar lying in the darkness on the railway line, several yards from the crossing. It appeared that Police Constable Templar had been killed instantly and fell where he had been run over by a train. There were extensive injuries to the head and body. His watch was broken and had stopped at 8.45, which was the same time that a passenger train had passed over the crossing on its approach to Cardiff Station. The locomotive on that train, which was berthed in some sidings nearby, was examined and traces of blood and human remains were found on the front of the locomotive, consistent with having struck Constable Templar at the crossing.

On Thursday, 10 January 1867, an inquest was held into the death of Police Constable William Templar at Cardiff Town Hall. After the evidence had been presented, the Coroner in his summing up remarked that he could not see that anyone was to blame except the deceased himself, who had doubtless walked across the line, not seeing the passenger train until it was too late. The jury retired for a short time to consider their verdict, and upon their return, they delivered a verdict of 'accidental death'.

THOMPSON Richard. ACCIDENT
Richard Thompson, age 30, was a railway policeman employed by the Lancaster and Preston Junction Railway Company. He was stationed at Lancaster Castle Railway Station. From the formation of the railway company in 1840, railway constables employed by the company performed a variety of duties, including those of train guards and ticket collectors in the event of staff shortages. This continued until 1859, when the railway company was officially absorbed into the London and North Western Railway and the police establishment became part of the LNWR Police Force.

On the afternoon of Saturday, 4 September 1858, Constable Thompson worked a goods train from Lancaster to Preston in the capacity of assistant guard/brakeman. After completing that duty, he caught the 9.20pm train from Preston back to Lancaster, volunteering to assist in the collection of tickets on his return journey.

When the train arrived at Galgate Station, just three miles from Lancaster, Constable Thompson went to the two middle carriages on the train to examine tickets (the train was non-corridor). After checking tickets in the two carriages, Constable Thompson made his way back along the platform to the carriage of the train where he had been travelling. As he approached his carriage, he shouted 'alright' to the guard of the train and the station master who were standing on the platform, indicating them to signal the train driver to proceed. As the train slowly moved along the platform, Constable Thompson opened his compartment door and climbed onto the running board of the carriage, but in the darkness, he lost his footing and slipped whist trying to enter the carriage, just as the train was leaving the end of the platform. Constable Thompson fell to the ground and was dragged along the track by the train. A carriage wheel severed his arm, almost amputating it. He suffered severe head injuries after striking his head during the fall and was killed almost instantly. A local doctor attended the railway station soon afterwards and certified death. On Monday 6 September 1858, a Coroner's Inquest was held and the jury returned a verdict of 'accidental death'.

TUBBS George. ACCIDENT
At about 4.40 am on Tuesday, 8 April 1890, George Tubbs, aged 59, a police sergeant with the London and South Western Railway Police, was on night duty at Nine Elms Goods Depot in London. For some reason, he decided to climb into a brake-van which was in motion during shunting operations. Whilst doing so, his coat became hooked up on a protruding point's lever which pulled Sergeant Tubbs to the ground. The wheels of the brake-van then passed over both legs. Sergeant Tubbs was conveyed to hospital where surgeons deemed it necessary to perform an immediate emergency operation to amputate both legs below the knees. George Tubbs died whist the operation was being carried out. A verdict of 'accidental death' was later recorded.

WARBURTON George. ACCIDENT.
At 10.30am on Monday, 14 May 1860, a coal train consisting of thirty-seven wagons left Merthyr Tydfil destined for Neath on the Vale of Neath Railway line. Shortly after leaving Merthyr, the train approached Abernant Railway Station which had a level crossing alongside, manned by a railway policeman. As he approached the level crossing, William Ball the engine driver, saw that the semaphore signal alongside the track was showing line clear for him to proceed. Standing in front of the crossing and facing the train, was

28-year-old George Warburton, a railway policeman employed by the Vale of Neath Railway Company who was in charge of the crossing. Constable Warburton held out his left hand, indicating to driver Ball that it was safe to proceed.

As the train came within 100 yards or so of the crossing, driver Ball noticed that Police Constable Warburton had omitted to open the crossing gates to allow his train to pass through and they were still closed across the track. Constable Warburton should have opened the gates for the train to pass, before he set the semaphore signal to the line clear position.

Driver Ball sounded his whistle several times to warn Constable Warburton, who then turned around and looked towards the crossing gates. After seeing that they were still closed, he ran towards them. Driver Ball shut off steam and applied the brake on the engine, but the weight of the train continued to propel it towards the crossing.

Police Constable Warburton succeeded in opening one of the gates, but before he could fully open the second gate he was struck by the locomotive and knocked to the ground. His body was dragged along the track some fifty yards before the train came to a halt. The mangled remains of Police Constable Warburton's body were later recovered from beneath the engine. A subsequent inquest returned a verdict of 'accidental death'.

Appendix D

BRITISH TRANSPORT POLICE LIST OF CHIEF CONSTABLES[30]

Arthur Charles WEST OBE, KPM.
Former Chief Constable of British Transport Commission Police, Arthur West OBE, KPM, was the first Chief Constable of the British Transport Police when it was founded on 1 January 1963. West retired at the end of August that year and Bill Gay succeeded him with effect from 1 September 1963.

William (Bill) Owen GAY. QPM, MA (Oxon).
Served as Chief Constable from 1963 until 1974.

Eric HASLAM. OBE, QPM.
Served as Chief Constable from 1974 until 1981.

Kenneth OGRAM.
Served as Chief Constable from 1981 until 1989.

Desmond O'BRIEN. OBE, QPM.
Served as Chief Constable from 1989 until 1997.

David WILLIAMS. QPM, LLB.
Served as Chief Constable from 1997 until 2001.

Ian JOHNSTON. CBE, QPM.
Served as Chief Constable from 2001 until 2009.

Andrew TROTTER. OBE, QPM.
Served as Chief Constable from 2009 until 2014.

Paul CROWTHER. CBE.
Served as Chief Constable from 2014 until his retirement in 2021.

Lucy D'ORSI.
The first ever female Chief Constable of the British Transport Police appointed in February 2021 and is the current Chief Constable.

BIBLIOGRAPHY

Appleby, Pauline. *A Force on the Move* Images Publishing (Malvern) Ltd. 1995.
BTC Police. *Police Journals* (Quarterly Magazines). 1949-62.
British Transport Police. *Police Journals* (Quarterly Magazines). 1963-90.
Gairns, J.F. *Railways* Ward, Lock & Co Ltd, London. 1925.
Gay, William O. *Communications and Crime* Barry Rose Publishers, London. 1973.
Head, Viv. *Policing South Wales Docks* Amberley Publishing, Stroud. 2018.
Layton, M. & Rogerson B. *Police Dog Heroes* Amberley Publishing, Stroud. 2016.
Layton, M. & Rogerson B. *The Hooligans Are Still Among Us* Amberley Publishing. 2017.
Lewin, Henry Grote. 'Railway Mania and its Aftermath' *Railway Gazette*, London. 1936.
Satchwell, Graham. *Great Train Robbery Confidential* The History Press. 2019.
Simmons, J. & Biddle G. *British Railway History* Oxford University Press. 2000.
Simmons J. *The Railway Traveller's Handbook (1862)* Reprint Adams & Dart. 1971.
Stackpoole-Ryding, R. *The British Transport Police Illustrated History* Amberley. 2015.
Whitbread J.R. *The Railway Policeman* George G. Harrap & Co. London. 1961.
Wier, Nigel. *The Railway Police* Author House Publishing. 2011
Wragg, David. *GWR Handbook (1923-1947)* Haynes Publishing, Yeovil. 2010.

NOTES

1. Statistics from British Transport Police website; https://www.btp.police.uk (Figures obtained in the spring of 2020 before the effects of the coronavirus pandemic).
2. Establishment figures for 1923 from Appleby, Pauline, *A Force on the Move* 1995 Images Publishing (Malvern) Ltd.
3. Gairns, J.F., *Uncle Dick's Puffer; Book 'Railways'* Ward, Lock & Co Ltd, London. 3rd Edition revised ch.3, p.37. Published 1925.
4. Fatal accidents information courtesy of the British Newspaper Archives.
5. Statistics for the year 1845. Grote Lewin, Henry, *Railway Mania and its aftermath*, *Railway Gazette*, London 1936.
6. Mentioned in the *Manchester Evening News*. Monday 10 August 1903. Courtesy British Newspaper Archives.
7. Referred to in television documentary *Railway Murders* episode 3, shown on Sky TV Yesterday Channel. Sunday 2 May 2021 and book, J. R. Whitbread The Railway Policeman. 1961, Harrap Publishers.
8. A letter dated 1 March 1848, showing that Thomas Manton of the Stockton and Darlington Railway changed his title from Superintendent to Chief of Police. The original letter has been preserved in the National Archives at Kew under reference number SAD8/238.
9. Particulars reported in the *Taunton Courier and Western Advertiser*, 2 January 1849 and *Bell's New Weekly Messenger* on Sunday 7 January 1849. Courtesy British Newspaper Archives.
10. Railway track miles in 1852. British Library learning timeline item number 106197.
11. Railway route mileage in 1900. National Archives.gov.uk (cabinet papers).
12. Number of railway companies operating in 1900. National Archives.gov.uk (cabinet papers).
13. Number of civil police forces operating in 1900 listed in National Archives.gov.uk and https://www.bbc.co.uk/bitesize/guides/z9f4srd/revision/5.

14. Number of civil police officers operating in 1900 listed in National Archives.gov.uk and https://www.bbc.co.uk/bitesize/guides/z9f4srd/revision/5.
15. Goods stolen in transit on the Stockton & Darlington Railway in 1826. Reported in the *Durham County Advertiser* on 18 November 1826. Courtesy British Newspaper Archives.
16. Incident reported in the *Leeds Patriot & Yorkshire Advertiser* newspaper dated 24 December 1830. Courtesy British Newspaper Archives.
17. Case reported in the *Cambridge Independent Press* dated 29 July 1848. Courtesy British Newspaper Archives.
18. Case reported in the *Manchester Times, Manchester Evening News* (both dated 17 June 1882) and several other newspapers. Courtesy British Newspaper Archives.
19. Case reported in the *London Evening Standard*, 18 April 1868 and numerous other newspapers. Courtesy British Newspaper Archives.
20. Courtesy the Railway Accident Archive.
21. Case reported in the *West Middlesex Herald* newspaper on 21 March 1857 and numerous other newspapers. Courtesy British Newspaper Archives.
22. Case reported in the *North Wales Chronicle* dated 12 September 1891 and numerous other newspapers. Courtesy British Newspaper Archives.
23. Passenger numbers and revenue statistics can be found in the GNR Company records held at the National Archives, Kew. https://www.nationalarchives.gov.uk/railways
24. The copies of all railway byelaws contained within this book are courtesy of the National Railway Museum in York.
25. Railway track mileage and passenger numbers courtesy National Archives. https://www.nationalarchives.gov.uk/railways.
26. Establishment figures for 1923 from Appleby, 1995.
27. The copies of all railway byelaws contained within this book are supplied courtesy of the National Railway Museum, York.
28. Details of British Transport Police, constituent forces obtained from the following sources; Research carried out by the British Transport Police, History Group. https://www.btphg.org.uk. Index compiled by Ed Thompson is displayed on the BTPHG website. Further research carried out by the author of this book. Information sources include British Newspaper Archives.
29. Details of nineteenth century railway and dock policemen killed whilst on duty obtained from the following sources. Research carried out by the

British Transport Police, History Group. https://www.btphg.org.uk. A Roll of Honour listing officers killed whilst on duty is displayed on their website. Information gathered by a number of individuals, including: Anthony Rae, Kevin Gordon, Viv Head, Glyn Thomas, Martin McKay, Steve Beamon. Various sources of the research include British Transport Police records, Police Review magazine, railway and dock policing records, British Newspaper Archives.
30. List of British Transport Police, Chief Constables. Courtesy of British Transport Police History Group (BTPHG) - https://www.btphg.org.uk.

INDEX

Arthur Charles West OBE, KPM, 26, 122, 124
Attempt to assassinate Queen Victoria, 96

Bow Street Runners, 13
Box Tunnel, 8
Bristol and Exeter Railway Company, 132
British Transport Commission Police, 122, 167
British Transport Police, 124
BTP Constituent Forces (Appendix B), 190-209
Bullseye oil lamp (image), 22

Cardiff Bute Dock Company, 145
Charles Wheatstone, 41
Chief Constables, BTP list (Appendix D), 226
City of London Police, 24
Colonel Norman McKay Jesper MC, DSO, OBE, ERD, 26

Definition of Time Act 1880, 46
Detective Sergeant Robert Kidd (image), 100

Early police truncheons (images), 18
Early police uniforms, 16

Edith Smith (First British policewoman), 158
Electric telegraph, 41
Elijah Winstanley, 100

Firearms, 178
Flag warning signals (image), 37
Franz Muller (image), 90
Furness Railway Company, 160

George Hudson, 9
George Hudson (image), 10
Grand Union Canal, 147
Great Eastern Railway Company, 134
Great Train Robbery, 59
Great Western Railway, 164
Great Western Railway Police, 164

Hull and Barnsley Railway Company, 161, 162

Irish Mail Train, 58

John Tawell (image), 45
Judge Samuel Boteler Bristowe, 96

Ladder gang, 102
Ladies only compartments, 90
Lineside sentry box (image), 40
Llanelli riots, 153
Locomotion Number 1 (image), 5

London City Police, 24
London, Brighton & South Coast Railway, 127
Lucy D'Orsi, 124, 158

Manchester, Sheffield and Lincolnshire Railway, 127
Margaret Hood (first railway policewoman), 118, 158
Middleton Railway, 2, 7
Midland Railway Company, 150
Mumbles Railway, 3
Municipal Corporations Act 1835, 14

North British Railway Riots of 1846, 33
North Eastern Railway Company, 155
North Eastern Railway Police, 162
North Staffordshire Railway Company, 139

Obstructing the railway, 69
Oystermouth Railway, 3

Parish Constables, 12
PC Joseph Byrne, 102
PC Marsh, 105
PC Richard Pace, 30
Penal Servitude Act 1857, 60
Pickpocketing, 60
Police Cadets, 173
Police Cutlass (image), 19
Police ranks, 23
Police Sergeant 102 Allinson and dog Jim (image), 119
Police Uniforms, 16
Post Office mailbags, 58

Railway accidents, 74
Railways Act 1844, 113
Railway Bye-laws (Appendix A), 181
Railway Clauses Consolidation Act 1845, 113
Railway construction, 28
Railway Mania, 8
Railway navvies, 28
Railway navvies (image), 28
Railway Regulation (Gauge) Act 1846, 164
Railway time, 45
Railway (Conveyance of Mails) Act 1838, 57
Regent's Canal and Dock, 147
Richard Trevithick, 2

Sarah Hart, 43
Sir Charles Rowan KCB, 24
Sir Richard Mayne KCB, 24
Sir William Forthergill Cook, 41
South Wales Railway Company, 142
Southampton Harbour Force Police Force, 132
Special Constables Act 1831, 35
Stealing coal, 56
Swansea Dock Company, 148
Swansea Harbour Trust Police Force, 147

Tadworth Police Training Centre, 169
Taff Vale Railway Company, 142
The Railway Regulation Acts 1840 & 1842, 113
Thomas Briggs (murder), 90
Thomas Manton, 25
Tyne Dock, South Shields, 153

Voluntary Women's Force, 158

William Bertram Richards MVO, 26
William Huskisson, 5
William Huskisson (image), 6

William Kearsley, 100
William Own Gay, OBE, KPM, MA (Oxon), 124, 226
William Owen Gay (Photo), 125
Women's Police Service, 158